ME THE PEOPLE

RANDOM HOUSE
New York

Me

THE PEOPLE

OR,

ONE MAN'S SELFLESS QUEST TO REWRITE THE

CONSTITUTION OF THE UNITED STATES OF AMERICA

BY

Kevin Bleyer

WITH A FOREWORD BY

Kevin Bleyer

AUTHOR OF

ME THE PEOPLE

OR,

ONE MAN'S SELFLESS QUEST TO REWRITE THE

CONSTITUTION OF THE UNITED STATES OF AMERICA

BY

Kevin Bleyer

☆ ☆ ☆

Published in the United States by Random House, an imprint of
The Random House Publishing Group, a division of Random House, Inc.,
New York.

RANDOM HOUSE and colophon are registered trademarks of
Random House, Inc.

The portrait of Associate Justice Antonin Scalia on page 137
is by Nelson Shanks and is currently on loan to the
Harvard University Law School.

The photo on page 247 is by Brian Lary.

LIBRARY OF CONGRESS CATALOGING-IN-PUBLICATION DATA
Bleyer, Kevin.
Me the people: One man's selfless quest to rewrite the constitution of the
United States of America / by Kevin Bleyer.
p. cm.
Includes bibliographical references.
ISBN 978-1-4000-6935-4
eBook ISBN 978-0-679-60412-9
1. Constitutional law—United States—Popular works.   I. Title.
II. Title: One man's selfless quest to rewrite the constitution of the
United States of America.
KF4550.Z9B55 2012
342.7302'9—dc23   2011052582

Printed in the United States of America on acid-free paper

www.atrandom.com

246897531

FIRST EDITION

Book design by Simon M. Sullivan

To the flag of the United States of America,
And to the republic for which it stands.

I couldn't have done it without you.

☆ ☆ ☆

The following is a work of unassailable scholarship. Any errors, omissions, or exaggerations were made only to prove my point.

Whether this is a feat of visionary genius is not for me to say. It is only for others to notice.

☆ ☆ ☆

☆ ☆ ☆

CONTENTS
OR, AN 𝕰𝖓𝖚𝖒𝖊𝖗𝖆𝖙𝖊𝖉 𝕽𝖊𝖌𝖎𝖘𝖙𝖊𝖗 OF
THE WISDOM REVEALED HEREIN

☆ ☆ ☆

THE UNITED MISTAKES OF AMERICA
THE NEW AMENDMENTS TO THE NEW CONSTITUTION

FOOTNOTES TO HISTORY
Seventeen More Amendments to Address Three More Problems
Booze, Servants, and Suffrage

The warmest friends and the best supporters the Constitution
has do not contend it is free from imperfections; . . .
the remedy must come hereafter.

GEORGE WASHINGTON, 1787

Let us . . . correct the crude essays of our first and unexperienced,
although wise, virtuous, and well-meaning councils. . . . Let us provide
in our Constitution its revision at stated periods.

THOMAS JEFFERSON, 1816

While our problems may be new, what is required to overcome them
is not. . . . What is required is a new declaration of independence,
not just in our nation, but in our own lives.

BARACK OBAMA, 2009

I got this.

KEVIN BLEYER, 2012

THEIR BELOVED BELL WAS IN JEOPARDY.

It had hung dutifully for decades, pealing hourly from its steeple above the Pennsylvania State House, breaking the peace of the Philadelphia streets only to remind its citizens that time had marched on and all was well. But these were no longer peaceful times. It was 1777, a year after America had declared her independence from the British Crown, and only days after her lionhearted general George Washington had suffered a withering defeat at the Battle of Brandywine. All signs were that Philadelphia, the revolutionary capital, might well be the next to fall. Fearing that the king's men would melt any metal they found into British cannons, a few American patriots confiscated their own bell—soon to be known, appropriately, as the Liberty Bell—and hid it in the safest place they could find: under a pile of horse manure. The gambit worked. The marauding redcoats never got their British hands on our American Liberty.

The lesson learned back then rings as clear today: Sometimes, in order to save something we cherish, we have to shit on it.

USA FIRST CLASS FOREVER!

Don't mock the Constitution! Don't make fun of it. Don't suggest that it's not American to abide by what the founding fathers set up. It's worked pretty well for over 200 years.

Senator Barack Obama, 2008

Hey guys—we should hide the Liberty Bell under a pile of manure!

Well-meaning American revolutionary soldier, 1777

FOREWORD
If Not Me, Who?

P AY ATTENTION. THIS IS IMPORTANT.

A man named Rexford Guy Tugwell, who actually existed—and whose cartoonish name, therefore, I did not make up—spent the last thirty years of his life trying to rewrite the Constitution of the United States. Before his death in 1979, he composed thirty-two separate drafts of a revised Constitution, a new and improved set of guiding principles he hoped would be appropriate to the modern times, accepted by his government, and embraced by his nation.

He failed.

His attempt, it pains me to gloat, was widely regarded as the lunatic ravings of a misguided crank, not least because Tugwell, if not quite a raving lunatic, was widely regarded as a misguided crank. Although he completed his self-imposed fool's errand and published his draft with a reputable publisher who frankly should have known better (it rhymes with Marper's Hagazine), his proposals were far too *nutballs* for even the indulgent sensibilities of the 1970s:

Replace the fifty states with twenty republics. Elect the president to one nine-year term. Add two branches of government. Eliminate the Senate. Rename the United States of America "the Newstates of America."

Yeah, I know.

Nutballs.

He had fooled many people, even presidents, for decades. Armed with a degree in agricultural economy from Wharton in the 1920s, Tugwell was a vocal part of Franklin D. Roosevelt's so-called "Brain Trust" and served as an architect of the New Deal in the 1930s. He was even featured on the cover of *Time* magazine in 1934, five years before Hitler was so honored. You know, back when it meant something.

Then things got weird. Tugwell, a devotee of the literature of "revolt and reconstruction," became the first (and, mercifully, only) head of FDR's notorious Resettlement Administration, a federal agency tasked with relocating the urban poor to the suburbs. Tugwell took to the gig like a pig to mud; it wasn't long before he and the agency were attacked for being socialist and utopian and just a little bit *nutballs*—something about a crazy notion "to relocate the urban poor to the suburbs." (There were other early signs of his troubling lack of judgment. During a 1927 junket to the Soviet Union, Tugwell missed a six-hour meeting with Joseph Stalin because he lost track of time while touring a collective farm; to repeat, Tugwell was too busy *studying Communism* to meet with *Joseph Stalin*. It is not hard to see why people took to calling him "Rex the Red.") Unable to convince people he wasn't totally nutballs, while simultaneously being totally nutballs, Tugwell resigned from his position in FDR's administration. Apparently taking his desire to get off the fast track far too literally, he went to work for the American Molasses Company—whose name, it must be said, I also did not make up. For two long years as a molasses magnate, Tugwell lived a sweet, sweet life.

One last hurrah in American politics beckoned, when New York mayor Fiorello La Guardia appointed Tugwell chairman of the New York City Planning Commission—which, we can assume, is why all the "darker" pigeons are now uptown. Here, too, Tugwell ruffled feathers, insisting publicly that his commission was no less than "the Fourth Power of Government"—news to both Mayor La Guardia and Park Commissioner Robert Moses. Again, he lasted a mere two years, or as it was officially declared, one million, fifty-one thousand, eight hundred ninety-seven New York minutes.

His options exhausted, Tugwell went south. In 1942, he became the governor of Puerto Rico, having received zero votes and having won no election; at the time, the Puerto Rican governorship was an appointed position, and FDR was more than happy to appoint him—and point him—as far away as possible. For four years as governor of the small tropical archipelago—we can presume—Tugwell lived a *vida muy, muy loca*. Some measure of his success might be surmised by the fact that soon after he left office, the position became an elective one; the people of Puerto Rico insisted on their right to choose their leader.

It was then, as the 1950s approached, that Tugwell began having bright ideas. The twentieth century was already half over, and as the nation marched toward its 200th birthday, he began to feel that its creaky Constitution was nothing to celebrate—that our "basic laws," inadequate to our modern needs, needed total "reassessment." So, much like Alexis de Tocqueville, but exactly the opposite—Tocqueville traveled throughout America to learn its virtues; Rex the Red ditched America to catalog its faults—Tugwell began to write a series of articles, which turned into a small library of books, which turned into one heck of a delusion of grandeur: that he, the guy who missed the meeting with Stalin, who had spent years making a sweetener for baked beans, and who was best known as the former governor of Spanish-speaking Puerto Rico, should rewrite the Constitution of the United States of America.

A mere thirty years later, he had rewritten our preeminent founding document. No one noticed. At the time of his death, he was a little-known academic living in Santa Barbara, a footnote in Puerto Rican history books.

While I mock his failure, I admire his cojones. For Rexford Guy Tugwell, agricultural economist, pseudo-Communist, actual person, nutball, may have been a misguided crank (everyone says so), yet he tried—and failed—to do what I have yet only failed to try.

That ends now.

ME THE PEOPLE

ME THE PEOPLE
An Order to Form a More Perfect Union

E HAVE MADE A TERRIBLE MISTAKE.

And by *we*, I mean *you*. You have made a terrible mistake. As a citizen of the United States of America, you have put your faith in a four-page document written by farmers, scrawled on animal skin, disseminated more than two centuries ago, conceived in desperation in the aftermath of war, composed in the language of the country it was intended to spurn, and, not for nothing, scribbled by hand with the quill of a goose.

And because you have made a terrible mistake, and because—lamentably—*you* and *I* together count as *we*, "we" have made a terrible mistake.

We the People.

But really, I blame you.

When Alexander Hamilton said, "The people are turbulent and changing; they seldom judge or determine right," he wasn't talking about himself. He wasn't talking about *we*. And certainly not *me*.

He was talking about you.

You the persons.

You have been told, promised, and guaranteed—and since you seldom judge or determine right, you have foolishly chosen to believe—that the Constitution is your great protector, as flawless in its foresight as it is eloquent in its expression, equal parts holy water, force field, security blanket, instruction manual, and swiss army knife—delivering a more perfect union, establishing justice, insuring domestic tranquility, providing for the common defence, promoting the general welfare, and securing the Blessings of Liberty.

The Killer App of governance.

But ask yourself, if the Constitution is such an astonishing document, such a landmark piece of literature, why no Pulitzer? Why no Nobel Prize?

If this supposed "American masterpiece" is so darn revolutionary, why was it never declared one of the "Ten Best Reads" of 1787? And did you even notice that "defence" is misspelled? How embarrassing. For all the Constitution's vaunted glories, it hasn't even been spell-checked. This is our Founding Document? (Quick, someone put that in a display case. It belongs in a muzeum.)

It is emblazoned on signs at political rallies, where it is as often quoted as it is misquoted. It is cited on the floor of Congress, by lawmakers who only defend the parts they like. It has been fetishized and refashioned as the pristine blueprint of a bygone era, a better era, an era we should long to return to, or at least mimic as closely as possible. In October 2010, *The Wall Street Journal* reported not just a growing obsession with the Constitution, but a spike in the sales of powdered wigs. On a particularly historic election night in 2009, no less than Speaker of the House John Boehner insisted that all the American people want is "a government that honors the Constitution" and, when he held up his pocket-sized version at a Tea Party rally in his home state, said: "I'm going to stand here with the Founding Fathers, who wrote in the preamble, 'We hold these truths to be self-evident, that all men are created equal.'" It was a pitch-perfect recitation, and the assembled crowd ate it up. Never mind that it was not the preamble to the Constitution or anything else. It was the second sentence of the Declaration of Independence.

John Boehner needn't be ashamed. In his ignorance, he is truly a representative of the people. According to a 1987 study, eight out of ten Americans believed, as he did that day, that the phrase "all men are created equal" is in the Constitution. Almost nine in ten swore that "*of* the people, *by* the people, *for* the people" is in the Constitution, too, even though it is *of* the Gettysburg Address, *by* President Abraham Lincoln, and *for*-crying-out-loud-didn't-anyone-ever-teach-them-that? Most egregious: Nearly half thought that "From each according to his ability, to each according to his need" was written by James Madison, not Karl Marx. (Although they couldn't have fingered constitutional author Madison in a lineup of the Framers and would no doubt have guessed Karl Marx was Groucho's brother.)*

Same as it ever was. Way back in 1847, only sixty years after the Constitution was adopted, the governor of New York, Silas Wright, was al-

---

* In 2006, according to a Zogby poll, more American teenagers could name the Three Stooges than the three branches of government.

ready grumbling, appropriately, that "no one familiar with the affairs of our government, can have failed to notice how large a proportion of our statesmen appear never to have read the Constitution of the United States with a careful reference to its precise language and exact provisions, but rather, as occasion presents, seem to exercise their ingenuity . . . to stretch both to the line of what they, at the moment, consider expedient." Which is a fancy way of saying what Senator Robert Byrd echoed in 2005: "People revere the Constitution yet know so little about it—and that goes for some of my fellow senators."* For two centuries, we have been expected to abide by it, live by it, swear by it—some of us, officially—yet we have no idea what it says.

So is it any wonder, I ask you, that President George W. Bush once called it, and I quote, *a goddamned piece of paper?*

Not to me.

Because unlike you, I googled that quote just now. Apparently it is "apocryphal"—which I *also* googled, and learned is another way of saying "not true." Never happened. Bogus. Evidently, a few years ago a left-wing muckraker spread the rumor that when one of the president's aides advised him not to renew the PATRIOT Act—on account of it being unconstitutional—the president said, "Stop throwing the Constitution in my face. It's just a goddamned piece of paper!"

Oh sure, there is some *truthiness* to it—but it is, nonetheless, a lie. The forty-third president of the United States never said that the Constitution he swore an oath to uphold "to the best of his ability, through rain, or sleet, or gloom of night" (note to self: google "presidential oath of office") was just "a goddamned piece of paper." After all, it couldn't possibly be a goddamned *piece of paper*—not when our *third* president had already, and long ago, declared it "a mere thing of wax." Thomas Jefferson, not long after the Constitution was in force, lamented aloud that the justices of the Supreme Court had already usurped the right of "exclusively explaining the Constitution" and therefore could, as the nation's first judicial activists, "twist and shape [it] into any form they please," like so much revolutionary Play-Doh. By calling dibs on the first constitutional metaphor, Jefferson has beaten Bush to the punch by two hundred years. It is no goddamned piece of paper, Mr. President; it is a mere thing of wax.

Fine. But even if the Constitution isn't a goddamned piece of paper,

* Let us hope that none of those senators were among the one in five Americans who claimed that the First Amendment guarantees them "the right to drive."

could the case be made that President Bush *treated* it like one? Sure it could. Most presidents do. That President Bush, and other presidents, have regarded the Constitution as a goddamned piece of paper is impossible to deny. The moment they take their hands off the inaugural Bible, having publicly sworn undying fealty to the Constitution, they secretly resent its existence.

For a head of state, the Constitution is a pain in the ass. It limits their powers and dampens their ambitions. There is an entire section—Article II—devoted to restricting what the president can, and dictating what the president must, do with his day. (Imagine if there were an entire section in our country's founding document insisting that *you* "shall receive Ambassadors" at *your* home.) It's no surprise that presidents try to cut constitutional corners, and it's no wonder that American history is riddled with egregious examples. Minor infractions, such as:

The Alien and Sedition acts of 1798—courtesy of President Adams

The suspension of habeas corpus—compliments of President Lincoln

The Palmer Raids and the suppression of free speech after World War I—thoughtful gifts from President Wilson

The internment of Japanese Americans during World War II—a considerate contribution care of President Franklin Delano Roosevelt

Trumped-up trials for treason during McCarthyism—bons mots from Presidents Truman and Eisenhower

The wiretapping of dissenters during Vietnam—delicious truffles served up by Presidents Johnson and Nixon

So when President Bush ultimately decided to renew the possibly unconstitutional PATRIOT Act, it may have been, historically speaking, the most presidential thing he ever did. He turned a goddamned piece of paper into a mere thing of wax.

As he often said, September 11th changed everything.

★ ★ ★

To suggest that violating the Constitution is somehow uncommon, or unpresidential, or, worse, un-American overlooks an inconvenient truth: namely, that if not for a flagrant violation of the Constitution—known more charitably as the Louisiana Purchase—by none other than Thomas Jefferson, we'd hardly recognize the country we see on so many elementary school maps. America wouldn't be America. If the third president of the United States hadn't shrugged off the document he had sworn to protect "by hook or by crook" (note to self: *seriously man*, google the presidential oath of office already) and doubled the size of the nation with the stroke of a pen—even though the Constitution gave him no such authority—the western coast of America would be the eastern bank of the Mississippi. We would be crowning thy good with brotherhood from sea to shining St. Louis.

Jefferson knew it, too. In embarking on the most aggressive executive action in history, he was quite aware he was sticking his neck out too far. The Constitution might not approve. "The Executive," he wrote, referring to himself, "in seizing the fugitive occurrence which so much advances the good of the country, *have done an act beyond the Constitution.*"*

Jefferson rationalized his decision, telling himself that his act of subversion was a vote of confidence in his fledgling nation—"I did this for your good," he wrote, plainly. His guilty conscience even spurred him to devise an excuse if the pitchfork-wielding guardians of the Constitution came knocking at his door. "I thought it my duty to risk myself for you." It is a startling admission for any president of the United States: His sworn assignment was (thank you, Google) to "preserve, protect and defend" the Constitution; his higher duty was to thwart it.

Like presidents to follow, Jefferson bargained with himself that this was a *one-time deal.* No precedent was likely to be set, since *we the people* would never allow it. "The good sense of our country," he insisted, "will correct the evil of construction when it shall produce evil effects." Spoken like a man who has never watched reality television. (One gets the sense that Jefferson, whose America was filled with citizens of "good sense," and Hamilton, who believed that people "seldom judge or determine right," didn't exactly hang with the same crowd.) Still, as Jefferson saw it,

---

* The italics are mine, the defiance of the Constitution is *all his.*

only by violating the Constitution—by no means a presidential act—could he double the size of our Republic as it struggled to spark to life—a *very* presidential act. If expanding the size of America is wrong, he didn't want to be right; it was his duty to risk himself for us.

So as tempting as it may be, We the People shouldn't point the finger at our presidents as they drive by in their bulletproof Suburbans on the way to their affairs of state and/or impeachment proceedings. They're not the problem. Rather, at this defining moment in history, we must point the finger *at* history and admit an unalienable fact that has become all too self-evident:

It's the Constitution's fault.

It's flawed. Broken. Practically *begging* to be violated. One might even call it "radically defective"—especially if one were, say, the noted constitutional historian Sanford Levinson of the University of Texas Law School. In his estimation, "a substantial responsibility for the defects in our polity lies in the Constitution itself." See? Even constitutional scholars agree: It's the Constitution's fault. It has utterly failed in its simplest of duties: to solve all our problems, secure all our freedoms, and answer every single question put to it. Is that too much to ask?

So let me dispel some myths.

No, President Bush, the Constitution is *not* a goddamned piece of paper, no matter what you didn't say; if anything, God would praise a document that gave Him so much credit.

And sorry, Thomas Jefferson, the Constitution is not a "mere thing of wax"; you're thinking of a "candle."

And James Madison—don't think *you're* off the hook, sir—when you called your Constitution "a dead letter, until life and validity had been breathed into it by the voice of the people," your feigned humility was self-evident; spare us your hot air.

Goddamned piece of paper, mere thing of wax, dead letter—it is none of these things. Rather, the Constitution of the United States of America, which supposedly guarantees everything from the Blessings of Liberty to an unabridged right to free speech, is in my expert humble opinion, a God-sanctioned, fully realized, blessed, immutable, rock-solid, entirely glorified, and purely calcified . . . piece of [censored].

And I say that with all due [redacted].*

---

* *See?* I've just proved my point.

★ ★ ★

Now, before you string me up for treason—as provided, conveniently, by Article III, section 3—keep in mind that I am not saying anything George Washington didn't say first. Just a day after he put his name to the Constitution, the Father of Our Country admitted his own contempt for the Framers' handiwork, decrying the final draft as a wishy-washy document that invited too many interpretations, a "child of fortune, to be fostered by some and buffeted by others."* Naturally, one might expect that the man who presided over the Convention that designed the Constitution, and who would become the first president in charge of defending it "come hell or high water" (note to self: I thought you googled this), and who was the very first to sign on its dotted line, would extol its many virtues. Not so. All he could offer was a punt: "What will be the General opinion, or the reception of it, is not for me to decide; nor shall I say anything for or against it." (Which is Founder-speak for *if you don't have anything nice to sayeth, don't sayeth anything at all*.) What was the General's most glowing review of the document on that day? And I quote: "It is the result of four months' deliberation."

Ouch.

He might as well have complimented the penmanship.

A week later, in a letter to the Anti-Federalist leader Patrick Henry—the same Patrick Henry who had famously demanded "liberty or death!" and who was now demanding one darn good reason to support this Constitution in the upcoming ratification debates—Washington still couldn't muster anything resembling a rave. "I wish the Constitution, which is offered, had been more perfect," he wrote. "But I sincerely believe it is the best that could be obtained at this time."

Mr. Soon-to-be-President, could you find *nothing* to applaud? If not the penmanship, then the margins? The tautness of the vellum? Something. *Anything*. Perhaps I could suggest the Unique and surprising, albeit Indiscriminate, use Of capitaliZation?

nO?

One suspects that when Washington stepped up to sign the document on that September day, he did so reluctantly. One almost imagines that as he held his quill with one hand, he held his nose with the other. Heck, one

---

* On this matter, he was quite correct. Say what you will about George Washington: He may have had wooden teeth, but he had great vision.

doesn't have to almost imagine. All one has to do is take a closer look, because that's exactly what happened:

WASHINGTON WEPT HERE
Scene at the Signing of the Constitution of the United States, During
Which Occasion Did General George Washington Register His Most
Evident Disapproval, *by Howard Chandler Christy*

Washington wasn't the only one holding his nose. Fellow Virginian Edmund Randolph refused to sign entirely, unhappy with the "dangerous
power given ... to Congress." George Mason and Elbridge Gerry also
gave an official thumbs-down. Ben Franklin consented only because he
could "expect no better." Even Madison, the so-called Father of the Constitution, felt the Constitution failed to "prevent the local mischiefs" that
got them into this mess in the first place.

Even a cursory reading of the Constitution in its original flawed form
reveals a self-evident truth George Washington could only admit reluctantly, many Framers tried to hide, and I shall now reveal: It's simply not
worth the sheep carcass it's printed on. With the benefit of two hundred
years of clear-eyed retrospect, its inherent defects are endless and obvious.
Beyond the fact that it's downright incomprehensible, even for the
Founders—from the beginning, the Anti-Federalist Patrick Henry thought
it "of such an intricate and complicated nature, that no man on this earth
can know its real operation"—in just the research I did to write this paragraph (and I have the footnotes to prove it), I have come to learn that despite filling a mere four pages, the Constitution contains a multitude of
mistakes. For starters (deep breath), it discredits the notion of *equality* (am

I right, suffragists?),* stays far too open to *interpretation* (am I right, enemy combatants?),† fails even to mention the word "slavery" (am I right, slaves?)‡ or the word "democracy" (the Framers found the concept too ... democratic)§ or the word "privacy" (a concept central to one of the most divisive issues in the American debate, the right to abortion),¶ plays *favorites* among the states (giving the tiny population of Wyoming as many senators as the massive state of California),\\ is blatantly *xenophobic* (give us "your huddled masses" but don't expect any of them to become "President Arnold Schwarzenegger")** and unnecessarily *ageist* (anyone can grow up to be president, but not until they're at least thirty-five years old), has no respect for the will of the *majority* (the president has lost the presidential election, votes-wise, at least twice),†† set the trap for a paralyzing stalemate in the first too-close-to-call presidential election of 1800 (and, not indirectly, the 1804 murder of its very own advocate, Treasury Secretary Alexander Hamilton, by Aaron Burr, its very own vice president),‡‡ misspells the commonwealth of *Pensylvania*,§§ and features at least four obvious *typos,* including the use of "it's" instead of "its" (my personal pet peeve) and a rogue *comma* in the Fifth Amendment that allows the government to steal your house (some say it's a rogue *comma,* others insist it's a *smudge*).¶¶ Not to mention perhaps the most distressing legacy of all: The Constitution, designed to "insure domestic tranquility," actually *caused the Civil War.*\\\\

As if typos weren't bad enough.

Some major, some minor, but these complaints are merely prologue—I believe the term of art is "preamble"—to the most embarrassing embarrassment of all regarding the Constitution of the United States: that in spite of its supposed American provenance and its claim to be the most American document ever produced, it is British.

Yes, British.

---

* The Constitution of the United States of America, 1787.
† Ibid.
‡ Ibid.
§ Ibid.
¶ Ibid.
\\ Ibid.
** Ibid.
†† Ibid.
‡‡ Ibid.
§§ Ibid.
¶¶ Ibid.
\\\\ Seriously, it did.

As in *England.*

As in *the country that got us into this mess.*

Despite the stiff-upper-lip service the Declaration of Independence gave to dissolving the Political Bands between this new nation and that olde one across the ocean, despite its proclamations of "repeated injuries and usurpations" at the hands of King George that so provoked the colonists, despite Thomas Paine's insistence that "an island cannot rule a continent," the Framers (who, I hasten to add, weren't even born in the United States), based their Constitution on, and thereby pledged their allegiance to, of all things, possibly the single most British thing they could get their American paws on: the Magna Carta.

Now, I know what many of you are thinking: *The Magna what-now?*

It's a fair question. Since Americans reserve their right not to understand their rights, let alone have any idea where they got their rights, allow me to briefly explain: The Constitution is the Magna Carta on steroids. Way back in 1215 on the plains of Runnymede, not far from where Windsor Castle now stands, an assembly of English barons, tired of paying scutage (a fee in lieu of military service) to a cash-strapped and increasingly despotic King John, demanded that their natural rights, which had been

OUR "UNIQUELY AMERICAN" CONSTITUTION: DID YOU KNOW . . . IT'S *BRITISH?*
Compare the Magna Carta, the basis of English law (left), to the supposedly "American" document it inspired, the Constitution of the United States (right).

Scholars agree: They even look *the same.*
Ask yourself: If you couldn't read, could you tell the difference?

handed down through the generations, finally be *written* down, confirmed with the royal seal, and sent to each of the counties to be read to all freemen. Thus was born the Magna Carta, or "Big Carta," and it established that no man—not even the king—was above the law.

Now skip ahead exactly five and half centuries. When the English Parliament enacted the stamp tax of 1765—launching the notorious era of "taxation without representation" that so rankled the Founders—the Massachusetts Assembly quickly referenced the Magna Carta in declaring the tax "null and void." While I applaud the canny method—they used the Englanders' own laws against them—I can't help but point out that it was shockingly shortsighted. The Magna Carta was the basis of all English law, yet in building their uniquely American doctrine, the Framers thought nothing of stealing its tenets, referring specifically to the Magna Carta and its rule of law in declaring the Constitution "the Supreme Law of the Land." The Constitution of the United States was, in this way, a declaration of *de*pendence—to the very country it was trying to shun.

In other words, not long before the Founders defeated the British, they defeated the purpose.

It all makes perfect sense when you consider the fact that George Washington was actually a British spy. Oh, I'm sorry—had you not heard that historical tidbit? George Washington, the first president of the United States, the "indispensable man" of the American Revolution, the revered general who presided over the Constitutional Convention and helped draft one of the founding documents seen above, was a *spy for the British*. It is an indisputable fact. Letters printed in *The Aurora*, the eighteenth-century newspaper edited by Benjamin Franklin's grandson, revealed that Washington, who had suspiciously failed to prevent the British from occupying Philadelphia in 1777, had taken bribes from his overlords in England and was intent on selling out his fellow countrymen for cold hard cash.

George Washington? More like *Benedict Arnold*. (Revolutionary War snap!)

Granted, the rumors may have been hogwash. *Admittedly,* it's possible it was all just a tactic to discredit Washington by those who wished to see him replaced. And okay, fine, I *suppose* the letters were later determined to be forgeries, written by fellow Founders with whom he had fallen out of favor—Thomas Mifflin and Benjamin Rush, the first American playa-haters. So maybe the indisputable facts are disputable. But we live in a different time now, a time when evidence is barely admissible in court, a time when no matter how many birth certificates he produces, President

Obama wasn't born in the United States, a time when no matter how many gay daughters he produces, Vice President Dick Cheney is Darth Vader. So as far as George Washington being a spy or not, I think we can all agree that just raising the question is evidence of its merit. In the end, I'm not saying Washington *was* a spy; I'm just saying that it's an accusation worth considering carefully and propagating thoughtlessly. Heck, I have no reason to believe George Washington was a spy—or, more to the point, *wasn't not* a spy—and for that matter, it's a testament to the Constitutional freedom of expression that he failed to successfully torpedo (what with him being a British spy and all) that we can ask these questions openly, honestly, and without regard to their being in any way true. The point is: Reasonable minds can disagree about whether George Washington, the father of America, was a spy for the British.

(Mr. President, I realize my defence [*sic*] of your patriotism is weak, but please understand, *I sincerely believe it is the best that could be obtained at this time*. I sure *you* can understand. Or should I say *ye*.)

So when you consider all the facts—that George Washington was a spy for the British, that the American Constitution he helped devise was based on the British Magna Carta, and that it therefore contained within its four pages a parade of flaws, a pageant of peccadilloes, a procession of indiscretions and indignities allowing executive, legislative, and judicial malfeasance only a king could love—it's no wonder that the revolutionary radical Patrick Henry famously characterized the new Constitution not as forming "a more perfect union," but as "squinting towards monarchy." From the very beginning, it reeked of meat pies and crumpets. Check your history books, my fellow Americans: It's right there in blacke and whyte.

★ ★ ★

To those who shudder at the thought that anyone might tinker with a founding document, I submit to you: The history of America is one of constant rewrites. I don't mean American history is constantly being rewritten; rather, historic Americans were constantly rewriting things. You name it, the Framers reframed it. George Washington famously rewrote a sixteenth-century set of Jesuit precepts into his own laws of personal etiquette—"roll not the eyes"; "kill no vermin, or fleas"; "do not laugh too loud." Benjamin Franklin, beating his contemporary Noah Webster to the punch by almost ninety years, drafted new definitions for old words, including more than two hundred colorful synonyms for "drunkenness"—*bewitch'd, wamble crop'd, smelt of an onion, with his flag out*. (To say nothing of Franklin's fanatical need to rewrite his Poor Richard's Almanack *every* damn year. The man was clearly incapable of picking a tidal schedule and sticking to it. Either that or he was totally *wamble crop'd*.) Most ruthless with a red pen, however, was Thomas Jefferson. One might expect the man who wrote the Declaration of Independence—and who later condemned the final, edited, 25 percent shorter version as a "mutilation" of his work—to support an original author's vision on principle. Just as one might expect Jefferson, the man who had advocated for the separation of church and state, to think it improper to—brace yourselves, Puritans—*rewrite the Ten Commandments*. Yet, Jefferson did precisely that, offering his own revised Decalogue to trump Moses's—with remarkably trivial injunctions compared to "You Shall Not Murder." Among Jefferson's decrees: "Take things always by the smooth handle." "Never buy what you don't want because it is cheap." "No man ever regretted having eaten too little; eat sparingly." His list may not instill the fear of God in a sinner; but it does strike mortal dread in any dinner guest.

Lest anyone deem his act a mere lark, Jefferson doubled down on his blasphemy by taking the sacrilegious step of rewriting the Bible—not once, but twice. He felt the teachings of the Bible had been corrupted by organized religion—like the Constitution today, it had been co-opted by those with axes to grind. Specifically, Jefferson had grown skeptical of the Gospels, which he thought were "unlettered" and "ignorant," and over time had been tainted by bad memories and misunderstandings. So his first version, *The Philosophy of Jesus,* was a stark distillation of Jesus's wisdom, "the most sublime and benevolent code of morals which has ever been offered to man," which Jefferson constructed by "cutting verse out of the printed book, and by arranging the matter which is evidently His, and which is as distinguishable as diamonds in a dunghill." (You heard right: That's Thomas Jefferson, on record as describing the Bible, or at least the parts he disliked, as a "dunghill"—otherwise known as a pile of shit.)

Years later, unsatisfied with his first try, he even offered a sequel, *The Life and Morals of Jesus of Nazareth.* Armed with a razor blade—yes, an actual razor blade—he literally cut verses from the gospels of Matthew, Mark, Luke, and John and rearranged them in chronological order, mingling the redacted passages to create a single coherent narrative, albeit one that conspicuously left out all the verses dealing with virgin birth, miracles, the Resurrection—what's known as the *strict mysteries,* or *Bible-y parts,* including the Divinity of Christ, the Baptism, and the Eucharist—as well as every other detail Jefferson deemed supernatural, or fantastical, or just made him roll his eyes. No turning water into wine, no healing the sick, no raising Lazarus from the dead. No divine intervention, no heavenly cures. As if Jefferson were asking, "Who believes this stuff? I mean, *Jesus Christ*—the guy's not a miracle worker." Needless to say, this Frankenstein version, which came to be known as *The Jefferson Bible,* was so blasphemous, so sacrilegious, so against the will of God (and, one assumes, so *boring*) that for many years it was given as an official welcome gift to every newly elected member of Congress.

Jefferson's message: Just because it's the Bible doesn't mean you have to treat it like, you know, *the Bible.* Even a sacred text can be brought in for repair. And if even a president refuses to treat the Bible like the inviolable word of God, why should I, a mere citizen with a word processor, treat the Constitution so?

I shouldn't. I should feel free to rewrite, revise, and razorblade the Constitution to my heart's content. And as long as I'm careful to remove all the boring, inessential, and irrelevant parts, to make it, as Jefferson said of his effort, "short and precious," I see no reason why Congress wouldn't one day pass it out as party favors.

After all, one of the many virtues of our unique American narcissism is our unrelenting belief that *our version will be better.*

Let me at it, our national motto.

Give me a shot.

From Ambassador to France Thomas Jefferson in 1786 ("a little rebellion now and then is a good thing") to Defense Secretary Robert Gates in 2009 ("no other country in the world is so willing to change course"), we Americans know that what makes us great is that we're constantly insisting that we're greater.

Anything you can do, We the People can do better.

ONCE MORE, FROM THE TOP

THE MOST GLARING, and glorious, example of this self-evident, inalienable truth? The Constitution *itself* was one big rewrite. Remember the Articles of Confederation? Neither do most. It was America's first "constitution," the Founders' original attempt at laying down a law governing this new country—but one that proved insufficient to the needs of the nation. I shall divulge its many defects soon enough, but suffice it to say that under the

Articles, debts were left unpaid, disputes weren't resolved, and states squabbled over taxes and commerce. America was, as Madison later described, in a "gloomy chaos." If it weren't for those meddling Federalists— Alexander Hamilton, John Adams, and James Madison among them—who made a compelling case for stronger central government, there would *be* no Constitution for United States presidents to swear to defend at their inaugurations. There would, indeed, be no United States presidents.

And yet, when the Framers convened in Philadelphia in 1787, many intended solely to bring the Articles in for a tune-up. To tighten a few screws, change the oil, rotate the tires. They saw no reason to junk the Articles simply because the country was on the wrong track. James Madison, though, had a different idea: He sold them for scrap and started from scratch. For this reason, it is said the Constitution he wrote was more than a revision; it was a revolution. It was a wholesale revision of our guiding laws. But it was also something so much less: just the latest draft. Merely the second version of the first stab at defining our most basic principles.

It is time—high time—for a third. Two hundred long years have passed since George Washington predicted "the people of America" might find the Constitution "less perfect than it can be made." Our country is young, but our Constitution is old—the longest-lasting written national constitution in the world. Our citizenry is vibrant and vital, but let's face it, many of our Founding Fathers were antediluvian and ancient. (Benjamin Franklin was a creaky eighty-one in 1787, so old he had to be carried to the sessions of the Constitutional Convention in a sedan chair. Some say he only signed the Constitution because it was on his Bucket List.) We have gotten good at being America and we have naturally inflated our sense of ourselves and our society, but our Constitution needs to be adjusted for that inflation. Not simply brought in for maintenance. More than nipped. More than tucked. No longer should we settle for confusion about what the Constitution says, or means. No longer should we give politicians free rein to exploit it, hide behind it, or find loopholes in its imperfections.

My fellow Americans, the time for "more perfect" unions has passed. *We the People* deserve perfection, and *Me the People* shall deliver it.

★ ★ ★

At this point, despite the fact that between the two of us I'm the one doing the heavy lifting here, you might still be wondering why I, Kevin Bleyer, should be allowed to rewrite the Constitution. Granted, I may not have majored in Constitution Writing in college, but neither did James Madison, and *he* got to write one. And true, I may have no experience founding a country, but I ask you: Did any of the signers of the Declaration of Independence? I think not.

Therefore I am.

To be sure, there are dozens of reasons why I should be in charge here, but for starters let me just say that *I hold these truths to be self-evident:* that All Men Are Created Equal, and that I Was Born to Do This.

But if you want to me to be more specific:

Self-evident truth #1: I've read the Constitution.

You haven't. Not recently, anyhow.

Self-evident truth #2: I care enough.

Specifically, I care more than you do. I'd even bet I have read more books about the Constitution in preparation for writing this book than you have before reading this book. Not to mention, one of us actually wrote this book; the other is just reading it.

Self-evident truth #3: I have no shame.

Unlike the Founders, who used a litany of anonymous pseudonyms— Publius, Pacificus, Helvidius, Virginian, Africanus, Citizen of the World— when they wrote essays defending their arguments, I am perfectly content to use my given name. And not just because all the good pseudonyms— Lady Gaga, Mr. T, Meatloaf, Seal, Wonkette, Hulk Hogan, Twiggy, Ludacris, Conan O'Brien—are already taken.

Self-evident truth #4: I am but one man.

This isn't a democracy, people. And that's a good thing. The Founders didn't trust democracy—even Jefferson said it was "impracticable beyond the limits of a town." And they walked the walk. Only thirty-something delegates attended the Constitutional Convention on a given day; strictly speaking, "we the people" were less than a few dozen old white guys who presumed to speak on behalf of an entire nation. In fact, the problem with the final Constitution, according to Ben Franklin, was precisely that it was a group effort. "When you assemble a number of men to have the advantage of their joint wisdom," he said, "you inevitably assemble with those men, all their prejudices, their passions, their errors of opinion, their local

interests, and their selfish views. From such an assembly can a perfect production be expected?" No, it can't. So I'll take it from here, thanks.

SELF-EVIDENT TRUTH #5: I AM OLD ENOUGH.

When he wrote the Constitution, James Madison was a mere thirty-seven
years old. Delegate Charles Pinckney, who later claimed *he* wrote the Constitution, was twenty-nine. But the youngest delegate to the Convention,
Jonathan Dayton, was a scant twenty-six. Let the record show I am old
enough to be his slightly older brother. The one with the good judgment,
and the awesome record collection.

SELF-EVIDENT TRUTH #6: I AM YOUNG ENOUGH.

As the historian Joseph Ellis points out, the Framers are "a finite number
of long-dead men." Surely they won't mind if someone else steps up to the
plate. Someone living, say. After all, it was none other than George Washington himself who, in a 1787 letter to his nephew Bushrod—yes, Washington had a nephew named Bushrod—wrote, "I do not think we are more
inspired, have more wisdom, or possess more virtue, than those who will
come after us." He was talking about me. *I* came after him. I am inspired,
and wise, and virtuous. Like the Founding Fathers before me, I am like the
Founding Fathers before me.

Washington said so himself.

And it was none other than Thomas Jefferson who, when he took it
upon himself to write the Constitution for the new Louisiana Territory,
admitted he did so in the same spirit as do I—"with boldness more than
wisdom"—and who decades earlier even mentioned me in a letter to James
Madison explicitly advocating the principle of constitutional revision: "By
the law of nature, one generation is to another as one independent nation
is to another. . . . The earth belongs to the living and not the dead." You
heard the man: the living! Not the dead! His description fits me *to a T.* I
am alive, which is more than can be said of some Founders I can think of.

Among my many qualifications, one distinguishes me from all others. Of
all the pretenders to the throne, of all the people who would rewrite history
in order to secure a better future, whether he be James "Father of the Constitution" Madison or Thomas "My Bible Is Better" Jefferson or Rexford
Guy "Nutball" Tugwell, I am, indisputably, the most recent. I am the "living
generation" Jefferson would be so proud of, if he were alive to see us today.

And by *us*, I mean *me*. After all, I am you, only more so. And it is precisely because I am you, and therefore no better than you, that I am more

qualified than you to speak on behalf of you. Which is why I am going to rewrite the Constitution, and you are not. It all makes perfect sense.

Am I too late? Possibly. Two centuries of inertia have taken their toll. Wars have been fought. Climates have changed. Laser printers have been invented. The "innovations of time," as Jefferson put it, called for updating the Constitution long ago. But at this defining moment in America, I am reminded of an old Chinese proverb: "The best time to plant a tree is twenty years ago; the second-best time is *now*." The lesson is obvious: If we plant a tree *now*, just imagine how many new Constitutions we can print up when, in twenty years, we cut it down.

There's no time to waste.

In order to form a More Perfect Union, we need an order to form a more perfect union. So let me be your quill, your soapbox, your veto pen, your bully pulpit, your lamplighter, your flamethrower, your fellow American, your goodwill ambassador, your Quorum of One, your heroic savior, and your humble servant.

Like Thomas Jefferson before me, I think it my duty to risk myself for you.

E Unum, Pluribus . . .

★ ★ ★

Abraham Lincoln knows what I'm talking about. On the day he was to sign the Emancipation Proclamation, President Lincoln was willing in mind, but not in body. "I believe, in this measure, my fondest hopes will be realized," he told his good friend Joshua Speed, who rarely left his side. "If ever my soul were in an Act, it is in this Act."

Yet, that morning at a New Year's reception, Lincoln had shaken the hands of a thousand of his fellow citizens, and knew the toll it had taken on his own. Speed urged Lincoln make haste and sign the pronouncement, but he demurred. "If I sign with a shaking hand," Lincoln explained, "posterity will say, '*he hesitated.*'" So he waited until he could take up the pen and sign with a clear, strong, and unwavering signature.

In that spirit, I, too, take up a pen and sign, with my full soul and my unwavering signature, a commitment by *Me the People* to *You the Persons* that *I the Patriot* will rewrite a new Covenant, a new Constitution, fashioned for our new times.

Never let it be said I hesitated,

Kevin B. Bleyer

THE
NEW
CONSTITUTION OF
THE UNITED STATES OF AMERICA

———

THE PREAMBLE
TO THE NEW CONSTITUTION

It's Greek to Thee

E THE PEOPLE of the United Flight 3247 from New York to Amsterdam, in order to catch a connecting Delta flight into Athens, had a range of reasons for taking a trip to Greece: establish suntans, ensure non-domestic tranquility, provide for the common photo ops, promote the general tourism industry, and secure the tchotchkes of democracy for ourselves, our posterity, and our mantels back home.

Only one of us hoped to establish a new Constitution for the United States of America.

Only one of us boarded his flight unconcerned with where to get the best souvlaki or the dirtiest deck of "Greek Erotic Art" playing cards, but obsessed with how to rebuild our American foundation from Greece's toppled columns and crumbled pediments.

Only one of us secretly knew that by the time he had studied the structure of Athenian government, after he was done dismantling the foundations of Greek democracy, when he had stolen and scavenged the best parts of the famous ancient city-states, these famous ruins would be in ruins.

Kevin Bleyer.

Seat 7B.

This should have happened long ago. By Thomas Jefferson's math, the Constitution of the United States should have been rewritten eleven times by now.

The third president of the United States, and, as such, one of our Founderest, believed the Constitution he helped birth should "naturally expire at the end of nineteen years." From his distant perch in Paris, where he was serving as minister to France—and perhaps not coincidentally, where he was having an affair with a married woman sixteen years his junior—he wrote to his good friend James Madison, "The earth belongs always to the living generation. . . . No society can make a perpetual constitution." (And certainly no single man—especially one busy flirting with teenagers.) Never mind that Madison had just spent two years shepherding the document through ratification, hoping to make his constitution as perpetual as possible; in insisting on revisions every nineteen years, Jefferson meant business. "If it be enforced longer," Jefferson insisted, "it is an act of force, and not of right."*

Although he wasn't successful in convincing Madison of the wisdom of his suggestion—since 1789, by my math, there has been only one Constitution—Jefferson's diagnosis was nevertheless accurate: The Constitution we've been living with has been dead for over two centuries.

Flat-lined.

Kaput.

But thankfully, not yet buried.

Which is why, on this day in August, I'm sitting in coach on a plane to Athens. To single-handedly revive the Constitution of the United States of America. To turn Madison's "dead letter" back into something resembling a "living document." To breathe new life into our most cherished founding charter.

Really, it's the most I can do.

★ ★ ★

I do not judge my fellow travelers. Under usual circumstances—when not, say, rewriting the American Constitution—I am as superficial as they are. When I flew to Africa, it was to see the animals. When I visited Moscow, it was so I could take pictures in Red Square. My trip to Ireland was as much about the Celtic music and the Guinness as the Troubles. They were vacations, and if I picked up any history along the way—hey, gravy.

I am an American, after all, and it is an unmistakable feature of American Exceptionalism that we Americans know what's important: namely, *we Americans*. We are, in the words of genuine British person Eddie Izzard, "the self-choosing chosen people." So certain are we about our special status in the world that we take pride in how little interest we show in things that *aren't* American. We revel in the fact that we don't understand, can't locate on a map, or almost deny the existence of, other countries. If it's Greek to us, it's Greek to us—even if, strictly speaking, it's Chinese.

---

* Jefferson even proposed an immediate addition to Madison's Constitution: a sunset clause, an automatic trigger to be included that would ensure every new generation be allowed to rewrite the Constitution—*their* Constitution—to add whatever bells and whistles are necessary to make its freedoms ring anew. It should, he thought, be open source, public domain, remixable by every new generation—like Bieber sampling a Kanye version of an Otis Redding tune.

Mind you, this is no mere supposition on my part; our lack of global awareness is a measurable, statistical fact. In 2010, when asked what percentage of our gross domestic product should be sent as humanitarian aid to foreign countries, 92 percent of Americans responded, "Wait a minute— there are *foreign* countries?"* *We the People* take no heed of *They the Foreigners*. We make no bones about our lack of interest in our fellow man, and we offer him no apologies—because, we figure, our fellow man lives halfway around the world, and really, what's he gonna do about it?

It is much easier to feel unique when you assume that you are alone.

It wasn't always this way. Americans of the Founders' generation weren't the domestic navel gazers we have come to be. On the contrary, they were enchanted by a particular part of the world most had never visited, nor ever coud visit: namely, ancient Greece, and its ancient Greco-Roman partner, Rome. In the late eighteenth century, even for the American revolutionaries who had, let's say, more pressing local concerns, involving redcoats and Hessian mercenaries, Greece and Rome were on the brain. Commoners in the eighteenth century leafed through the works of Homer and took their history from Livy and Thucydides. Citizens of what would become the nation's capital meandered down the banks of the Potomac, which they affectionately called the Tiber, after the river that flows through Rome. They were far more likely to name their horses Gracchus and Plutarch than Trigger or Silver. They called their slaves Claudius, Jupiter, Caesar, and Pompey—and even the slaves, though they lacked for education, were familiar with their namesakes. Greece captivated the most common citizen. According to Fergus Bordewich, a talented historian whose parents clearly hated him, Americans of the eighteenth century "embraced their idealized vision of Rome . . . with a credulity that, from a twenty-first-century vantage point, itself seems quaintly antique." Quaintly antique, perhaps, but totally impressive, too.

For their part, the Founders' interest in Greece and Rome was more than mere pandering to the masses; they meant business. It bordered on the obsessive. Thomas Jefferson, who insisted that architectural plans throughout the capital city steal from the ancients down to the size of the ancient Roman brick—"twenty-two inches long, eleven inches wide, and two inches thick"—saw a study of the distant past as a pathway to a glorious future. He "believed with an almost religious passion," Bordewich writes, "in the power of the colonnades, domes, and marble porticoes to ennoble the human spirit and sharpen the intellect." To design many of the buildings in the capital,

* According to a poll conducted by Some Company I Made Up.

Jefferson handpicked Benjamin Latrobe, who, despite being British, was a self-described "bigot" on behalf of Athenian aesthetics. Rome found a home in D.C. as well; when shown the blueprints for the "Congress House," Jefferson took a red quill to the design, crossing out the two words and replacing them with one—"Capitol"—to directly invoke the famous temple of Jupiter Optimus Maximus—perhaps thinking, *We're stealing the Romans' precedent for popular government, we may as well steal their name.*

Jefferson believed in nothing less than a kind of Greco-Roman feng shui. It explains the countless eagles, the marble columns, the Latin and Greek mottoes, the V'S VSED IN PLACE OF U'S WHICH MAKES THEM SO HARD TO VNDERSTAND. He and his fellow Founders borrowed all the Athenian stylings they could to create something perfectly American: an Epcot of Democracy.

★ ★ ★

But in 1787, a decade before D.C. became D.C., the real action was in Philadelphia. And although he was overseas during the pivotal drama of that summer, Jefferson made his presence felt there, too. In the months leading up to the Constitutional Convention, as James Madison prepared for his role shepherding the proceedings in Philadelphia, barely a day went by when Jefferson didn't show up in Madison's mailbox. He sent Madison missives with postmarks from around the globe, news of innovations and modern miracles he had discovered on his travels. Each care package held a wonder of the world intended to expand Madison's horizons: phosphorus matches ("by having them at your bedside with a candle, the latter may be lighted at any moment of the night without getting out of bed"), new cylinder lamps ("thought to give a light equal to six or eight candles"), a government report on mesmerism, a pamphlet on animal magnetism, and the latest reports on developments in the high-flying world of hot-air ballooning.*

But Jefferson knew that the best way to influence Madison was to appeal to his mind. So he sent Madison books—trunkloads of encyclopedias, textbooks, and broadsides, more than two hundred volumes in all. There was no ulterior motive; they were sent merely to deepen Madison's understanding of republican governments throughout history—to guide him through the ruins of the past, including the Helvetic Confederacy of fourteenth-century Switzerland and the Germanic and Belgic confederacies of the seventeenth century. And, of special note: the Amphictyonic and Achean confederacies of Greece.

* With a thrilling account "of Robert's last voiage thro' the air!"

Now, I don't know what half of those words mean (certainly my spell-check is none too happy with them), but the last one rings loud and true. "Greece." Jefferson, who spoke Greek fluently, had a hunch that a study of Grecian government would prove particularly helpful. As he saw it, Greece was "the first of civilized nations [which] presented example of what man should be." He knew (though no doubt it would have been hard for the blissfully ignorant on my flight to believe) that long before Philadelphia was the birthplace of democracy, Greece was the birthplace of democracy.

The books Jefferson sent only whetted Madison's appetite. Madison wrote back to Jefferson asking that he send along more treatises on ancient and modern republics, specifically "the Greek and Roman authors where they can be got very cheap." (Add "stingy" to the list of Madison traits.) He made copious notes about each confederacy, cataloging the keepers and clunkers (those displaying an "intolerance of religion" and suffering a "weakness of the Union," for starters), and he published his findings in *Notes on Ancient and Modern Confederacies*, forty pages covering the minutest details about the Greek confederacies.

Madison's study paid off. After poring through Jefferson's books, he composed *The Vices of the Political System of the United States*, in which he concluded that all confederacies—ancient and modern—suffered from the same "imbecility" that plagued the American government under the Articles of Confederation: a weak central government unable to corral the power of the colonies. As the Constitutional Convention approached, he had his talking point: The thirteen original colonies must become united states.

★ ★ ★

It's one thing to do your homework; it's quite another to take a really cool field trip. (If my fifth grade curriculum is any guide, we can read books about dolphins all we want; only a trip to the aquarium inspires us to be marine biologists.) And that's where our Founding Fathers flubbed. Neither Madison, the father of the Constitution, nor Jefferson, who advised him along the way, *ever went to Greece*. Neither boarded a 757 (or even a hot-air balloon) to the birthplace of the democracy they were hoping to emulate. In Jefferson's travels throughout the Mediterranean, all roads led to Rome (though he made it only as far south as Milan). No roads led to Athens. Madison, a hypochondriac, never even crossed the Atlantic, fearing that a sea voyage would be bad for his health.

They may have believed that Greece was "the first of civilized nations" to present an example "of what man should be," but *really, how would they know?* They steeped themselves in Greece, but they never stepped, themselves, in Greece. They knew not whereof they spoke.

So when I boarded that plane headed to the birthplace of democracy,* I wasn't just revisiting the ancient past or racking up frequent flyer miles. I was remedying a 230-year-old oversight.

In just ten days.

My time would be tight, and the stakes high. I had to get this right. To help my chances, I had even sought out the advice of the most prominent Greek I knew, a woman who has never lost her Greek accent despite having lived in America for twenty years. My email to Arianna Huffington was appropriately lengthy—epic, you might say—explaining in great detail that I was rewriting the Constitution (careful to add, of course, that there was no need to thank me), and then inquiring what I should study while in Greece, who I should talk to, and where I should visit. Not long after came her response:

Oooh. I loooooove Crete.
Sent from my BlackBerry

I chose to assume not that she was too busy to help, or that she didn't take my project seriously, but rather that, like Jefferson, *she, too,* knew that just seeing Greece firsthand was all that my spirit and intellect would need to be sharpened and ennobled. Or was it ennobled and sharpened? I forget. Either way, I'm pretty sure that's what she was getting at.

But it was a start. Crete or Bust. It would be a featured stop on what was quickly becoming a full agenda I was eager to undertake—so that when I turned in my rewritten Preamble, I would be able to say: I have taken the Grand Tour of Democracy. I have circumnavigated the Parthenon. I have watched the changing of the Parliament guards. I have knelt with the monks of the monastery above Megalochori. Like an athlete from antiquity, I have marched into the Panathenaic Stadium (where, as you can see, I placed first. I was always very skilled at imaginary sporting events).

Unlike Madison, I have seen the sunset over Santorini, taken the ferry to Heraklion, gazed into the turquoise waters of Crete (thanks, Arianna!), felt the humid breezes of the Costa Navarino, and bobbed among the salty cerulean waves of both the Aegean and Ionian seas. I have consumed my body weight in souvlaki, eaten capers in Kalamata, feasted on figs, and downed so many olives that this morning I'm pretty sure I pissed a martini.

---

* Bleyer's voiage thro' the air!

*The author, having vanquished his challengers in that
sport in which they were, evidently, competing*

I have explored the cave where Nestor hid the cattle he had stolen from his brother Apollo. I have fancied myself an Olympian in Olympia and a Spartan in Sparta. I have ridden a donkey to the birthplace of Zeus.

I have risked airsickness, seasickness, sunburn, flight delays, and jet lag.

I have climbed, spelunked, excavated, imbibed, and inquired.

I have eaten. I have prayed. I have loved.

Unlike Jefferson, I have seen firsthand "the example of what man should be."

(Clearly, I'd have to hurry. Democracy may have developed over 2,500 years, but I don't have that kind of time. My *voiage back thro' the air* is on Sunday.)

But you get my point: Unlike Madison as he prepared to write *his* Constitution, unlike the Framers of 1787, I will have felt firsthand "the power of the colonnades, domes, and marble porticoes"—including those that had toppled millennia ago.

In my mission to revive the United States Constitution, I would leave no stone unturned, no matter how ancient.

ACROPOLIS NOW

My first stop on this mission to revive the United States Constitution brings my first hiccup: The Acropolis is closed.

The author, seen here putting Thomas Jefferson to shame

It had been welcoming visitors for millennia—just not this particular morning. It seems I have arrived in Greece just in time for democracy to kick in, in the form of a series of general labor strikes—seven this year and counting—to protest harsh austerity measures imposed by a government contending with massive debt. (For years, the economy of the world has been crumbling—and as it has since antiquity, Greece has been leading the way.) So, on my first day, with sunscreen applied, sandals donned, and courage mustered, after a rather taxing walk up Areopagus Hill toward the entrance of the Parthenon, I am turned away like a common tourist. Like someone who wasn't hard at work saving America.

"Open at noon," says the man at the ticket booth, as he points at a sign on the glass, written in English: FOUR-HOUR STRIKE, CULTURE MINISTRY. Rather than let me in to see the Acropolis up close, the country's public service workers have abandoned their stations and convened just outside Parliament, where they are busy chanting slogans and reciting poetry in Syntagma Square. (I learn later that *Syntagma* Square translates to *Constitution* Square, commemorating two Greek soldiers who stormed the palace in 1843, confronted their Bavarian occupiers, and demanded a new constitution be written in thirty days. Gotta say, I've never met them, but I like their style.)

I try not to get frustrated: America has been waiting two hundred years to be rescued, what's a few more hours? Still, for all his trials in returning to Greece—a Cyclops, a beast with six heads, a kingdom of cannibals—I doubt Odysseus had to deal with ticket takers worried about their pensions.

But he didn't cry about it, so neither will I.

Stiff upper lip, Bleyer. Keep it together. You're in Greece now, the land of the Stoics—act like it.

Yet—as I quickly find some shade to watch the protest—I consider that I might shed a tear if I weren't so damn dehydrated.

★ ★ ★

"History doesn't repeat, it rhymes."

MARK TWAIN

For all the talk about its Spartan stoicism, Greece is a country that, from antiquity on, hasn't exactly shrunk from shows of passion. It is a country whose history is told through the epic verse of Homer's *Iliad* and *Odyssey,* whose ancient Panhellenic games featured poetry competitions alongside javelin and discus throws (well, not *too* alongside), and whose prime minister at the time of my visit, George Papandreou, despite being born in Minnesota, despite being the buzzkill who imposed the recent austerity measures, famously wooed his wife with Greek love songs (and the occasional Bob Dylan tune) in late-night serenades.

In the roll call of important professions, the Greeks have always known their priorities, with *poet* at the top of the heap. "The poets are the interpreters of the Gods," said Socrates. "Poetry is nearer to vital truth than history," added Plato. Aristotle, too: "Poetry is finer and more philosophical than history; for poetry expresses the universal."

So then: If our Constitution is so darn Greek, if our Greek-inspired Preamble is expected to express the universal rights we hold dear, by all rights it should be poetry on parchment. If Jefferson's Declaration of Independence is saluted for summoning Milton's "rules of ancient Liberty," it would seem only appropriate that Madison's Preamble should at least get the Constitution started with a little bit of pizzazz.

And yet, I've looked closely. I read it a few times. And I've noticed: There's no Greek in it. No poetry. It has no hint of Homer, Euripides, or Aeschylus—or if there is, it is buried too deep for any casual reader to notice. And by that I mean: It doesn't even rhyme.

So I know this about my new Preamble: At the very least, it would rhyme. My new Preamble would give you a reason to sit up and take notice.

Heck, if we're going to be comparing Preambles—and I say, *let's!*—the Preamble to Madison's Constitution ("We the people of the united states, in order to") pales in comparison to that of Jefferson's Declaration of Independence ("When in the course of human events, it becomes necessary"). I ask you, out of the blocks, which has more oomph? As Christopher Hitchens reminds us, when Lincoln rose to address the mourners at Gettysburg and came to ponder "whether the American ideal could long endure, it was to Jefferson's Declaration of Independence ('four score and seven years' before 1863) and not to the federal Constitution that he applied his moral attention." Indeed, Lincoln made no mention of that *other* preamble, the one written so memorably "three score and sixteenish years ago."

No, Lincoln was swayed by the force of Jefferson's jeremiad:

> When in the course of human events, it becomes necessary for one
> people to dissolve the political bands which have connected them with
> another and to assume among the powers of the earth, the separate
> and equal station to which the Laws of Nature and Nature's God
> entitle them, a decent respect to the opinions of mankind requires that
> they should declare the causes which impel them to the separation.

Jefferson knew how to grab his reader by the scruff: with a little old-school zazz.

Yet just five years later, Jefferson was already defensive about the accusation that "America has not produced one good poet"—a charge levied by the Abbé Raynal, a French Enlightenment writer who probably should have just minded his own business. Jefferson wouldn't disagree. He conceded that, of all the innovations America had produced (hey, they can't all be phosphorus matches), it had yet to produce even a single world-renowned rhymester, promising, *Well, just you wait.* "When we shall have existed as a people as long as the Greeks did before they produced a Homer, the Romans a Virgil, the French a Racine and Voltaire, the English a Shakespeare and Milton, should this reproach be still true, we will enquire from what unfriendly causes it has proceeded, that the other countries and quarters of the earth shall not have inscribed any name in the roll of poets." In the meantime, mind your own beeswax, Frenchie.

Unlike Greece, we had only been open for business eleven years. But that didn't change the fact that in the days leading to the Constitutional Convention, when he was frantically trying to inspire Madison to greatness and Greekness, even Jefferson had to admit: We had no poet.

Which explains how we ended up with this:

> We the People of the United States, in Order to form a more
> perfect Union, establish Justice, insure domestic Tranquility, provide

for the common defence, promote the general Welfare, and secure the Blessings of Liberty to ourselves and our Posterity, do ordain and establish this Constitution for the United States of America.

Uh-huh.

Anyone still awake? I'm sorry, but I nodded off by word twelve. Perhaps that's what they were going for, with all that soporific talk about "tranquility." All I know is that halfway through the first paragraph, the Constitution of the United States already sounds like adults talking in muted trumpets to the Peanuts characters. "In order to do this, this, this, this, and this, we're doing this."

Wah wah wah, wah wah ordain and establish *waaaah.*

Never mind that government has largely failed to deliver on every one of these to-dos, proving that our Constitution is based on a litany of empty promises.

Did you listen closely? Not a single rhyme.

"Not one good poet" is right.

★ ★ ★

Which brings me back to your previous author, James Madison.

For all his accolades, Madison was hardly considered a poet. And he know it. (See? How hard can it be?) Compared to the other delegates, he was not exactly a wordsmith. He didn't have a way with language like Jefferson, nor is he remembered as a great orator—an Alexander Hamilton, a Gunning Bedford—who could command a room with either vigor or volume.

In truth, he wasn't much of a presence at all. For someone who cast such a long shadow, James Madison was a small man. "A hundred pounds only if he had a hat full of rocks," it was said. "No bigger than half a piece of soap!" The so-called Father of the Constitution, the famed Virginia delegate to the Constitutional Convention, the man behind the "Virginia Plan" establishing our uniquely American government, had yet another notable distinction: He was tiny. Like, Tom Cruise tiny. If one had to choose shoulders on which to rest the New World, they would not belong to little Jimmy Madison.

Atlas he was not.

To many penny-ante patriots in the first part of the twenty-first century—who believe reflexively that our Founders were all giants among men—this is shocking news. I admit that I, too, found it alarming. Yet we need only glance at any of his official portraits for proof:

Official Portrait of James Madison,
the Tom Cruise of 1787, *by*
John Vanderlyn (1816)

James Madison, Prior to the Invention
of the Adjustable Easel, *by*
Gilbert Stuart (1821)

According to his friends, Madison stood five feet six inches. According to his enemies, no more than five four. And according to one report, presumably that of an ex-girlfriend, he barely cleared five feet. Even on his tippy-toes, Madison fell an inch short of his wife, Dolley, whose predilection for wearing "high feathers" and turbans at society balls and state functions made her husband seem even shorter—they were the Nicole Kidman and Tom Cruise of the revolutionary era, a walking optical illusion. Dolley herself called James "the Great Little Madison." Any patriot would find it a tough pill to swallow: The Father of the American Constitution was downright Napoleonic.

Personally, I find it surprising that such a minuscule man would so vigorously defend *proportional representation.**

* *[Fife-and-drum rimshot!]*

Why is his height so jarring to our modern sensibilities? Why does it matter that when Madison (reached up to) put his hand on the inaugural Bible in 1809, he would enter the annals not only as our fourth president, but as our shortest? Because we've come to demand in our leaders a certain stature. Surely when it comes to presidents, we respect—that is to say, we elect—only upright men of great proportion. Consider the recent occupants of the executive suite. Barack Obama, six feet one inch. George W. Bush, an even six feet in cowboy boots. Bill Clinton, six feet two inches when upright, as was George Bush the Elder. Ronald Reagan, six feet one inch. Even Jimmy Carter, at five nine and a half, made Martin Van Buren (five foot six) look like Michael Dukakis (three foot five).

The Oval Office may as well have a sign: *Must Be This Tall to Enter.*

There is a simple reason we seek giants to lead us: We the People have gotten ourselves into this mess; we rely on grander men with larger backs and stiffer spines to carry us out. In the words of the colonial preacher John Winthrop (five foot six), the first governor of the Massachusetts Bay Colony, whose famous sermon "A Model of Christian Charity" roused the colonists in 1630: "When a man is to wade through deep water, there is required tallness." We require tallness. If not figuratively, then literally. After all, these days we're in more than deep water; we're in deep shit.

We desperately need someone to look up to.

Yet, unlike history, I do not judge Madison for his height. I cannot; as a man lacking in some stature myself—literally and figuratively—it would be the height of hypocrisy. Which reminds me:

SELF-EVIDENT TRUTH #7: I'M TALL ENOUGH.

Nor, I must add, do I begrudge him his taste for taller women. Much like Madison, I, too, have dated a taller woman ("over six feet tall from top to bottom," it was said!). I called her Dawn, for two reasons: (1) that was her name, and (2) from my perspective, she spent a good part of the day eclipsing the sun. Although she wore neither feathers nor turbans, she would, on many occasions, wear high heels of the style fashionable in the early twenty-first century. I won't deny that I was tickled by the unique pairing, and the quizzical, envious stares it invited (she stoops, he conquers!) but I grant that, like James & Dolley and Tom & Nicole before us, we cut a ludicrous figure. Even I had a hand in doling out the ridicule: When she framed a picture of us walking hand in hand on the beach, I had no choice but to add a Post-it note: "Not to scale."

No, I judge James Madison for the rest of James Madison. His height, after all, was not his only shortcoming. There was also his personality. He was humorless, monkish, a "cloistered pedant," "mute, cold and repulsive," seemingly incapable of smiling. The wife of one of his fellow delegates in Congress, Mrs. Theodorick Bland, found him "a gloomy, stiff creature" who had "nothing engaging or even bearable in his manners—the most unsociable creature in existence." (Surely it is a special class of insult to be called dull by a woman named Bland.) New Englander Fisher Ames found him a man of "rather too much theory. . . . He is also very timid and seems evidently to want manly firmness and energy of character." (In fact, Madison, who often wore all black even on cheery occasions, was known to sink into dark depressions, beginning in his early twenties, when his deep ambition collided with the prospect that he might never be more than a gentleman farmer in what he called "an obscure corner of land" in Virginia. So we can add *entitled whiner* to his list of traits.) Madison was "self-consciously inconspicuous," writes historian Joseph Ellis. "His style, in effect, was not to have one." In the historian Richard Beeman's appraisal, he was "extraordinarily shy in nearly all social situations, particularly ones in which attractive women were involved." It didn't help that he was "prematurely balding" and "frequently brushed the few remaining wisps of hair at the top of his head downward to hide his bald spot"—ladies love that. This is a man who was known to avert his gaze from a woman's, to trail off incomprehensibly at the end of sentences, to banish himself to the dark corners of the room at the annual Christmas mingle. During official business—including the Philadelphia Convention that was to cry freedom to the world—it was said that Madison's voice was so weak and inaudible, stenographers would complain they couldn't understand a word he was saying.

Well then, allow me: *Seriously?!* This *is the "Father of the Constitution"?*

In our modern times, men like Madison make no mark. As Beeman puts it, charitably, "Only in the eighteenth century, where intellect and depth of character"—that's the charitable part—"were at least as highly valued as wit, telegenic good looks, or 'manly firmness,' could a person like Madison have achieved public prominence."

For me, a single anecdote offers the measure of the man: In 1783, before Dolley came into the picture, James Madison had set his sights on Catherine "Kitty" Floyd, a young woman less than half Madison's age (to which I offer no defense, or even comment; I can stomach a discrepancy in height, but half his age? *C'mon*). The attraction was mutual, but Thomas Jefferson—Madison's wingman at the time—suspected that his friend was *seriously blowing it, dude.* He wrote to Madison urging him to propose marriage to the teenager posthaste, assuming, I suppose, that any woman named Kitty wasn't going to stick around forever.

Madison's response was worthy of a Harlequin romance, as written by Henry Kissinger: "Your inference on the subject was not groundless. Before you left us I had sufficiently ascertained her sentiments. Since your departure the affair has been pursued." But wait, it gets steamier. "Most preliminary arrangements," he continued, his tongue darting left and right, his hips thrusting with every syllable (okay, I made that part up), "will be postponed until the end of the year in Congress."

Oh, James, you wild man.

★ ★ ★

This is the dreamer who is supposed to stir our passions for a more perfect union?

Well, actually no. As it turns out, James Madison is not to be blamed for our Preamble; he didn't write it. Its ponderous language is the work of Gouverneur Morris, the New York merchant whose task in the convention hall was that of the "amanuensis," a Latin term meaning *dude who actually held the quill.* Even Madison, the declared Father of the Constitution, admitted that "the finish given to the style and arrangement of the Constitution, fairly belongs to the pen of Mr. Morris"—most famously, the style and arrangement of the William Preamble.

Unlike Madison, Morris was a man of many words (he rose to speak a record 173 times on the floor of the Convention and "delighted in oratorical pyrotechnics"), very little self-restraint (he was "well-proportioned," even compared to the other fat Founders), and many indulgences (he "never passed up an opportunity for amorous adventure"). Even among big personalities at the Convention, he stood out. "Mr. Gouverneur Morris . . . winds through all the mazes of rhetoric, and throws around him such a glare that he charms, captivates, and leads away the sense of all who hear him," wrote Georgia delegate William Pierce, clearly jealous.

As fellow authors of the Constitution, Madison and Morris were an odd couple—the Felix and Oscar of the 1790s. In fact, although by the nature of my current enterprise I readily identify with Madison, I easily find in Morris a kindred spirit. He was the id to Madison's ego, and while I must honor the fastidious Madison, who sped home each night to transcribe his impressions of the Convention proceedings, I can't help but identify with the libertine decadences of Morris, who, with his rakish misdeeds, more than earned his reputation as the "Founding Rogue"—a reputation that long preceded his attendance at the Constitutional Convention.

Whereas Madison studied political philosophy at Princeton, Morris wrote his bachelor's and master's theses on "Wit and Beauty" and "Love." (I can relate; I once wrote a Valentine's Day card longer than any essay I wrote in college.) Whereas Madison scarcely went on a date in his college years, Morris never passed up an opportunity to mingle with the fairer sex. (I can respect that; while no Casanova, I was no monk.) If Madison was the father of the Constitution, Morris was the handsy uncle.

Morris's own diary is filled with steamy, poetic, very un-Madisonian accounts of his musings as a ladykiller: "She had the remains of a fine form and a countenance open and expressive . . . but they were wearing fast away," he wrote in 1798. "Neither had nature quite lost her empire, for the tints, which love in retiring to the heart had shed over her countenance, were slightly tinged with desire. I thought I could, in a single look, read half her history."

So yeah, we're of a feather, Morris and I.

I even imagine that Morris would applaud my current project—that of rewriting the Constitution single-handedly, with counsel but no veto from outside sentiments—mainly because Morris, like many of his fellow delegates, was an unrepentant elitist. He cared little for the opinions of others, "a respecter of very few persons." In the words of Madison himself, Morris was a man who did not "incline to the democratic side." After being bullied by his fellow New Yorkers, he relocated in Philadelphia, all the while, as Beeman puts it, "disdaining the democratic tendencies that allowed ignorant bumpkins to take the place of virtuous men."

Ditto.

Perhaps the most interesting and unusual—if least relevant—trait that I, the man rewriting the Constitution, share with Morris, the man who wrote the Preamble: Both he and I are missing significant body parts. (Did anyone see that coming? I suspect not.) He, the lower half of his left leg; me, the big toe of my left foot. My story of loss is simple: While traveling through East Berlin in the 1980s, a few years before the Berlin Wall came down, I caught my shoe in the exposed gears of an East German escalator— a Communist escalator!—and despite the valiant efforts of the American embassy to rush me across Checkpoint Charlie in time to save my crushed toe, well, this little piggy went to the market in the sky.

As for Morris's accident, the details are murkier. One story has it that his leg was run over by a horse carriage—too far from his fancy Philadelphia physician to have it fixed. But another explanation—deemed apocryphal by so-called historians—contends that he shattered his limb upon leaping from a window to escape a jealous husband who caught Morris engaged in "a great compromise" with the man's wife. This is the story I choose to believe. Sounds like the Morris I know. Besides, I'm a romantic. I may only have nine toes, but I'm all heart.

Does shared trauma necessarily make us kindred spirits? No. But it does give us something unique to talk about at cocktail parties (assuming, that is, that we never show up at the same one).* And not surprisingly, Morris was no stranger to cocktail parties, where, unashamed, he wore his false leg like a fashion accessory, never complained about the discomfort it brought, and made jokes about it at his own expense—many of them, it is said, quite ribald. (None will be reproduced here—this is a family book, and I haven't yet reaffirmed the First Amendment right to free expression.) Morris was more than willing to continue hitting on women despite his disability, leading his friend John Jay to comment that although Morris's missing leg was "a tax on my heart," occasionally he was "tempted to wish that he had lost *something* else." (I'm assuming his thumb?—again, this is a family book.)

One might ask of our Founding Charter: If its introductory Preamble, its most famous passage, was written by a man with a peg leg, doesn't that give our Constitution hardly a leg to stand on? Wouldn't we want to put our best foot forward? At least, shouldn't we have leaned on someone that doesn't invite so many bad puns?

Not so. Be it known that Gouverneur Morris, while clearly imperfect, was brave, and passionate, and ebullient, and—like me—the perfect man for the job of making a more perfect union.

Which again reminds me:

SELF-EVIDENT TRUTH #8:
NOT HAVING A TOE DOESN'T MEAN I CAN'T WRITE A CONSTITUTION.

In the end, there is only one way Morris, the peg-legged amanuensis, fell short. He failed to transfer his evident passion or humor into his intro to the Constitution. He snuck no poetry into the Preamble.

---

* Another party trick? I could produce from my wallet an impressive collection of two-dollar bills, while Morris might brag that it was his idea to use the word *cent* instead of the oh-so-British *penny*.

Morris wasn't afraid to be sneaky, either; he once added an unauthorized semicolon to Article I that would have greatly expanded the power of the government to impose taxes—true story—only to be thwarted when fellow delegate Roger Sherman noticed what he was up to. Nor was he afraid to step on the toes of Madison; he once wrote in his diary of seeing Dolley in a lowcut dress and wondering if she was "amenable to seduction."

Peg-legged Morris didn't merely have the opportunity to be poetic, and the will, he had obvious motive; there is, after all, great poetry in suffering. One of the most poetic letters ever penned by a Founder, Thomas Jefferson's famed "Of Head and Heart," was composed by Jefferson entirely with his left hand (and his pained heart), as he had crushed his right while leaping over a fence in order to impress a woman, the wife of an artist he met in France. It was to that woman he wrote, in part,

> Seated by my fireside, solitary & sad, the following dialogue took
> place between my Head & my Heart:
> HEAD. Well, friend, you seem to be in a pretty trim.
> HEART. I am indeed the most wretched of all earthly beings.
>   Overwhelmed with grief, every fibre of my frame distended
>   beyond its natural powers to bear, I would willingly meet
>   whatever catastrophe should leave me no more to feel or to fear.

Ooomph. It was the longest letter Jefferson had written to that point, and it was a passionate account of his growing obsession with a married woman.

Don't get me wrong, Morris's Preamble is a nice laundry list of noble aspirations. It sufficiently lays out what exactly we should expect of our Constitution. But it's all head, no heart. There's nothing epic about it. Gouverneur, I ask you, where's the poetry? Where's the protest? At the very least, where are the rhymes? What—did you run out of times? (See? Again, was that so hard?)

★ ★ ★

Let's not forget, the Constitution of the United States is as much a revolutionary document as was the Declaration of Independence. Jefferson's pen may have cast off the yoke of the British and invited the Revolutionary War, but the Constitution had an even more unfathomable task: Admit that the experiment in self-government—i.e., America—was failing.

It said: *That's it, we're shutting down the Acropolis. We're going on strike.*

It said: *We're going to see if we can't make this thing a little "more perfect."*

It said: *Instead of relying on our crumbling foundation, we're going to keep building, because even an extremely historic artifact sometimes needs an extreme makeover.*

The Scaffolding of Democracy

Yet the most revolutionary sentiment in the entire document is not what the Preamble proposes. It is *who* is doing the proposing. The truly revolutionary, the truly American—and to some, the utterly contestable—sentiment contained in these rebel phrases is buried in plain sight, right there in the first three words:

We the People.

Patrick Henry, the Virginia governor who "smelt a rat" in Philadelphia and boycotted the proceedings and who would later deem the completed Constitution to be "squinting towards monarchy," was already wrinkling his nose by word three. "Who authorized them," asked Henry, "to speak the language of, We, the people, instead of We, the states?"

It was a fair question. The Annapolis Convention had sent the delegates to Philadelphia only "for the sole and express purpose of revising the Articles of Confederation, and reporting to [the Continental] Congress . . . alterations," not to fundamentally shift power from the states to the people. Congress had called for recommendations, not revolutions, and when the delegates acted like demagogues, Patrick Henry had every right to cry foul.

He needed to be convinced, and the Preamble, as written, wasn't cutting it. On this, I share Patrick's concern. The Preamble was destined, by mere circumstance of placement, to be the overture before the symphony, the opening bars of the song that would be America, and yet: There's no music in it. For all its claim of being memorable, it strikes no chord. If we are being honest, we would admit that the only reason we know it by heart is that it has been beaten into our brains.

Gouverneur, if I may: Where are the Wit, Beauty, and Love on which you wrote your master's thesis? Where are the "mazes of rhetoric" that charmed your fellow Founders? Perhaps it is too much to expect a few dozen words to sum up the centuries, but your Preamble was inspired, roused, and energized by "We the People"; the least it could do is return the favor. Are we not "amenable to seduction"?

As I sit here, in the shadow of the Acropolis, listening to the passion of protesters demanding their democracy—and hallucinating that I can understand any of it in my growing heatstroke—I can't help but wonder, had the Preamble just a little more poetry, it might have been just a little more convincing. Perhaps Patrick Henry would have sung along instead of heckling.

With that in mind, I have brushed the dust from my eyes, wiped the sweat from my brow, and composed a new Preamble worthy of our country. I think you'll be pleased. It even rhymes.

(You know, like Homer.)

Your New Preamble

We the People of these States now United,
(More perfecter now than we were when divided)
But seeking perfection, with ev'ry election,
And aware that our welfare and system of justice is
Based in part on Emperor Augustus's,
Of Thee We Sing.
Now: Let's do this thing.

THE LEGISLATIVE BRANCH
An Imbalance of Power

Con-gress is the opposite of *pro*-gress.
KEVIN BLEYER

Yeah, I said it.
KEVIN BLEYER

HE CONSTITUTION BEGINS with a whimper.

For a country that began with a Shot Heard Round the World, its founding document starts with what can only be called, in good conscience, a dud.

I'd like to give James Madison the benefit of the doubt. I'd like to presume his ears were still ringing from the gunfire at Lexington and Concord, and, like a hungover soldier the morning after a well-lubricated victory parade, he tiptoed into his Constitution-writing room—lest his own footsteps aggravate his migraine—sat down at his Constitution-writing desk, dipped his Constitution-writing quill into his Constitution-writing inkwell, and tried not to cause any sort of ruckus.

It is the only explanation for the words on page one:

All legislative powers herein granted shall be vested in a Congress of the United States.

★ ★ ★

Sssssh, Mr. Madison. *Quiet.* We wouldn't want to do anything truly revolutionary. Best not draw any attention. After all, we're only trying to *centralize power in a national government* over here.

What was Madison thinking? *Was* he thinking? Had he never heard of the American president? At that pivotal moment of our country's founding, Madison and his fellow Framers had all the powers of "leader of the free world" to explore, yet they devoted their first attentions, their first efforts, and the very first Article of their prized Constitution to the clear also-ran in the competition for the American imagination: *Congress*. To a ragtag gang from every corner of the country who play a distant (and discordant) second fiddle to the one, central figure recognized and revered around the world— a world he visits in his *very own jumbo jet*, mind you. In Madison's Constitution, the Legislative gets top billing over the Executive, over the guy who commands an entire military? Who gets a Secret Service code name?

Everyone has a Congress. But how many countries have an American president? I doubt China has ever had an American president. I ask you, is there a single six-year-old who declares, "Mommy, when I grow up, I want to be a three-term backbencher from Iowa's 14th District"? No, sir, there is not.

So to Madison, I say, *shame*.

You could have tackled the distinctly American invention of the presidency. Instead, you set right to work picking the lowest-hanging fruit.

Not so fast, you might say. The president would be nothing without the Congress, you might say; the president may have an army to lead, you might say, but Congress can choose not to pay for it. You might even say, as many have, that while the president may wield "the sword," it is Congress that carries "the purse." But are you even listening to yourself? Since when does a purse beat a sword? If there's one thing we've learned in life's great game of Rock, Paper, Scissors, it's that *sword* beats *purse*.

Think about it: A sword can cut a purse. Or cut the person wearing the purse. And I don't care if "it takes a purse to buy a sword." I don't have to buy a sword. Weren't you listening?

I already *have* a sword.

It's that thing I'm cutting your purse with.

Right off the bat, then, I know what I must do: I shall swap the First and Second Articles of the United States Constitution.

What? you ask.

You can't do that, you protest.

Too late, I answer. *I just did*. And I'm going to have to ask you to yield back the balance of your time to the Speaker. I'll take it from here.

Should you wish, feel free to skip ahead to the next chapter, the exciting chapter, the one about *The President of the United States of America*.

I'll wait.

★ ★ ★

[*Pause*]

★ ★ ★

Exciting stuff, right?

Meantime, I welcome you, my fellow Americans, not to the new Article I, but to the new Article II of the new United States Constitution: the (yawn) Legislatuzzzzzzzzzzzzzzz.

ARTICLE II:
CONGRESS, THE OPPOSITE OF PROGRESS
(YEAH, I SAID IT)

THE QUESTION REMAINS: Why *did* Madison lead with Congress?

As I see it, here's what happened. Even though they had cobbled together grand ideas from ancient Greece and Rome, from not-as-ancient England, and from other world governments—a smidge of democracy here, a dash of republic there—the Framers imagined a government that, from the start, was intended to feature a central, all-American ingredient: the *separation of powers*. Three distinct branches of government as important to our national identity as red, white, and blue are to our national flag. (Never mind, patriots, that a tripartite system of government was first tried in Greece, developed by the Romans, refined by the English, and established as a political philosophy by a French philosopher (and satirist!) named Charles-Louis de Secondat, baron de La Brède et de Montesquieu. Or that the flags of more than two dozen other countries are red, white, and blue—including those of North Korea, which is hardly a friend of our country, and the Faroe Islands, which is hardly a country.)

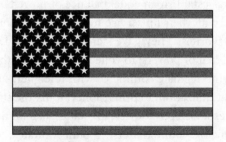

The flag of the United States

*Before this became the flag of Liberia, it
was the wet dream of Texas.*

*Despite indications, is not true that Betsy Ross designed this
prototype flag while drunk. It is true, however, that Western
Samoa adopted it as its official flag in 1949.*

For a country that hoped to enter the world stage with a bang, the *separation of powers* was, admittedly, counterintuitive: multiple branches of government, working hard to make sure no one branch became too powerful. From the beginning, when Madison wrote "A National Government ought to be established, consisting of a supreme Legislative, Executive & Judiciary," he believed that by divvying up the chore wheel among three branches, peace and unity would naturally spring forth. To put the country on good, balanced footing, immunized against the despotic and tyrannous power shifts that had doomed so many countries throughout history, all they had to do was establish an equal balance of power.

They didn't. For all their lip service to wanting "co-equal" branches, the Framers played favorites. They gave star billing to the Legislative Branch and gave it an arsenal of powers: to collect taxes; to pay the country's debts; to borrow money; to regulate commerce with foreigners and Indians; to establish rules of naturalization; to print money; to fix the standard of weights and measures; to establish post offices; to establish a national capital; to grant copyrights; to penalize counterfeiters; to punish pirates; to fund armies; to maintain a navy; to raise a militia; and to declare war—and, just to be safe, to make all laws "necessary and proper" to get it all done. The Founders clearly believed Congress was the most important branch; in their hands, it would get the most ink, the most prominent placement, and the most power.*

Perhaps this was to be expected. Many of the delegates to the Constitutional Convention had served in the Confederation Congress before heading to Philadelphia. James Madison, before he became "the Father of the Constitution," was Congress's longest-serving member. Naturally, they thought their day jobs vital to the success of the country. If God made man in His own image, certainly a lowly congressman would, too. Ask a mechanic to design a house, you can be sure it'll have one kick-ass garage.

Clearly, the delegates didn't read their own press. Or pay much attention to the Billboard Charts of 1776. No doubt they would have remembered this little ditty about their Continental Congress:

> *These hardy knaves and stupid fools,*
> *Some apish and pragmatic mules,*
> *Some servile acquiescing tools,*
> *These, these compose the Congress!*
>
> *When Jove resolved to send a curse,*
> *And all the woes of life rehearse,*
> *Not plague, not famine, but much worse—*
> *He cursed us with a Congress.*

A poem about the plague, back when people actually *got* the plague. It was an especially vivid indictment.

By Jove, every century has taken its turn to indict Congress. The nineteenth century had Mark Twain: "Suppose you were an idiot and suppose you were a member of Congress. But I repeat myself." The twentieth, Will Rogers: "Every time Congress makes a joke it's the law, and every time they make a law it's a joke." One twenty-first-century wordsmith, a man of abundant gravitas and unparalleled wit, was known to point out that "if you really think about it, *Con*-gress is the opposite of *pro*-gress."

---

* Just take a look at Article I. (Don't read it; just look at it.) *Long*, right? According to the historian Richard Beeman, word count doesn't lie. The organization of the Articles, with Article I by far the longest, was "a clear signal about the priorities of the framers of the Constitution." (Consider: *This* book is creeping up on twenty thousand words, and it's already pretty darn important.)

Yeah, you heard me.

Stupid fools and pragmatic mules—these composed the Congress from its very first session. In its inaugural decade under the Constitution of 1787, when the Legislative Branch was still teething, rules governing its conduct were so loose that fistfights among representatives would break out on the floor. Even visitors to the gallery weren't safe; Georgia congressman James Jackson was known to wave his pistol at onlookers, threatening to shoot them if they made too much noise. Not that much work was being done, either; Congress in the 1790s was so dysfunctional that one out of every three senators resigned in boredom or disgust before their terms were over. *Acquiescing tools is right.*

It was this Congress, filled with gunplay, fistfights, and quitters, that so clearly, and so mistakenly, captivated the Framers.

★ ★ ★

My complaint is not with the way Congress reigned in those early decades; rather, it is how Congress was composed in the first place. Not by design, but by defeat.

Had newspapers in the eighteenth century run headlines—before Ye Olde Craigsliste put such papers out of business, the front pages of the *Pennsylvania Packet* in 1787 were dominated by classified ads—any self-respecting editor in charge of crafting the banner headline on the morning after the signing of the Constitution would have had no choice but to deliver the bad news in bold, 1776-point type:

CONSTITUTION COMPROMISED!
Embarrassed Delegates Return Home in Defeat, Disgrace (Disguise?)

September 18, 1787—Yesterday, unable to come to a consensus on possibly the most important decision they will ever make, the delegates to the Constitutional Convention fled Philadelphia having signed a document that officially affirms their utter failure to stand up for something. In a lily-livered concession—what will come to be known, we assume ironically, as the "Great" Compromise—the delegates from states both large and small abandoned their heartfelt principles and betrayed their fellow statesmen, devising a new hybrid Congress that will satisfy no one save Dr. Frankenstein. The lower chamber, or "the House

of Representatives," will be populated according to proportional representation, while the upper chamber, to be
called "the Senate," will be assigned the arbitrary number
of two Senators from each state. Why such a hybrid?
James Madison could not be reached for comment. He
was last seen trying to escape notice by donning his powdered wig backward (that olde tricke) as he scurried to
the city limits, muttering, "Which way to Virginia?"

To be sure, when Madison, the Father of the Constitution, stepped forward to sign the document he had just helped birth, he may have been
endorsing a new Constitution for his beloved country, but he was also no-
tarizing his own failure. In the previous four months, not just many but
most of the revolutionary ideals he had insisted should be included in the
new Constitution had either been voted down or dismissed outright, most
painfully his prime directive for this new American republic, his rallying
cry, his original reason for even coming to Philadelphia: that the Congress,
the whole Congress, should be composed of men sent to serve by their fellow Americans. It was just such a "pivot," as he described the idea, that
would distinguish America from the very system it had just rejected in
principle and defeated in war. Unlike in England, where only the House of
Commons was elected, in Madison's America *all* legislative power—both
House and Senate—would be vested in *We the People*.

That is, if the delegates in the Pennsylvania State House that summer
could be sold on the idea.

★ ★ ★

Madison had a hunch that this debate—over how *we the people* would be
represented in our government—would become the central front in the
battle over the Constitution. At first, he was hopeful his fellow delegates
would see the wisdom of his approach, sign on from the get-go, and maybe
they'd be home by lunch. When they did not, Madison was forced to make
an even more dramatic pivot: from fighting for what he cared about to
abandoning his own standards. Madison was once asked by an impatient
man outside the Convention, "Mr. Madison, could you please tell us, what
are the principles—if there are any—to be of American government?"

"Yes, there are three," Madison answered. "Compromise. Compromise.
Compromise."

Peg-legged Morris shared Madison's chagrin, declaring his reservations about the completed draft in typically chauvinistic terms: "I not only took it as a man does his wife"—or in Morris's case, likely someone else's wife—"for better, for worse, but what few men do with their wives, I took it knowing all its bad qualities."

Exactly why Madison, Morris, and their fellow delegates managed to let such "bad qualities" slip in—on page one, no less—and how history has somehow convinced itself that the deal they struck that summer was a "Great Compromise" when it could easily and more accurately be called a "Great Defeat"—that's worth a trip to the scene of the crime.

How did we base the most revered statement of American principles on a compromise?

I can't excuse it; I can try to explain it. So on behalf of America, I'll board the Megabus from New York City to Philadelphia, Pennsylvania, to search for clues at Independence Hall—where the Constitution was devised, debated, and written—and try to find some answers.

PHILADELPHIA, HERE I COME

DESPITE ITS NAME, the Megabus displays no superheroic qualities. It's your basic double-decker: Paint it red and it might be found bouncing around Piccadilly Square. Still, as we roll along, I fancy myself a heroic Founding Father eager to cast off such Briticisms, summoned from New York to Philadelphia—the same route James Madison took in May 1787, I'll have you know—to ratify a new covenant for a new America, in *style*.

I consider that it took the Founders weeks to get from their home states to Philadelphia, the cauldron city of our burgeoning American experiment. They risked disease (I would presume), highway robbery (I would imagine), the resentment of their homebound colonial wives (I would wager). Me? I'm gonna get there in less than two hours while surfing the Internet. (The Megabus has free wi-fi.) It makes me grateful that President Dwight D. Eisenhower established the interstate highway system as part of the Federal-Aid Highway Act of 1956. (Like I said, free wi-fi.) And I'm gonna do all it for a buck. (Yet another distinction of the Megabus: If one purchases a ticket early enough, or chooses an unusual departure time, say, Saturday at twenty-six o'clock, it costs only one dollar.) When I handed over the crinkled one-dollar bill upon boarding, I'm pretty sure I saw a crinkled George Washington glare at me.

No doubt he was marveling at how far we've come.

And, thanks to me, *how far we'll go.*

★ ★ ★

Halfway to Philadelphia, I realize: Something is amiss. We're cruising past neighborhoods filled with homes filled with families filled with moms, dads, sisters, brothers, citizens—millions of my fellow Americans, all of whom will be liberated and enriched by my efforts. Yet none of whom know what the hell I'm up to.

Even more shocking, I have no one to blame but myself. I've overlooked perhaps the most vital step in any declaration of independence: a Declaration of Independence.

It's mandatory, really. Just as Jefferson wrote in *his* Declaration—"a decent respect to the opinions of mankind requires" that the colonies submit their reasons for rebellion "to a candid world"—I too should give my fellow Americans a thoughtful heads-up.

That's what this revolution needs: a press release.

So with only thirty miles to go, with Philadelphia as my north star and I-95 as my set course, with a slightly bumpy voyage only the Framers could appreciate (naturally, I presume Thomas Jefferson wrote his draft on horseback)—and with the recent revelation that my laptop has maybe twenty minutes of juice left, tops—I quickly compose my declaration of independence from the unlikeliest of tyrants: the American Constitution.

"FOR IMMEDIATE RELEASE—*When in the Course of Human Events*"—seems as good an intro as any, definitely worth borrowing—"*it becomes necessary for One Man*"—that's me!—"*to dissolve, dismantle, and discarde the Political Bands which have, let's face it, been duteously discredited and duly discounted*"—a little heavy on the alliteration, but it'll do—"*and offer his Boundless Wisdom, Bountiful Insight, and Rhetorical Eloquence on behalf of an entire nation*"—I'm really rolling now—"*necessity demands that he rewrite the Constitution of these United States of America.*"

Nice touch, I think. This isn't *me* demanding. This is "necessity."

"*A new Covenant need be written, and should be written, and shall be written, and that* One Man—"

I hesitate for a moment. Why be coy?

"*—and that* Kevin J. Bleyer, *affirmed gentleman, scholar, penman, wordsmith, mathlete, World Traveler, prospective homeowner, hopeless Romantic, deep thinker, infamous scribbler, Award-Winning Satirist, Peerless Leader—*"

Am I coming on too strong?

"*—and humble servant—*"

Much better.

"*—shall be the one to write it.*"

So far, so good. But is it enough? Seems short.

As the battery monitor on my laptop turns red, I look up Jefferson's Declaration again to see if there's anything else I may have missed. I scan the impenetrable cursive until my eye reaches the end of the document, and I'm reminded of the genius of Jefferson's manifesto: The bottom quarter of the page is nothing but signatures. Frilly ones, pedestrian ones, illegible ones, vaguely familiar ones, and yes, JOHN HANCOCK. Appreciating that there is strength in numbers—and clearly a pioneer in fiddling with margins—Jefferson made certain his Declaration was fifty-six strong. Fifty-six delegates from the thirteen states who believed in the case for rebellion, were willing to declare it publicly, and didn't mind being page filler so Jefferson could reach his word count.

With my battery blinking now, I scan my address book for my own band of boldfaced brothers, a broad cross section of authentic Americans, representative not of a vast experience in revolution—or any, really—but of the wide swath of what it means to be a true patriot in twenty-first-century America. The list quickly grows to two, then three, then five, then ten. Of my eventual fifty-six potential signers, I've got twenty email addresses on hand, and a few others courtesy of a Google search. A good start, it seems to me. The many that will become the multitude. The mob that will become the movement. My "soldiery," as George Washington would have called them; extraordinary Americans doing their duty as ordinary troops.

Persuading such an army won't be easy, I remind myself. But at that moment, I somehow contrive just the right words to muster us all. "The summer soldier and the sunshine patriot," I say aloud, "will, in this crisis, shrink from the service of their country; but he that stands by it now, deserves the love and thanks of man and woman!" An ideal sentiment. Then I remember that those are Thomas Paine's words, not mine. (No wonder they sounded familiar.) But the fact that he said them back in 1776 makes them, I submit, an even More Perfect Sentiment. I'm sure he won't mind.

As the Megabus slows to a stop directly in front of Independence Hall, where the Constitution was debated, written, and submitted over the course of four months in the summer of 1787, I press *send*.

"The die has been cast," John Adams wrote, having heard news of the

Sons of Liberty dumping tea into Boston Harbor. "The people have passed the river and cut away the bridge."

The revolution has begun.

HOW A BILL BECOMES A FLAW

"Is this the cemetery?"

"What?" I ask.

"Is this the cemetery?" she asks again, like I should know what the heck she's talking about.

I don't.

"Sorry?"

"The cemetery from *National Treasure*? Is that it?"

Finally, some context. Still, I'm not sure why this woman is asking *me*. She saw me get off the Megabus with her. She knows I'm not a local. Yet she's asking *me*. I can only assume she noticed my general air of authority.

"I really don't know," I say.

"But it's here somewhere, right?"

I have no idea whether it's here somewhere or not, but I'm tempted to say: *Look, lady, this isn't a movie set. This is Independence Hall. The Declaration of Independence was signed here. The Constitution of the United States was written here. Washington Slept Here.* (He didn't, but you get my point.) *History is the star attraction here, lady. Not Nicolas Cage.*

I say none of this, of course. Instead, I swallow my disdain and point her across the square toward what appears to be a grassy knoll. Not just *any* grassy knoll, mind you, but *the* grassy knoll—I learn later from a park ranger—where they filmed the cemetery scene from *National Treasure*. Even the staff has given up the fight.

Truth is, I'm fairly certain I have seen *National Treasure*. If I recall correctly, at one point I even possessed a torn ticket stub to its sequel, *National Treasure 2: Book of Secrets*, although for the life of me I can't remember having seen it, or if I did, what it was about. Best guess: something about a treasure, and a book, and secrets. I do vaguely remember the plot of the original: In order to save the Declaration of Independence, Nicolas Cage announces he's going to steal the Declaration of Independence—by saying, if memory serves, "I'm going to steal the Declaration of Independence"—and then (spoiler alert!) he steals the Declaration of Independence. In fact, he steals the Declaration of Independence from the people who were already protecting the Declaration of Independence, because they don't believe him that someone else is about to steal the Declaration of Independence. The movie teaches a vital life lesson, one that resonates with my current mission: Sometimes the only way to protect something you care about is to swipe it from the people who were already protecting it because, well, because *you know better*.

Also, because there may be a treasure map on the back.

So like any great actor, or even Nicolas Cage, I had my motivation. *I know better*. It is why I have waited in line with the tourist hordes for forty-five minutes to enter Independence Hall, where the delegates were dispatched by Congress "for the sole and express purpose of revising the Articles of Confederation." The country was faltering, and the states were quarreling; it was their task to make nice. Their orders were limited: only "to devise such further provisions as shall appear to them necessary to render the constitution of the Federal Government adequate to the exigencies of the Union." They were only to provide "alterations." Instead, they used their power to, as Thomas Paine put it, "begin the world over again."

Because *they knew better:* Someone had to Save America.

★ ★ ★

It is August. In Philadelphia. Which is to say: It's hot. Judging by the disposition of the overheated tourists tired of waiting in line for entry into Independence Hall, the air is thick with revolution. To a man, we are eager to storm the State House—if only to regulate our core temperatures back to something resembling normalcy. Gotta be honest, when the guide waves us in and we finally enter the mercifully cooler State House—austere yet magnificent, grand but frankly kinda smallish, and long since renovated to make the experience palatable to sweaty tourists—I marvel that Benjamin Franklin's many wondrous inventions somehow did not include *double-paned windows,* or that Thomas Jefferson's Declaration of Independence did not claim the right to "life, liberty, and the pursuit of air-conditioning." If it were me, that would have been a dealbreaker.

But as the blast of cold air greets me—and the threat of revolt subsides—I regain my wits and realize: I've arrived.

So this is it.

It all happened right here.

What *exactly* happened right here, well, that's a different story. In truth, we don't know—we cannot know—everything that took place inside these walls that summer of 1787. William Jackson, the young convention secretary whose job it was to keep the official journal of the proceedings and record the votes, proved to be an utter failure. Thirty years later, when Secretary of State John Quincy Adams tried to assemble a convention journal from the "official" record that Jackson had kept, he found that Jackson's notes were nothing more than random details, and that he had thrown away "all the loose scraps of paper" given to him by the delegates. Perhaps sensing a slacker in their midst, the delegates did consider a Plan B. South Carolina delegate Charles Pinckney proposed that a committee be appointed specifically "to superintend the Minutes," but the delegates voted the proposal down. (Or as secretary Jackson recorded it, "I like puppies.")

Only James Madison, the "monkish pedant" who cared about these things, felt it his duty to keep copious notes, which he recorded at night while his fellow delegates were carousing throughout the town. His nightly chronicles are the only decent account of that summer in Philadelphia. Decades later, Madison claimed he took the notes as a contribution to Posterity, "to preserve as far as I could an exact account of what might pass in the Convention." But let's be honest: Is Madison even to be trusted? As a Virginian, he was a fierce advocate for the large states and the mastermind behind proportional representation, the central debate for much of the summer. His notes, no matter how copious, couldn't help but be biased. What's more, they weren't published until a full fifty years after the Convention—enough time to burnish countless revisionist rewrites. Like Patrick Henry before me, *I smell a rat.* We should trust Madison to be an honest accountant of the Constitutional Convention no more than we would trust a prosecuting attorney to serve as stenographer of his own trial.

Yet Madison's notes are the only account we have. Without them, we'd all be guessing what transpired, because in those pivotal months of 1787, total secrecy ruled. At the outset of the Convention, it was agreed that it be held entirely in secret, with "nothing spoken in the house [to] be printed, or otherwise published or communicated without leave." The premise behind the rule of secrecy was to make the Philadelphia Assembly Room a think tank of respectful deliberation rather than a hotbox of partisan debate—it would, as Madison promoted it, "secure unbiased discussion within doors, and prevent misconceptions and misconstructions without." A *safe place.*

Thus, from day one, the delegates shut the doors, shuttered the windows, put out the No Trespassing sign, closed the Book of Secrets (so as not to reveal their National Treasures), and made a pact that (a) news of what transpired within the Convention would be on a need-to-know basis, and (b) no one outside their clubhouse needed to know.

No one meant *no one.* When James Madison's own father asked how his son was getting on, little Jimmy told him to butt out, revealing only that "nothing definitive is yet done." When Benjamin Franklin left the Assembly Room each evening, the convention assigned two men to tail him to ensure he wouldn't stop by a common house and blab what he had observed that day—Poor Richard was a very poor keeper of secrets. And when a copy of a sensitive report—their Book of Secrets, we should assume—was found lying on the floor of the Assembly Room, evidently dropped by a careless delegate, it was quickly given to Convention president George Washington. Washington waited until the end of the day's session, rose resolutely from his seat, and upbraided the anonymous delegate who "has been so neglectful of the secrets of the Convention as to drop . . . a copy of their proceedings." As the General rose to his full six feet two and one-half inches, the stomachs of the delegates surely sank. "I must entreat [the] gentleman to be more careful, lest our transactions get into the news papers, and disturb the public repose by premature speculations."* He threw the report down on the table in front of him, and with a final reprimand—"Let him who owns it, take it"—he bowed, picked up his hat, and marched out of the room. No one stepped forward to claim the document on that day—or any other. The Case of the Anonymous Report was never solved.†

I don't want to say the delegates' embrace of confidentiality was hypocritical. I don't have to; the Constitution they wrote, which promotes candor throughout, says it all. Article I requires each chamber of Congress to keep a journal and "publish same, excepting such parts as in their Judgment require Secrecy." Article II demands that the president "from time to time give to the Congress Information of the State of the Union." And although Article III shies from insisting that the Supreme Court let us peek inside their robes, their Bill of Rights demands that all criminal trials in this country be not only "speedy," but also "public." Thanks to their Constitution, we've become a nation that espouses "open government" and demands, if not expects, "transparency" among our politicians and elected officials.

Just not among the delegates convened here in 1787.

Not everyone was happy about the vow of silence. Thomas Jefferson, already feeling out of the loop in France, wrote to Adams, horrified that the delegates "began their deliberations by so abominable a precedent as that of tying up the tongues of their members. Nothing can justify this example but the innocence of their intentions, & ignorance of the value of public discus-

---

* The rumors are true: George Washington had a real problem with premature speculations.

† The delegates also followed a rigid "No Snitching" policy.

sions." Had they not read his Declaration, just a decade previous, promoting "a decent respect" to "a candid world"? Jeffersonian candor, it seemed, was so 1776. Under Madison's watch, the goings-on in the Pennsylvania State House in the summer of 1787 would be Invitation Only.

Delegate George Mason described such rigid confidentiality as "a necessary precaution to prevent misrepresentations or mistakes; there being a material difference between the appearance of a subject in its first crude and undigested shape, and after it shall have been properly matured and arranged." Point taken—first drafts *can* contian a *lot* of errers—but the decision turned the rest of the New World into a rumor mill. George Washington had feared that *any* news might spur "premature speculations"; well, *no* news spurred outright fantasies. Absent any solid leaks from the assembly, an anonymous pamphleteer in Connecticut even spread word that the delegates sequestered behind closed doors had decided "to tread back the wayward path" and return America to a monarchy. He spun the theory that the Framers had found no one among them qualified to govern the country and, worse, were planning to summon the second son of George III "to have him crowned King over this continent."*

Jefferson saw all this coming, and was horrified by it. This was the man who, in his preamble to the Virginia Statute of Religious Liberty, wrote that "truth is great and will prevail if left to herself." This was the man who had such a "decent respect to the opinions of mankind," and who not only "declared the causes" of revolution but invented the first copying machine, the first revolving bookstand, and this thing:

The polygraph, "the finest invention of the present age," according to its inventor, Thomas Jefferson. It made instant copies of handwritten letters for quick distribution—and indicated if you were lying about your involvement in a string of murders in 1762.

* Centuries later, that same pamphleteer spread the rumor that President Obama was a Muslim.

We can hold yet another truth to be self-evident: If Thomas Jefferson were alive today, he would have a Twitter account.

@TJeffs1776: endowed by cre8r w unalienable rts! #life #liberty #pursuit of happiness

And as I stare at the windows here in the Assembly Room, kept shut by the Founders to avoid prying eyes, I resolve not to repeat the delegates' "abominable precedent," and instead to follow Jefferson's lead. I will not shutter my windows. I will not work behind closed doors. Mine may be an exclusive clubhouse of one, but everyone will be invited to peek inside. Not only will this revolution be televised, it will be open-source. All the mighty powers of the Internet will be brought to bear in the service of the *Me the People* cause.

Facebook:

Status: Kevin is *currently fixing Congress.*

Twitter:

@kevinbleyer: I've got gr8 ideas for the Legisl8ure. All less than 140 chars. RT freely. Thx!

Flickr:

Had the Founders their own social networks—Facebooke.com, perhaps—they might have been more willing to share news of what exactly

they were constructing inside that Assembly Room: an innovative, Newtonian constitution, a system of equal-and-opposite forces—separated powers, checks and balances—designed to release pent-up energy while preventing political passion from tearing us apart. The Constitution they devised has been called "A Machine That Would Go of Itself," a self-propelling, counterweighted, perpetual-democracy contraption that would power the republic to eternal greatness.*

Perhaps that is true of the Constitution; the same cannot be said of the Convention that created it.

Well-oiled clockwork, it was not.

YOU SAY YOU WANT A DEVOLUTION

TWO AND A HALF CENTURIES before the delegates convened in Philadelphia to notarize the freedoms of the New World, a Englishman named John Heywood—the favorite playwright of Queen Mary—fled his homeland to seek a life of religious liberty. Like the Puritan John Winthrop, he knew a better life was to be found beyond the borders of England—although he ended up in Belgium, not Boston. Between writing plays and fleeing despotism, Heywood also managed a rather Jeffersonian feat: He collected all the proverbs in the English language, which he assembled in his succinctly titled book, *A Dialogue Conteinyng the Nomber in Effect of All the Prouerbes in the Englishe Tongue, Compacte in a Matter Concernyng Two Maner of Mariages, made and set foorth by Iohan Heywood.*

His proverbs are familiar in sentiment if not in spelling:

> *Rome was not bylt on a daie.*
> *For better is halfe a lofe than no bread.*
> *Euery man for him felfe, and god for us all.*

He may as well have been writing a history of the Convention in Philadelphia.

> *Rome wasn't built in a day.*
> *Half a loaf is better than none.*

---

* As might be found, say, in a movie starring Nicolas Cage.

Every man for himself, and God for us all.

Each proverb would apply perfectly to the Constitutional Convention at some point that summer in 1787. But at its outset in May, one piece of pith rings truest:

Of a good begynnyng comth a good end.

A good beginning makes a good ending.

All is well that endes well.

By now, I've made it perfectly clear that the Convention did not end well. (See: *Constitution of the United States, The*). It stands to reason, then, that it did not begin well.

For starters, it barely started. James Madison arrived in Philadelphia eleven days early—not to be careful or prompt, but to be conniving and to plot. The Virginian had grand designs about how to remake government—a system that included direct representation in both houses of Congress that came to be known as the Virginia Plan—and like an athlete training at altitude, he figured the extra time in Philadelphia would gain him a competitive advantage. He'd wow 'em with a quick start out of the blocks while others were still finding their way around town. By the time they got their footing, he'd have left them in the dust.

Or so he thought. Madison's road to Philadelphia may have been paved with the intention to outsmart his colleagues; for his fellow delegates, it wasn't paved at all. By May 14, the day the Convention was scheduled to begin, only a few delegates had arrived. Madison had no quorum. No doubt to his chagrin, the only newsworthy event in Philadelphia on that day—at least as the *Pennsylvania Herald* reported it the next morning—featured the exploits of a notorious town drunk.*

He might have expected some absences. Despite the obvious need for real government reform, many delegates thought the convention was ill-

---

* Not that the drunk's exploits weren't newsworthy: He had approached a young lady "of delicate dress and shape," announced that he "did not like her so well *before* as *behind*," but would still request "the favour of a kiss." The woman dismissed him handily, replying, "With all my heart, Sir, if you will do me the favour to kiss the part you like best!" As he walked the streets of Philadelphia, Madison had to wonder: Were the delegates saying the same to him? That he could kiss their ass? Historians disagree.

advised, or worse, doomed. Even George Washington, a proud man, worried that getting too cozy with the Convention would mar his pristine reputation. At the very least, as if it were a party hosted by the least popular kid in class, no one wanted to be the first to arrive. Unwilling to admit the worst, Madison blamed "the late bad weather" and the bad roads for their absence. Or, wait—did he forget to put the address on the invitations?

Whatever their reasons, it took twenty-two days for enough delegates—representing seven of the thirteen states—to reach the quorum necessary to get under way. (A quorum is one thing; a full house is another. At no time during the entire summer were all fifty-five delegates present in the Philadelphia Assembly Room at the same time, which puts the lie to any unilateral claim today that, on any particular issue in 1787, "all the Founding Fathers believed [fill in the blank]." It's just as likely the delegate from Vermont was out that day.) When the Convention was finally called to order on May 25, Madison, the least popular kid in class, had been stewing for more than three weeks. Ever the overachiever, he was prepared—overprepared, even—but for all the lines he had memorized, his Convention would follow no script.

★ ★ ★

The Convention may have taken three weeks to come to order, but it took no time at all to fall apart. On the first Monday, the delegates voted down a proposal to do what should have seemed obvious and necessary: namely, "to call for the yeas and nays and have them entered on the minutes"—which is to say, to keep track of what the heck was going on. Delegate George Mason argued that forcing delegates to put their votes where their mouths were "would be an obstacle to a change of . . . opinions." Then, they adopted a motion to act as a so-called Committee of the Whole, which allowed any delegate to reconsider, at any time, any motion that had previously been voted on. The consequence would seem obvious to anyone who has ever played Whack-a-Mole: Ideas would pop up and be struck down, only to rear their heads again when any delegate felt it necessary. With votes left unrecorded, even those issues that seemed settled were fair game for reconsideration. Thanks to the Committee of the Whole, as the summer unfolded, the larger Constitutional Convention became little more than a Committee of the Don't Hold Me to This. The goal was greater consensus; the result was endless argument.

And there was plenty to argue about.

The central debate throughout the summer pitted the proponents of the

Virginia Plan, delegates from primarily large states who insisted the Senate be populated by proportional representation, against the advocates of the New Jersey Plan, primarily small states' men who called for an equal number of senators from each state. For four months, it was this disagreement—the composition of the Congress—that consumed the Convention and divided the delegates: Team Virginia versus Team Jersey.

When Madison (Team Virginia!) began the Convention by revealing his Virginia Plan, it stunned the delegates. Many on Team Jersey couldn't believe their ears. Madison wasn't proposing mere alterations; he wanted to scrap the Articles of Confederation altogether and adopt a truly national, fully representative government.

Earlier that morning, they had—in some haste to get things moving—already voted to establish a "supreme Legislative, Executive, and Judiciary," rejecting the cherished principle of federalism on which their American Republic had been founded and embracing what could only be called a more British government. (What a difference a decade makes; they were rebelling against their previous rebellion.) Thus, Madison had already launched a revolution—independence from the Articles of Confederation—without saying a word or firing a shot. Now he was describing his bold blueprint for a new government. To Team Jersey, this wasn't just revolutionary, it was revolting.

When Patrick Henry said he "smelt a rat," this was the rat.

Instead of surrendering to Madison's genius, rubber-stamping his plan, and calling it a government, Team Jersey . . . called it a day. Madison had just dropped a bomb in the halls of the Republic, and they needed time to absorb the blow. With nerves jangled, the delegates agreed to adjourn and reconvene the next morning with, according to Madison's notes, a simple item on the agenda: nothing more, and nothing less, than "to consider the State of the American Union."

★ ★ ★

Actually, there was one more thing.

As the delegates were leaving the Assembly Room that afternoon, delegate Charles Pinckney of South Carolina insisted that he, too, had a plan for a new government, and that the delegates should consider his plan when they considered the state of the American Union the next day. It was this request that led Pinckney to, in later years, claim authorship of the Constitution. But it's not clear he ever had a plan—certainly Convention secretary Jackson, who was busy liking puppies, failed to keep a copy of any Pinckney proposal. Historians have called the delegate from South Carolina "a sponger" and "a plagiarist," a "pathetic" man who made "extravagant claims" to burnish his reputation. Madison himself insisted that Pinckney's alleged plan was but a figment of his imagination. We might give Pinckney the benefit of the doubt—Madison, after all, had a vested interest in clearing the path for his Virginia Plan—if not for the fact that he was a known liar: Although he was twenty-nine years old at the time of the Convention, he claimed to be just twenty-four—conveniently, two years younger than the actual youngest delegate, Jonathan Dayton of New Jersey. It was a lie he stood by; many years later he even recalled "the deep diffidence and solemnity which he felt, being the youngest member of that body." Pinckney was a man determined to make his mark on history, either by *making* his mark on history, or by telling people he had. It's hard to say why he thought being the youngest delegate would do the trick; but it's easy to see that the official portrait he submitted to the Convention was overkill:

Charles Pinckney, supposed author of the "Pinckney Plan," seen here
With Pacifier, "proof indisputable that I'm younger than everybody
else here no matter what they say." Portrait by Gilbert Stuart.

Suffice it to say, this is the kind of behavior James Madison had to deal with. And if history was being written by the Great Men of the Convention, little Charlie Pinckney wanted his footnote.*

---

* And here it is. (Go get 'em, Charlie!)

★ ★ ★

Not surprisingly, for the delegates about to do nothing less than "consider the state of the American Union," one night's sleep didn't do the trick. Little Charlie Pinckney set the mood of the morning, insisting that the whole Convention was out of order. They had, he reminded them, been sent to make amendments to the Articles of Confederation, not toss it out entirely, and if the delegates behind the Virginia Plan were intent on abolishing state governments, then "their business was at an end"—only hours after it had begun. He was going to take his ball, and his vote, and go home. The Convention might have ended there, if the peg-legged amanuensis Gouverneur Morris hadn't leapt—well, not *leapt* exactly—to the Virginia Plan's defense: "In all communities," he boomed, "there must be one supreme power and one only."

With that, the debate was on: between Team Virginia and Team Jersey, between those who believed in a strong national government and those whose allegiances were to their thirteen sovereign communities. "We the People" versus "We the States."

The signature play of Team Virginia—*proportional representation,* the idea that the composition of the legislature should be tied to population— was one of Madison's most cherished proposals. But it wasn't cherished by all.

Certainly not by the captain of Team Jersey. William Paterson, the former attorney general of New Jersey who would become the face of the New Jersey Plan, was committed to state sovereignty, and simply did not trust the political judgment of "the people." Proportional representation, therefore, would not do. Paterson didn't trust the people to do much of anything, for that matter. As New Jersey's top prosecutor during the Revolution—that is to say, when he really should have had more important things on his mind—he spent much of his time prosecuting his own citizens for fornication. And when not stopping other people from having sex, he was shutting down many of the state's taverns. Later, as New Jersey's governor, he advocated legislation outlawing the playing of billiards. Under Paterson's rule, there would be no sex, liquor, or nine-ball.

So much for the pursuit of happiness.

(And, frankly, for everything we now associate with New Jersey.)

The teetotaling, coitus-averse, billiard-phobic Paterson remained silent for the first two weeks of the Convention, content to take notes as the other delegates argued. But as soon as the arguments began to coalesce,

William Paterson of New Jersey, seen here
not having sex or playing pool

and Paterson sensed things were moving in a nationalist direction he didn't support, he could no longer bite his tongue (he had, after all, also outlawed the biting of tongues). He rose to address the assembly, and directly indicted his fellow delegates: They weren't just breaking their promise; they were breaking the law. They had failed in their sworn duty merely to amend, not replace, the Articles of Confederation. "The idea of a *national* government," he had it on good authority, "never entered into the mind" of the states that sent their representatives to the State House—and as Captain of Team Jersey, he would have none of it. "New Jersey will never confederate on the plan before the Committee. She would be swallowed up. I would rather submit to a monarch, to a despot, than to such a fate." It was no idle threat, his; this is a man, after all, who could keep people from indulging in snooker.

When he insisted that any vote on the matter be postponed, the committee instead adjourned for the weekend, defeated, after two weeks of no progress. (They adjourned like this quite often. Quitting while you were behind seemed to be the theme of the summer.)

The next two weeks were a mess of abandoned resolutions. Questions of representation, of how slaves should be counted, of whether "states ought to have weight . . . in proportion to their wealth"—all solutions were bandied about, debated, and discarded. On what would become the peskiest of questions—um, just who is this Congress going to be, anyway?—Benjamin Franklin offered a unique formula: Each state could be given an equal number of delegates, but each delegate would be allowed to vote independently. To Franklin, it seemed a sensible middle ground—so sensible, in fact, that delegates dropped it without comment.

Compromise was not yet on the table. There were no cries of mercy. The delegates still hadn't given up.

★ ★ ★

The southern states were just beginning to feel their oats. Temperatures in Philadelphia had soared past eighty degrees. The Assembly Room was a dutch oven—further evidence, it seems to me, of their lack of judgment. Shouldn't we question the genius of supposed visionaries who choose midsummer in Philadelphia to hold a convention? And then, in the name of secrecy, nail the windows shut? And then, in the name of style, wear powdered wigs?

Hmmm, where should we hold our convention?

I know! A sweat lodge!

Fine, but only if we get to wear our wigs!

Naturally. But wait—wouldn't that look foolish?

You're absolutely right. Best we nail the windows shut, too. Passing out from heatstroke is one thing—

But to be *seen* doing so—?

Can you imagine?!

Just the thought of it!

So we're agreed. Anyhow, is it hot in here, or is it just me?

The results might have been expected. As the larger New England states were starting to feel antsy, and perhaps ready to make a deal, the men from the southern states—many of them small, most of them slave-owning, all of them stubborn—were just getting warmed up.

Men like Luther Martin. Martin, who had been a star attorney in Maryland before being appointed attorney general, was selected by the small-state advocates for his skills as a prosecutor in the courtroom. He was known for winning many unlikely and unpopular cases. They had good reason to believe he was the man to represent their cause well.

The only problem? He was also a drunk.

In Martin's defense, it is worth a small detour in the narrative of the summer's devolution to reveal an inconvenient truth about the Framers of the Constitution: They were *all* drunks. Or, in the parlance of the day, drunkards. Aside from a few teetotalers—I'm looking at *you*, Mr. Paterson (although not in a way that would make you uncomfortable)—the amount of alcohol consumed in 1787 was staggering. The average American over fifteen years old threw back almost six gallons of alcohol each year, more than twice our modern consumption. Drinking was a ceremonial part of the day, and a companion at night. John Hancock himself kept a gallon of smuggled rum punch by his bedside, so that he might sleep well and dream of large signatures.

As custom, then, the delegates indulged. They began each morning with a "small beer" for breakfast—water and milk were considered unsafe, as if they needed an excuse—and they kept the party rolling during the day with hard cider and rum. By design, office hours for the delegates at the State House were a paltry 10:00 A.M. to 3:00 P.M., so that they could make happy hour at the local taverns—where many of the delegates not only drank every afternoon, but slept each night, and tended to hangovers each morning. Despite complaining about Philadelphia's acrid air and contracting an intestinal disorder that had to be treated by a local doctor, Connecticut's William Samuel Johnson made his bed at Philadelphia's City Tavern.* Two of the most respected men in the Assembly Room that summer, Washington and Franklin, brewed beer with as much gusto as they fought wars or managed feats of diplomacy. As for the Father of the Constitution, when he was president in 1809, James Madison tried to establish a National Brewery and a position in his cabinet for a Secretary of Beer. (He accomplished neither, for those keeping score of his many failures.)

It violates our current image of these demigods: One imagines them poring over textbooks in grand libraries in their search for truth, not hurling in an alley off Market Street. But the fact remains: Their assembly in 1787 was as much a convention as a "beer summit," and the Constitution was written—to borrow from Franklin's drinker's dictionary—by a bunch of *glaiz'd, wamble crop'd Philippians* who had *Rais'd Their Monuments, Seen the Devil,* and *Gone to Jerusalem.* If they are our Founding Fathers, we are all the Children of Alcoholics.

And the "Miracle at Philadelphia" was that the Constitution wasn't written on the back of a bar napkin.

---

* Where, a decade into the twenty-first century, one can still enjoy wassail served in pewter glasses and quite delicious "Martha Washington Style Turkey Pot Pie," cooked by a chef who is a close personal friend of country star Kenny Rogers, at least according to the picture of the pair displayed in the entryway.

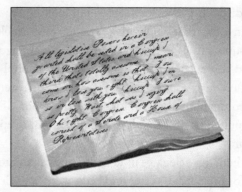

*Friends don't let friends drink
and draft constitutions.*

Even among a band of brewers, Luther Martin stood apart. "Of medium height . . . near-sighted, absent-minded, shabbily attired, harsh of voice . . . with a face crimsoned by the brandy which he continually imbibed," Martin had such a reputation for drunkenness that he became known as "the wild man" of the Convention. His fellow Baltimoreans loved to recount the tale of the time he bumped into a cow on Baltimore Street in the town center, mistook it for a gentlewoman, bowed respectfully and apologized to it, and then went on his way—no doubt pleased with himself, convinced he had just shown unerring politeness for all to see. His *cherubimical crump-footedness* (Franklin's words, not mine) also flowed into the courtroom, where, let the record show, his frequent presiding judge witnessed that he was "often intoxicated" during sessions. (Judge: "Order in the court!" Martin: "I'll have a vodka martini.")

When sober, Martin was a lucid, fierce opponent of the Virginia Plan, which would shift power away from the states, most notably from his beloved Maryland, and he was selected by fellow "states' men" to attack the Virginia Plan, which they saw as an unacceptable seizure of state power in the name of nationalism. They needed a passionate advocate to counteract such a desperate measure. They needed a lawyer to give the closing argument of a lifetime.

They got Dudley Moore. Or as Franklin might have seen him, a "Prince Eugene" who had "eaten a Pudding Bagg."

As Martin rose to speak amid the growing summer heat of June 27, he launched into such a long-winded ramble of animated disputation that even his allies lost patience with him. Robert Yates, otherwise a champion of Martin's Anti-Federalist position, was forced to admit that Martin's arguments were "too diffuse; it was not possible to trace him through the whole, or to methodize his ideas into a systematic or argumentative arrangement." What it lacked in cohesion—"I'm not as think as you drunk I am!"—it made up in length; Martin's rambling speech took up the full day.

He barreled through each of the Anti-Federalists' arguments: That the only purpose of a central government was to protect state governments. That "the people" who cast off the yoke of the British Crown had delegated authority to their own states, not to another central, monarchical government. That no one should mess with Maryland. He cited Joseph Priestly. He quoted John Locke. He whipped himself up into such a frenzy that he even started making drunken threats: If the three largest states continued to insist on proportional representation, he said, then the ten smallest states "should league themselves together" against them.

Then he got tired. Try as he might, he couldn't filibuster his own sobriety. As James Madison recorded it, Martin abruptly declared himself "too much exhausted . . . to finish his remarks," demanded that he be allowed to finish them the next day, and walked out of the State House into the streets of Philadelphia—where, we can assume, he bumped into a cow.

Some historians suggest that the small-state cause never recovered from Martin's drunken ramblings. What is certain is that Martin's diatribe really freaked Benjamin Franklin out, prompting him to make a speech in the Convention for the very first time, in which he reflected on "the small progress we have made after five weeks' close attendance." They were still "groping . . . in the dark."

Franklin, the revered elder statesman in the room, knew he needed to act. But even he was at a loss. So what, then, was his solution?

For a man of little religious faith, it was a shocking one:

Pray for help.

"How has it happened," he asked, "that we have not hitherto once thought of humbly applying to the Father of lights to illuminate our understandings?" He even appealed to the Convention's president. "God governs in the affairs of men," he told George Washington. "And if a sparrow cannot fall to the ground without his notice, is it probable that an empire can rise without his aid?"*

Such was the sorry state of the Convention, only five weeks in. Benja-

---

* In his handwritten copy of the speech that day, Franklin underlined the word "God"—not once, but twice. That's how <u>screwed</u> they were.

min Franklin, the world's most famous deist, was on bended knee. *May God help us all.*

He put forth a formal motion that "henceforth prayers imploring the assistance of Heaven, and its blessings on our deliberations, be held in this Assembly every morning, before we proceed to business, and that one or more of the clergy of the city be requested to officiate in that service." As Richard Beeman records it, "an embarrassed silence followed."

Everyone knew the stakes: If Franklin was calling for a priest, this Convention was on its deathbed.

Alexander Hamilton finally broke the silence, delicately pointing out that posting a casting call for a local clergyman, especially "at this late day," would "lead the public to believe that the embarrassments and dissensions within the Convention had suggested this measure"—which, of course, they had. Luckily, Hugh Williamson of North Carolina summoned a much more palatable reason why they couldn't afford to hire a priest: Namely, they couldn't afford to hire a priest. "The Convention [has] no funds." It's not that they didn't *want* to appeal to God; it's that Divine Intervention doesn't come cheap.

So it was settled: There would be no priest, no prayers, and little hope.

★ ★ ★

To some, the next morning appeared to offer a reprieve in the deathwatch; to others, what transpired that day was the final stake in the heart of the Constitution. It began as usual, with arguments entrenched on both sides. Then Connecticut's William Samuel Johnson took the floor. His cure was a drastic one: that both models for Congress "ought to be combined: that in one branch, the people ought to be represented; in the other, the states."

In other words: a compromise.

Quitter.

He oughta be ashamed. All around him sat Founding Fathers, men of steely resolve who embodied the virtues of bold, unbending intransigence (of, as Morris described it, "obstinate adherence" to their beliefs)—and yet here were Johnson and his Connecticut colleagues, eager to Cry Uncle.

Granted, we know this compromise—"divided sovereignty" between the states and a central government, now known as the *Connecticut* Compromise—ultimately won out; at the time, however, things got ugly. Pennsylvania's James Wilson threatened that if the small states were not willing to join the union under proportional representation, the large states would get along very well without them, thank you very much. Madison piled on, scoffing, "The party claiming from others an adherence to a common engagement ought at least to be guiltless itself of a violation." (*Oh, snap! I know you are, but what am I?*)

After a day of *Yo Momma* taunts, it's not hard to believe that "the fate of America," as peg-legged Morris wrote, "was suspended by a hair."

Benjamin Franklin tried to cool tempers in the increasingly heated room. "When a broad table is to be made," he grumbled, doing his best Wilford Brimley impression, "and the edges of planks do not fit, the artist takes a little from both, and makes a good joint. In the manner here both sides must part with some of their demands in order that they may join in some accommodating proportion."

But even Franklin, respected by all, could get accommodation from none, despite the nice story about how tables are made. Attitudes had overwhelmed platitudes. Gunning Bedford of Delaware then launched into the most vitriolic speech so far that summer, culminating in a sentiment that summed up his feelings about Pennsylvania, Massachusetts, Virginia, and the other large states: "I do not, gentlemen, trust you." And, he threatened, if the large states persisted in dismissing the small, "the small ones will find some foreign ally of more honor and good faith, who will take them by the hand and do them justice."

It seemed Delaware didn't need Virginia to dance with it. Delaware had a girlfriend in Canada.

At yet another impasse, the Convention adjourned.

About the only agreement they could make was that they were getting nowhere. As Gouverneur Morris recalled the mood, "Debates had run high, conflicting opinions were obstinately adhered to, animosities were kindling, some of the members were threatening to go home, and, at this alarming crisis, a dissolution of the Convention was hourly to be apprehended." *But other than that, sure, we're getting on famously. And how is* your *summer going?*

What kept the Convention alive, in fact, was how little some delegates cared about it. When there was a stalemate, again, over the proposal to give each state an equal vote in the Senate, three men were simply absent: Georgians William Pierce and William Few were headed to New York to cast a vote in the Continental Congress. A few tables over, the seat of Maryland's Daniel of St. Thomas Jenifer (yes, that was his name) was suspiciously empty, too. Until that day, Maryland had been divided on the question of representation, with Luther Martin, *in* (hiccup) *favor* of giving states an equal number of senators, and Daniel of St. Thomas Jenifer *against*. But when the vote to proceed was to be cast, Jenifer was gone, inexplicably missing from the Assembly Room, putting Maryland in the "yes" column and temporarily reviving a Convention whose demise had been "hourly to be apprehended."

So had it not been for a few conscientious objectors who were occasionally MIA from the Convention, there would have been no Constitution. For the survival of the Republic, we can thank the quitters.*

When even this didn't stick—and at this point, why would you expect it to?—the Congress assembled on that day did what Congresses have done for two centuries when they have no earthly clue what the heck to do.

No, not pray to God.

They formed a committee.

James Madison knew that committees were the most desperate of desperate measures, and "had rarely seen any other effect than delay coming from such committees in Congress." And it was a particular kind of embarrassment to Madison; he recognized that choosing only one delegate from each state to join the committee directly flouted the very principle he was trying to float: proportional representation. One might as well hire the Devil to man the Pearly Gates.

Madison's Convention wasn't going nearly as he had planned. When the delegates adjourned for the Fourth of July break, so that those who wished could distract themselves with "the celebrations on the anniversary of Independence," Madison attended none. He was in no mood for fireworks—he had just experienced six weeks' worth.

★ ★ ★

With the summer half over, the taverns still stocked, and the heat rising inside the State House, the frustrated delegates began to realize that not only might they not reach an agreement that pleased everyone; they might not reach an agreement at all. It is "doubtful," George Mason wrote, "whether any sound and effectual system can be established." Writing to Washington from New York, Alexander Hamilton spelled out their possible fate: "I fear that we shall let slip the golden opportunity of rescuing the American empire from disunion, anarchy and misery." In response, Washington wrote back with only pessimism: "In a word, I almost despair of seeing a favourable

---

* Whether Jenifer had secretly struck a deal with Georgia's Abraham Baldwin—an agreement to see to it that slavery be protected, say—well, let the conspiracy theorists conspire. Suffice it to point out, as soon as the vote was complete, Jenifer meandered nonchalantly back into the Assembly Room. He never explained his absence.

issue to the proceedings of the Convention," adding with some petulance, "and do therefore repent having any agency in the business."

When the committee finally offered its official report recommending an equal vote in the Senate and one representative in the House for every forty thousand inhabitants, even the man with the most to lose if the Convention were to fail was against the compromise. Madison took to the floor to defend proportional representation in the Senate yet again, begging the delegates not to "depart from justice in order to conciliate the smaller states." Gouverneur Morris, who, with his peg leg and his large mouth, had easily earned his status as Madison's hype man, joined the hyperbole, suggesting that "the whole human race will be affected by the proceedings of this Convention," and with so many eyes upon them, surely they would choose the "reasonable and right" thing to do. When even that didn't evoke a response, Morris became unhinged. Perhaps the heat, the stakes, the expectations of the world, and a diet of beer, rum, and cider spurred him on, but Morris threatened extreme measures. America "must be united," he rumbled, and if "persuasion does not unite it"—he paused, surveying his fellow delegates—"the sword will."

The sword will!

Was Morris threatening a sword fight, right here? A duel between Team Virginia and Team New Jersey? It would have been messy, no doubt, but it might have quelled talk of compromise right then and there. At the least, it would have spiced up those high school history textbooks.

The boring truth: Morris threw down the gauntlet; no one picked it up.

This maddening game of back-and-forth consumed July, with proposals on representation voted down as quickly as they were brought up: one senator from each state; two senators from each state; three senators; two senators, but only those who owned property; divide the nation into regions and apportion representatives accordingly; a sliding scale, with one senator for very small states (Delaware, Rhode Island) up to five for Virginia. There were dozens of solutions, but no takers.

For weeks, the delegates would drink in the morning and argue through the afternoon. And as if their own tempers—or talk of swordplay—weren't enough to disturb the delegates in the increasingly humid Assembly Room, they had another distraction: the raw stink of Philadelphia. Just a block away, the tanners and butchers of Philadelphia had set up shop long before the delegates arrived, and they didn't take down their shingles just because a few bewigged politicians needed a little peace. The butchers continued butchering, and the tanners continued their usual practice of throwing their used carcasses into the sewer along Dock Street, joining the excrement that flowed (or rather, didn't flow) down one of Philadelphia's main thoroughfares. The silver lining, perhaps—if a silver lining is to be found on rotting animal carcasses—is that the foul smell masked the delegates' own body odors; some didn't bathe for weeks.

Worse than the smells were the sounds. Immediately across the street from the State House stood the Walnut Street jail, where Philadelphia's most notorious miscreants were housed in odious conditions—dozens to a room, in crowded dormitories, next door to a bunch of *politicians,* no less—conditions so disgusting, in fact, that it led to the formation that same year of the Philadelphia Society for Alleviating the Miseries of Public Prisons. Many prisoners needed rehab after their rehab—not only were they angry, they were drunk. It is said that twenty gallons of liquor were brought into the prison daily by the jailer for sale to the inmates; those who couldn't afford any would barter the clothes off their back. So not only were they angry and drunk, they were naked. And in mid-July, they rioted—angrily, drunkenly, nakedly, and within easy earshot as the delegates tried to listen to nuanced arguments about the separation of powers. It had to affect the delegates' thinking; one might as well try to do a jigsaw puzzle inside a boxing ring.

But hey—at least the prisoners could riot. The delegates, who had their own heat, humidity, and daily torture to complain about, had no such remedy. When it looked as though the delegates would launch into yet another round of heated debate—this time over the matter of whether Congress should be given the absolute power "to make all Laws" necessary to enforce all *other* laws (which became the infamous "necessary and proper" clause in Article I, Section 8)—some just up and left. They had had enough.

Those who remained, complained. George Washington, usually the country's reliable straight man, now dripped with sarcasm, noting smugly that if the Convention were to fail, "the defects cannot with propriety be charged to the hurry with which the business has been conducted." John Rutledge grew incensed at the "tediousness of the proceedings," adding that if they didn't wrap up soon, they might as well plan to spend the winter in Philadelphia. John Adams would later compliment the Constitution as "the greatest single effort of national deliberation that the world has ever seen," but at the time it seemed the world might never see it. As summer began, they had greeted each other as liberators; now they hated each other as deliberators. Familiarity among the delegates bred both a clear contempt ("Every article is again argued over," New Jersey's David Brearley whined) as well as a burning desire for a change of scenery and company.

("I am as sick of being here as you can conceive," Elbridge Gerry wrote to his young bride, Ann, adding, "entre nous, I do not expect to give my voice to the measure"—French for "Between us, this whole things sucks.")

There was simply no end in sight. Even Madison's tank was on empty. The notes he penned so diligently each night grew noticeably shorter as August wore on. What began as an exhaustive diary of each delegate's contributions became brief, catty dismissals of their speeches and positions. Soon he was just drawing stick figures in the margins.

As the end of August neared, just when it seemed they might not stand one minute more in one another's company, John Rutledge proposed a stunningly homeopathic remedy: *longer* hours. Perhaps what they needed, he thought, was to work harder, to spend *more* time, not less, at one another's throats. Fewer breaks, more resentment. Rutledge, who until then had shown no signs that he wanted to be Hall Monitor in the Nerd Convention, proposed that they extend the session from their customary adjournment at three o'clock (no one ever accused the delegates of workaholism) to four o'clock, and that "no motion to adjourn sooner be allowed." His bright idea lasted about a week. Had it been enforced any longer, those rioting in shackles just outside the State House could well have been joined by a few in powdered wigs.

To the noise and heat from outside, add intense pressure from above. The Pennsylvania state legislature, due to reconvene on September 5, had come back into town expected to take their usual seats in the Assembly Room. But when they found the delegates locked in heated arguments (many lasting until three o'clock in the afternoon!) they agreed to move upstairs to the grand hallway of the State House until the Convention disbanded. Since the state legislature was quite aware that these delinquent delegates just a floor below were secretly redefining American government in a way that would have direct and possibly devastating effects on how such state legislatures operated, and worse, that they were *borrowing their office to do it*, it's hard to believe they relocated upstairs without complaint.

Educated guess? They stomped around a lot.

To be sure, no one was happy with the arrangement. However eager the Pennsylvania state legislature was to reclaim its Assembly Room, the Convention delegates were just as eager to hand it over. So with key decisions still unmade, and very little common ground unearthed, on September 8 the Convention appointed yet another committee, this one tasked "to revise the stile and arrange the articles which had been agreed to by the House." It was the only consensus the exhausted delegates could find:

Screw it, let's just start writing the damn thing.

For the next week, after adjourning for the day, the five members of the "Committee of Stile and Arrangement" wrote and edited a final draft that changed nightly, hostage to the latest whim of the Convention. They would set something to parchment, just to have it overruled by any blowhard with a wig on his head. At the precise point when they should have been chiseling an indelible charter, they had in their hands a bunch of cursive Jell-O.

A WikiConstitution.

More of an Etch-A-Sketch than a blueprint.

Just as the Committee of Stile started its double duty, and the delegates were eyeing the door, Virginia's George Mason, a man of terrible timing, voiced his wish that they add another heavy load onto their docket.

A bill of rights.

Mason, who in 1776 had authored Virginia's Declaration of Rights, knew that he was asking too much of the beleaguered delegates, and therefore tried to limp in, soft-selling his request: "A bill," he calculated, "might be prepared in a few hours." A bill of rights, completed in an afternoon? Who was he kidding? These people hadn't even written a Constitution in four months.

Nonetheless, Mason asked that his proposal be put to a vote. The debate on its merits lasted "no more than a few moments." Every single state delegation voted against it. That is how despairing they were over the possibility that they'd spend another day together: They couldn't even bother to address the fundamental rights of every American.

The bill of rights, which came to be known as the Bill of Rights, would have to wait for the ratification debates.

★ ★ ★

There was a new Constitution to consider, and that was enough. The Committee of Stile had turned in its recommended version—and this time, thankfully, mercifully, *finally*, there would be *no backsies*. Should the delegates agree to it, this would be their Constitution: one Preamble and seven Articles, full of grand ideas, huge mistakes, and, right there on page one, a "Great Compromise."

They were about to add their signatures to an extremely anticipated official document they had extremely mixed feelings about. So the delegates did what anyone might do under such pressure: They drank themselves silly. After they toasted the occasion, they drowned their miseries. They had spent four months compromising their values; perhaps they could drink their guilt away. They certainly tried. In the span of just a few hours, the fifty-five men who crowded City Tavern on Friday, September 14, 1787, guzzled enough alcohol to fell an army regiment: sixty bottles of claret, fifty-four bottles of Madeira, fifty bottles of "old stock," vats of porter, cider, and beer, and what has been described as "some" bowls of rum punch. They weren't just pledging their sacred honor; they were pledging a frat. So wild did the celebration get that City Tavern, a place quite familiar with drunkenness, took the unusual step of sending along a bill for "breakage."

Despite what must have been a monster hangover, the next morning the delegates tried to sober up to what they had done over the previous four months. Aware they were about to go public with their creation, Maryland's Daniel Carroll suggested the Convention prepare a general address to the

American people. The exercise, he thought, would consolidate and justify their best arguments to a suspicious populace. It also might help them get their story straight. (They would soon have a lot of explaining to do.)

Useful as such an address may have been, John Rutledge objected—not because it wasn't a good idea, but "on account of the delay it would produce." The thought of another minute in one another's presence, at one another's throats, was simply too wretched to contemplate. At least not sober.

We don't have to go home, but we can't stay here.

Before long, in spite of their lingering headaches—or perhaps because of them—the delegates were at it again, revisiting an issue that had already been decided: proportional representation. Only an official promise that "no state, without its consent shall be deprived of its equal suffrage in the Senate" finally put the debate to rest.

Then came the wildest idea of all, considering the Constitution had been agreed to. Virginia's Edmund Randolph still found the Constitution deficient in many of the ways voiced by the Convention that day, most blatantly in Article I, in the "indefinite and dangerous power given by the Constitution to Congress." He demanded that delegates to the upcoming ratification conventions be authorized to add amendments. George Mason joined Randolph's protest, and together they insisted they weren't interested in mere amendments after all. There was no use anymore in tinkering at the margins—a phrase here, and revised ratio of representation there. No, they had something much more revolutionary in mind.

A *second* Convention.

A *do-over*.

Once more, this time with feeling.

For the Framers in that room—who had to be thinking, *You've gotta be kidding me*—it was a harsh indictment from two Virginians they respected. They had begun the summer, as Thomas Paine spun it, endeavoring to seize "every opportunity and every encouragement before us, to form the noblest, purest constitution on the face of the earth." They had failed. And Mason was proposing the only salvation:

Let's start over.

We have it in our power to begin the Constitution again.

Randolph declared he would sign the Constitution only if it included an amendment calling for such a second convention. Think about that: One of the Framers of the Constitution wanted to put language *in the Constitution itself* admitting that the Constitution was, as Constitutions go, an inferior Constitution.

The Convention's official response to Randolph's proposal reflected less their disagreement with his premise than it did their sheer panic at having to stick around any longer. "All the states answered—no." The dissenters had been defeated. As Madison recounted it, "Col. Mason left Philadelphia in an exceeding ill humour indeed."

At last, the delegates called for a vote "on the question to agree to the Constitution, as amended." Finally, the question was on the table: *Is this really the best we can do?*

Madison recorded the moment: "All the States Ay."

★ ★ ★

Their job was done, if not done well. All that was left to do was sign on the dotted line—or in this case, scratch a goose feather dipped in oak gall ink onto a piece of sheepskin. For that long-awaited moment to arrive, they first had to designate a man to engross the official copy on parchment, a man whose status and accomplishments might personify just how they felt about this hard-fought, hard-won, and hard-to-swallow document. Would it be the devoted Madison? The respected Franklin? The "indispensable" Washington?

Meet Jacob Shallus, assistant clerk.

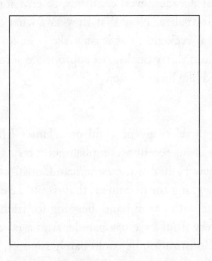

The unremarkable Jacob Shallus,
seen here not pictured

Doesn't ring a bell?
Of course not.

The delegates should have been falling over one another for the solemn duty, leaping at the opportunity to leave their mark on "the noblest, purest constitution on the face of the earth"; instead, presumably ashamed of the mess they had made, they pawned it off on a junior clerk to the Pennsylvania legislature. Gone were the proud days of 1776 when Thomas Jefferson, the "author of America," slaved at his desk writing the Declaration of Independence—*we mutually pledge to each other our lives, our fortunes, and our sacred honor*—doting over each dotted *i*, lingering over each crossed *t*, taking great care to make sure each *s* looked like an *f* for some reason. The Constitution of 1787 was a rush job fit for an assistant clerk.

We mutually pledge our lives, our fortunes, our sacred honor—and let's be honest, our apologies.

Thus it was that on Friday, September 14, the Convention gave the task of actually writing the Constitution no delegate could bear to defend to a man no American has ever heard of. (Or much cared to. Shallus's identity wasn't unearthed until 1937, long after we learned other important details, like which delegate once apologized to a cow.) Even though he held the pen, he left no impression, and made little mark on history.

He would be the perfect scapegoat. (Are we delegates to blame for this scourge? Nah, *Jake* touched it last.) The concepts that informed the Constitution had taken decades, even centuries, to envision. The details had taken months to formalize. Now that they saw what they had wrought, Shallus was given a weekend to at least make it look pretty. And for his efforts, they paid him thirty bucks. An appropriate sum. Any more and it would have seemed like hush money.

★ ★ ★

The next day was a relatively peaceful one. James Madison spent it as would befit a man of his recent accomplishment: trying to borrow a hundred bucks. The new Father of the American Constitution was broke. So on the day before signing the document that would save America, he went delegate to delegate with hat in hand, begging for train fare back to New York. It was a far cry from a victory parade. And a far cry from a victory; not only was it a Constitution he could barely support, it was a Constitution he could barely afford.

On the morning of Monday, September 17, the day the delegates were to sign the Constitution, it was read aloud in the Assembly Room. Best guess, it took about half an hour. Each delegate had been given a copy, so that those who wished to, and could bear to, might read along, careful to ensure that each of his pet concerns was included, and to cringe with each concession. James Madison must have felt especially cringey, as the document he was about to sign—which he had championed for so long—had very few of his fingerprints. His most vital concerns had been jettisoned, including that which he cared most about: proportional representation for all.

For Madison and many others, even after four months, those thirty minutes could not go fast enough. Benjamin Franklin must have known that it would be a moment of reckoning, because when the reading was complete, he stood up and produced from his pocket a speech that he had written over the previous weekend. Too exhausted to deliver his own words, however, he placed it into the hands of James Wilson, who read it aloud for him.

And what was Franklin's final thought to offer the roomful of delegates? What was his best pitch as they considered whether to sign? Only this: "When you assemble a number of men to have the advantage of their joint wisdom, you inevitably assemble with those men, all their prejudices, their passions, their errors of opinion, their local interests, and their selfish views. From such an assembly can a perfect production be expected?" He turned to Washington and gave his meekest endorsement: "Thus I consent, Sir, to this Constitution because I expect no better."

Really, Ben? Is that all you got?

Then, despite confessing that "there are several parts of this constitution which I do not at present approve," Franklin asked that "every member of this convention who may still have objections to [the Constitution] would, with me, on this occasion doubt a little of his own infallibility—and to make manifest our unanimity—by putting his name to the instrument." Clearly, even the eldest delegate would not be spared by this Constitution. It had reduced a revered old man to a common mendicant.

Franklin's pleading worked. No one, after all, wants to see a grown man cry. All but three delegates put their names to the instrument.

While the last delegates waited in line to sign, it is reported that Ben Franklin found the strength to stand, point at the back of George Washington's wooden chair—on which was carved a half-sun—and declare: "I have often in the course of the Session . . . looked at that behind the President without being able to tell whether it was rising or setting. Now at length"—four interminable months, to be exact—"I have the happiness to know that it is a rising and not a setting sun." The Constitution had been written, the sun had risen, it was the beginning of a new dawn. But on a day marking such abandoned principles, at a moment of such obvious compromise, it's a wonder he didn't say, "Heck, call it noon."

★ ★ ★

Now we understand how it all happened—or rather, almost didn't.

The Constitution wasn't a "Miracle at Philadelphia" written by an "assembly of demigods." On the contrary; what began as a measured, deliberate effort to rescue a beleaguered country became a perpetual unresolved-motion machine—a maddening cycle of nonbinding votes by a parade of toothless committees, marked by fits and starts, fights and "full stops," conducted by a combative group of exhausted, drunken, broke, petty, partisan, scheming, squabbling, bloviating, backstabbing, grandstanding, godforsaken, posturing, restless, cow-tipping, homesick, cloistered, claustrophobic, sensory-deprived, under-oxygenated, fed-up, talked-out, overheated delegates so distraught and despairing they threatened violence, secession, foreign allegiance, even prayer—and concluded, for those who didn't abandon the proceedings altogether, with as much premeditation and forethought as a game of musical chairs: the last, least abhorrent, mutually-somewhat-acceptable idea on the table when the music stopped—or the heat became too unbearable, or the liquor too strong, or the rioting too loud, or the pressure too intense, or the company too loathsome, or the wigs too uncomfortable, or the patience too thin—became the law of the land. As much the product of an "assembly of demigods" as a confederacy of dunces.

From page one, the Constitution is, by its own admission, a compromise. It is what you get when you drink beer for breakfast.

★ ★ ★

I'm not suggesting there's something inherently wrong with compromise. I'm *saying* it. I'm screaming it from the rooftops. We're America, dang it.

But even those who believe in compromise think of it as a necessary evil. "We accept compromise," write authors Eric Lane and Michael Oreskes, "because we feel we are represented in the decision." And due to "dysfunctions in the Congress that need to be fixed," most sensible Americans "no longer feel well represented."

Not just many; most. Far from feeling "well represented," two-thirds of Americans can't even name their congressman. And the one-third who can almost gag at the mention: Aside from a few weeks after the 9/11 attacks, the approval ratings of Congress have lingered somewhere between bedbugs and the Ebola virus. We glimpse them as cartoons in campaign commercials, but we see our representatives in the flesh only during biennial campaign events, when they drop by long enough to ask for our votes, clog our airwaves, kiss our hands, shake our babies, and spend obscene amounts of money telling us that Washington has a spending problem. The rest of the time, we see Congress not as our loyal representatives, but as "the bums" in Washington who constantly deserve to be thrown out, even though we can't muster the energy to do so: The turnout for midterm elections barely reaches 40 percent. Worse when it's raining.

Congress is now, in the words of congressional expert Norman Ornstein, "the Broken Branch." Whispered by more than a few in 1787, our reservations about Congress have become a chorus, with even sitting congressmen joining the choir: "We're incompetent!" thundered Senator Tom Coburn in 2010. "Frankly I wonder who the 23 percent of the American people are that trust us!" By late 2011, approval of Congress had dropped to 9 percent, leaving South Carolina's Lindsey Graham to resort to extreme measures: "It's so bad sometimes I tell people I'm a lawyer." Former Nebraska senator Bob Kerrey places direct blame for our current state of affairs on page one of the document they had all sworn to defend: "I have serious questions today as to whether or not Article I can sustain democracy in times that we're in."

It would be treasonous if it weren't so true.

Senators Kerrey and Coburn are merely reciting what James Madison and I have long understood: When you make compromises in the Constitution, you compromise the Constitution.

★ ★ ★

It's not our fault. The system has been designed to alienate us. Consider, to take just one example, the common practice of gerrymandering, the process of letting those in office redesign the boundaries of congressional districts, thereby ensuring their own reelection. Named after Massachusetts delegate Elbridge Gerry, who as governor in 1812 contrived a district for a political ally so unnatural it looked like a salamander—hence "Gerry-mandering"—the technique was, let's be honest, never a good idea.*

James Madison himself was almost a victim; in 1788, the man who helped design Congress was nearly gerrymandered out of the House by Patrick Henry and the Anti-Federalists who controlled the Virginia House of Delegates—just their way of saying *thank you* to the Father of the Constitution. Since then, it has become an even more noxious practice, a science so finely calibrated with demographic statistics and computer models that it makes a mockery of our elections. In 2006, thanks in large part to gerrymandering, the opposition party in fifty-five districts didn't even bother nominating a candidate. The deck was too stacked. The game too rigged. Why bother.

With gerrymandering, democracy has been flipped: Instead of the voters choosing their legislators, legislators choose their voters. Together with a lack of term limits, it has resulted in a class of "professional politicians" who can rely on a long career in Congress without needing to take their opposing constituents' desires into consideration. They can stay as long as they want and do as they darn well please—if their opposing constituents complain, they'll just get new constituents.

Is this democracy? Is this fair representation? Does the pope ask rhetorical questions?

Indeed, we are not well represented. We are not fairly represented. Yet thanks to our own alienation from the government and the complexity of the system itself, we feel powerless to do anything about it.

Until now.

THE FIX IS IN

THE CONVENTION MAY have taken four months to come up with a compromise that satisfied no one and—you heard the senator from Nebraska—doomed democracy. Proudly I say, I shall make quicker work of the task, compromise nothing, satisfy everyone, and save us all. The good news is that the time and effort the delegates spent wasn't totally wasted. They may

---

* Although it was much more popular than "gormadilloing," Massachusetts delegate Nathaniel Gorham's failed attempt to redesign every district into the shape of an armadillo.

not have revealed all the right answers—hey, we can't all be Nicolas Cage—but hidden throughout their debate are the right questions. Beginning with Ben Franklin's simple concern, posed early in the summer: whether "the number of Representatives should bear some proportion to the number of the Represented." If this is to be a government "of the people, by the people, and for the people," just how many people are we really talking about here? It was an important question—after all, these would be the men (and, much later, women) who had the powers to "exercise authority over dock-Yards," for goodness sake—and the delegates spent much of the summer debating it. A ratio of one representative for every forty thousand inhabitants seemed to please most, but Madison foresaw a problem: "The future increase of population" would, "if the union should be permanent, render the number of representatives excessive."

Delegate Nathaniel Gorham of Massachusetts tried a curious method to allay Madison's fears: "It is not to be supposed that the government will last so long as to produce this effect." *Don't worry, James. This government you just designed? It's doomed.*

Why, yes, it can be supposed. And while this vast country has gotten even vaster, Congress hasn't followed suit. When it was created in 1789, there were only 65 members of the House—approximately the size of a first-grade classroom today. Each congressman represented a mere 30,000 grateful citizens. As the population grew, so did the House—until 1910, when it was deemed that a legislative chamber of anything larger than 435 would be too unwieldy. But after the census of 1920, Congress established that the size of the House would be permanently fixed—not to 435, but to "the then existing number of Representatives"—an inconspicuous way to avoid admitting that 435 is an utterly arbitrary number, and hardly sacred. Had it held firm to the constitutional principle of one representative for every 40,000 people, Congress would have over 7,500 members today. Instead, the deliberative body pulled 435 out of its deliberative ass.

Today, a single member of the House represents 650,000 citizens—more than thirty times the number intended by the Framers when they invented Congress to be directly representative of its population. Far too many people for one man or woman to worry about.

Even with the fine scalpel of the gerrymander, we are too diverse to be represented by so tiny a ratio. As Madison put it, "No society ever did *or can* consist of so homogenous a mass of Citizens"—certainly no society of 650,000. "There will be rich and poor; creditors and debtors; a landed interest, a monied interest, a mercantile interest, a manufacturing interest."

We are blue state Republicans, and red state Democrats. We are cats and dogs, living together. And multiplying like bunnies.

There was a man in the Convention on that final day who saw this crisis coming. He had sat silently throughout the summer as issues of supposedly tectonic importance were debated and discussed, with none prompting him to raise his voice in either protest or affirmation. He had spoken not one word in the Assembly Room in over three months. But on that final day, he stirred. What panicked him?

Congress, that's what. And not the general, indefinite "dangerous power" given to Congress that so worried Edmund Randolph. For this man, there was a very specific concern: the ratio of congressmen to citizens. As he saw it, one representative for every forty thousand citizens "had always appeared to himself among the exceptionable parts of the plan." The ratio was too small. Average citizens, this delegate predicted, would be too far removed from their representative, too alienated from a government ostensibly "of the people."

That man?

George Washington.

The tall man in the front of the room.

As president of the Convention, his position "had hitherto restrained him from offering his sentiments on questions depending in the House," and, "it might be thought, ought now impose silence on him." But now that the Constitution was at the finish line—and he was no longer able to wash his hands of the affair—he thought the number of legislators "of so much consequence" that he couldn't bite his tongue. The future first president of the United States thought the ratio of representation in Congress too important to stay silent. His rep was on the line.

His bold, silence-shattering, earth-quaking solution? A slightly larger ratio: one representative for every—wait for it—*thirty thousand citizens.*

Huh? If Washington felt it important enough to break his record silence, why did he make such a meek adjustment? Even some of his contemporaries, far less great than he, demanded far greater representation. The very first amendment proposed to the United States Constitution, in fact, attempted to increase the number of representatives in Congress—it was one of the two "lost amendments" that were voted down from what otherwise would have been a twelve-amendment Bill of Rights (which, we can agree, is a much less pleasing number than ten). Over the years, there have been many suggestions to redesign Congress. The journalist Henry Hazlitt suggested replacing Congress with "a directorate of twelve men." George Will has suggested the nice round number of one thousand representatives. But leave it to nutball Rexford Guy Tugwell to have the wildest of solutions: "To make the Congress more representative in a nation whose problems are so generally countrywide . . . the lawmakers must have the nation, not local districts, as their constituency." (A congressman representing the entire nation?! Nutballs!)

Once again, where the Founders fall short, and Tugwell even shorter, I shall stand tall. No more compromises. No more tinkering at the margins. I don't care if you *were* the most adored president of the United States, Mr. Washington, there shall be no more futzing with the formulas. Mr. Madison, I don't care if you *did* lose your battle for proportional representation in both houses of Congress; no more whining. And Mr. Franklin, no more crowing about a Constitution "so near to perfection."

Perfection is at hand.

650,000 to 1? 40,000 to 1? 30,000 to 1?

No, sir.

Try 1 to 1.

From now on, upon adoption of this new Constitution, every American shall also be—a congressman.

What's that, Congressman? You say this sounds drastic, radical, totally insane? I agree—if by *drastic* you mean *bold,* if by *radical* you mean *awesome,* and if by *totally insane* you mean *only natural.* After all, this drastic, radical, totally insane solution is our logical next step on a path begun with the Constitution itself. We should recall that one of the most profound innovations of the Constitution of 1787, in fact, was the acknowledgment that the underlying principle of the Articles of Confederation of 1777— that newly independent Americans were capable of suppressing their individual self-interest to do the right thing for their country, even if it meant burdening themselves, or their state—was deeply flawed. It turns out that doing good just for heck of it, or for the country, is not our strong suit. With the Articles of Confederation, the Founders had misjudged our true motivations. Even George Washington was forced to admit, "We have probably had too good an opinion of human nature in forming our Constitution [of the Confederation]," he wrote. "Experience has taught us, that men will not adopt and carry into execution measures best calculated for their own good, without the intervention of a coercive power." Simply put: "We must take human nature as we find it." *It's only natural.*

General Washington should have seen it coming, frankly. From our founding we have been obviously selfish, in ways large—fewer than 1 percent of Americans were willing to join the army to fight for American independence—and small—we couldn't bear to fork over a few extra pennies to the British for a cup of tea. What the Founders sought in the Constitution was a new form of government based on an understanding and acceptance of what people are really like. (We're no angels. "If men *were* angels," Madison theorized, "no government would be necessary.") As Donald Rumsfeld might have put it, *You form a government with the people you have, not the people you might want or wish to have at a later time.* "What is government," James Madison asked, "but the greatest of all reflections of human nature?"

And what are people, I ask, but the most selfish of all creatures? Alexander Hamilton stated the obvious in 1787: "Men love power. . . . Give all power to the few, they will oppress the many. . . . Give all the power to the many, they will oppress the few." Allow me, then, to happily follow Hamilton's logic: *Give all the power to the all, they will oppress the none.* This is basic math, people.

Two-thirds of Americans can't name their congressman? Gone are the days when we trust strangers to represent us. Strangers who don't know our hopes, our fears, our dreams, our plans to construct a "public research university" in our basement. Tired of gerrymandering? Let us gerrymander completely, to districts of one. Elbridge Gerry will never know what hit him. *The people's house?* Let's prove it.

What's more, if we are fully represented, we won't malign government; we *are* government. Like a defendant choosing to represent himself, we'll have no one to blame but ourselves. As Thomas Jefferson himself said, the best democracy we can imagine is one that makes "every citizen an acting member of government," lest they "become inattentive to the public affairs." So no more half measures. No more fiddling with ratios. No more decrying excessive partisanship. What we need, what we deserve, is full representation. What we need is *every man for himself.*

As John Heywood might have written it, *Euery man for him felfe, and god for us all.*

The history of America, after all, is one of increased pandering to the individual, of giving greater and greater power to the people. We kicked it off, you may recall, by rebelling against an undemocratic king. Soon, Americans of every stripe were eligible to join the Confederation Congress—as long as one of their stripes was that of a rich, white, educated property owner. Then, an elite few (the Founders) paved the way for an elite few (the House) to appoint an elite few (the Senate). Both chambers grew, allowing more and more Americans to take part in governance. By 1913, with the Seventeenth Amendment, the people had even earned the power to elect their senators directly. We all had a say in choosing every legislator who represented us—because selfishly, we felt we deserved it.

By the 1970s, individual states—most notably California, the largest—began experiments in direct democracy, letting every citizen have a say in how they were governed through referenda and initiatives that allowed citizens to amend their state constitutions and state laws directly. Two years before Ronald Reagan was elected president, voters in the state he once governed were asked if they supported Proposition 13, which would, if enacted, limit how much they had to pay in property taxes. Not surprisingly, a citizenry eager to keep its money overwhelmingly voted yes. (Technically, I believe the options were "yes," "no," and "no, *duh,*" with "no, *duh*" hosting the blowout victory party.) Governor Jerry Brown called it "the strongest expression of democracy in a decade"—no doubt referring back to Proposition 12, which asked children if they wanted more candy.

And so on. Into the eighties (the "Me" Decade, you'll recall), voters in states across the country directly determined the outcome of issues as controversial as they are varied: property taxes, gay marriage, the right to an abortion, immigrant rights—even pedestrian concerns like auto insurance rates. As David Broder presciently observed at the time, "I do not think it will be long before the converging forces of technology and public opinion coalesce in a political movement for a national initiative—to allow the public to substitute the simplicity of majority rule by referendum for what must seem to many frustrated Americans the arcane, ineffective, out-of-date model of the Constitution."

"Before long" meant a mere couple of decades. Former U.S. senator Mike Gravel announced his 2006 candidacy for the United States presidency primarily on the platform of taking the initiative model nationwide—a version of Broder's "national initiative," which Gravel titled, cleverly, the "National Initiative."* One might wonder what his former colleagues in Congress might feel about Gravel's plan to make them irrelevant, but then, one might wonder about a lot of Gravel's actions.† But they got on board. In 2010, Republicans in the 111th Congress saw the mad genius of Gravel's idea and—in a brilliant combination of utter resignation and good ol'-

---

* Mike Gravel cannot be accused of lacking creativity. The former senator from Alaska once starred in a flabbergasting campaign commercial comprised solely of the candidate staring into the camera as he stood silently on a lakeshore—until, in a purely Dada-inspired moment, he picked up a large boulder, threw it into the lake, and walked slowly away.
† The lake thing, for starters.

fashioned political pandering—proposed U-Vote, which would give everyday Americans the authority to pick and choose which policies the government should fund. In other words, they would do Congress's job for them.

I applaud recent legislators for admitting they have a problem: namely, their utter failure to get the job done.* They have begun to honor an increasingly evident truth about our American character: that all along, self-interest has defined us as a nation. The trick is recognizing it, in taking human nature "as we find it," as George Washington advised, and making it work for us. By pandering to it mercilessly.

But as brilliant as the National Initiative and U-Vote are, they are merely ornamental. They don't address the root of the problem. There's an easier way, one that doesn't just let the people sneak around the "arcane, ineffective, out-of-date model of the Constitution." It brings the Constitution up to date with the people. So forget about ratios, referenda, and U-Votes. Forget about throwing the bums out.

Let's throw all the bums in. We cast off the king; now let us embrace the subjects.

Let us make every American a congressman at birth.

WE THE HARDY KNAVES AND STUPID FOOLS

> I am obliged to confess I should sooner live in a society
> governed by the first two thousand names in the Boston
> telephone directory than in a society governed by the two
> thousand faculty members of Harvard University.
>
> WILLIAM F. BUCKLEY, YALE GRADUATE

TRUTH IS, WE'RE NOT FAR OFF. Congress has always been populated by characters seemingly ripped from the phone book. Lawyers, CEOs, lawyers, accountants, lawyers, and more lawyers. Rhodes scholars, playwrights, schoolteachers, and convicted felons. Men of broad shoulders and wide stances. Women of great vision and greater hairdos. William Randolph Hearst, Joseph Pulitzer, David "Davy" Crockett. Gopher from *The Love*

---

* I must also applaud Texas governor Rick Perry, who proposed in his run for the 2012 presidency that Congress become a "part-time" job. The more part-time it is, the more people we'll need to do it.

Boat, Cooter from *The Dukes of Hazzard*. Sonny from *Sonny and Cher*. NFL wide receivers, MLB pitchers, and NBA stars. Priests and accused pedophiles. Ex-slaves. Future prisoners. Astronauts.

But 2010 was the year things got crazy. That's when the diversity of democracy really kicked in. That's the year a former witch who condemned masturbation didn't just run for senator from Delaware; she won a Republican primary. It's the year an unemployed man accused of felony obscenity for showing pornography to a teenager didn't just run for senator from South Carolina; he won a Democratic primary. It's the year a front-runner for senator from Nevada proposed bartering live chickens for medical care.

Granted, none of these characters were elected. (Somehow the witch's claim that "I'm nothing you've heard, I'm *you*" didn't quite persuade her fellow Delawareans, who, presumably, either were *not* witches or *were* relentless masturbators. Somehow the unemployed man's novel plan to rescue the economy by selling bobbleheads featuring his likeness didn't ultimately seem a workable plan to other South Carolinians. And somehow trading chickens for medicine, well, that's just plain stupid.) But they came pretty darn close. In the grand scheme to take human nature "as we find it"—rather than as we wish it to be—the midterm elections of 2010 were a tipping point.

If we're willing to give it a push, the Legislative Branch can finally become what it was intended to become, what Virginia delegate George Mason during the Constitutional Convention called "the grand depository of the democratic principle of the government." The junkyard of the American character, if you will. Because when the anti-masturbation wiccan Republican candidate for senator from Delaware claims to be just your average everyday American woman, she brings up a very solid point. (Not too solid a point, mind you. We'd hate to make her uncomfortable.) Summed up, as all nuggets of true wisdom are, in a campaign commercial: "They call us wacky. They call us wingnuts. We call us 'We the People.'"

She is "We the People" just like you and I are "We the People." Had she been elected, she would have had just as much right as any other Wiccan American to hold high office. And no less than President Ronald Reagan (not for nothing a B-list movie star who once co-starred with a chimpanzee) would likely have cheered her on. As he said in his first inaugural address in 1981, "From time to time, we've been tempted to believe that society has become too complex to be managed by self-rule, that government by an elite group is superior to government for, by, and of the people. Well, if no one among us is capable of government himself, then who among us has the capacity to govern someone else?" When searching for capable Americans to represent us, we shouldn't aim high or low; we should aim everywhere. "We hear much of special interest groups. Well, our concern must be for a special interest group that has been too long neglected: . . . 'we the people,' this breed called Americans."

Hear, hear, Mr. President. We should make "We the People" the most special of special interest groups. And we shall call that special interest group: *Congress*.

> ### YOUR NEW ~~ARTICLE I~~ ARTICLE II
> All legislative powers herein granted shall be vested in a Congress of the United States, which, so they will stop complaining, shall consist of everye man, woman, and childe upon birth, no matter how qualified, prepared, or interested in the gig. At least this way they'll pay attention.

Congratulations, Congressman.

FREEDOM RISING

MY JOB HERE IS DONE, I think, as I take a final look around Independence Hall. After all, I'm not here to wallow in history; I'm here to fix the future. And the future is across the street. While the Constitution may have been written in these vaunted halls, the tourist pamphlet seems to imply that the Constitution itself is kept at the National Constitution Center—across Chestnut Street, a mere five hundred yards away. (A perfect metaphor, I think, for how little we have advanced in two centuries.) One step closer to my rendezvous with destiny, and willing to subvert the very document behind our Rule of Law, I think nothing of jaywalking.

First impressions? For all its promise to make the Constitution "fun," the National Constitution Center is the opposite of Disneyland. There are no carnival games, no roving mascots, no log flume carved from George Washington's felled cherry trees—and no lines. There is, however, a gift shop, and Uncle Sam has gone all-in on merchandising. Polyester ties with Ben Franklin's face. Stuffed eagle puppets. "More Perfect Union" shot glasses. Almost blocking the entrance, impossible to miss, stands one of those mechanized penny-squishers, in which, for 51 cents, visitors can flatten Abraham Lincoln's face and take the newly ruined penny home as a souvenir.

Because nothing says "honor America's traditions" like the destruction of its currency.

I quickly peruse the gift shop bookstore, with its strange mix of notable historians—David McCullough, Jon Meacham—and polemic partisan-authors—Pat Buchanan, Glenn Beck. I am pleased that the Constitution Center makes such room on its bookshelves for fellow *men of letters*, but I assure myself that even these poseurs are scribbling at the margins. Unlike the Buchanans and the Becks, I'm not here to rewrite history; I'm here to rewrite the future. So I purchase a 99-cent "We the People" pencil—the closest proxy for a quill I'll likely find—and follow the signs to my manifest destiny: *Signers' Hall*.

The home of the Constitution.

Where, armed with my new quill-pencil, I shall make my stand.

Or my sit. (You know, depending on how they have the whole thing set up.)

★ ★ ★

The National Constitution Center is subdivided into Constitution-themed sections: Posterity Hall, Freedom Classroom, the Stars and Stripes Overlook. (If I were a less patriotic visitor, I'd wonder if the Founders might have found it tasteless.) As I pass through a hallway devoted to Freedom of Expression, a woman holding her daughter's hand steps into my path.

"Do you know the way to Domestic Tranquility?"

Simple, I'm tempted to say. *Follow me.*

I realize she's just looking for the section with the restrooms, so I give her my best guess. "Near the Delegates' Cafe?" And off she goes.

I shouldn't be surprised that Signers' Hall is located near the exit—like the finale of a Fourth of July fireworks spectacular, it is the star attraction. The main course of a five-star meal—if they gave it out right away, people wouldn't stay for the salad. And along the way, like the Sirens to Odysseus, there are installations and attractions that would divert those less resolute than I. A miniature television studio, complete with a green screen, where you can take the presidential oath of office ("and purchase a DVD copy for only $10.99!"). A mock jury box, where twelve of your peers can pretend to sentence you to prison ("while you learn about the Supreme Court!"). Interactive video screens inviting you to "touch the face" of your favorite Founding Father. (If I were a less patriotic visitor, I'd be certain the Founders would have found it disrespectful.)

There is also a show. *Freedom Rising,* which comes with the price of admission, is a cross between a planetarium, a laser light extravaganza, and an experimental one-man show of *Our Town.* Imagine a 3-D version of a Ken Burns movie, with an actor playing the role of "historical foot-age." It is oddly compelling. Even stirring and inspirational. The lone actor, choruslike, occasionally slips into the audience to make visitors feel like a part of the production, and before long, just as she recites perhaps the best-known phrase in American history—"We the People"—the music swells, and the text of the Constitution is projected directly into our faces.

We have become the living parchment on which the Constitution is written.

"*You*, the People," she says.

And I just know, she's talking about *Me.*

Me the People.

I immediately get up and head for the exit. The time is now.

In the lobby, I find the nearest security guard.

"I'm here to rewrite the Constitution," I say.

No doubt impressed by the force of my words and the grit in my gaze, he points me the way.

"Signers' Hall. 'Round the corner."

★ ★ ★

Signers' Hall is empty, save for a few dozen life-sized brass sculptures of the Framers in various revolutionary poses. I'm glad they're here. *Witnesses to history,* I think. In the middle of the room sits a large desk with a yel-lowed paper on top. *This must be it.* I approach gingerly, respectful of the moment. Here it is before me, the two-hundred-twenty-something-year-old foundation of our country, inches from my reach. Waiting to be rescued from its own flaws.

Within minutes, I will take a gigantic leap for mankind. By rewriting the Constitution, I will be a new Founding Father for a new era. People will line up to "touch my face" and crush my currency.

But just as I'm about to apply my "We the People" pencil, I notice a second, larger page lying next to the first. There's a question emblazoned across the top—"Would *you* sign this Constitution?"—and what appear to be hundreds of signatures in every illegible scrawl imaginable. Black ink. Blue ink. Crayon.

This isn't the Constitution at all; it's a reproduction, displayed so that visiting tourists and students can feel what it's like to sign a piece of parchment. This exhibit is for schoolchildren.

It's *pretend.*

I look around to find the hidden cameras. *Is this their idea of a joke?* This has got to be their idea of a joke. (For proof that it is a cruel joke, see next page.)

I track down the security guard who led me astray back in Posterity Hall. "I'm not here to sign a *fake* Constitution," I tell him, poking my quill-pencil in the air. "I'm here to rewrite the real one."

"Oh yeah?" he snorts. "Well for starters, you're in the wrong city."

What?!

"The Constitution isn't in Philadelphia," he says. "It's in D.C. So is the Declaration of Independence and the Bill of Rights."

And it is then, standing only feet from Independence Hall, feet from where the Constitution was conceived—so close to Domestic Tranquility I can taste it—that I practice my God-given right to Freedom of Expression.

"Fuck."

I knew I should have paid more attention to Nicolas Cage.

★ ★ ★

At yet another crossroads, I think again of Lincoln.

In 1840, after a series of personal and professional defeats—including a broken engagement to Mary Todd—Abraham Lincoln was beset by depression. As if by habit, his good friend Joshua Speed rushed to his bedside. "Lincoln, you must rally or you will die!" Lincoln would hear none of it, dejected and forlorn as he was by his evident and repeated failure. "I would just as soon die—right now," he said, "than live a minute longer."

But history records that Lincoln did *not* die. (At least not right *then,* anyway.) Rather, he rose from his bed and redoubled his efforts. Why? As he told Speed, "I have not done anything to make any human being remember that I had lived." There was still work to be done, and Lincoln was intent on being the man to do it. (And on being known for having been the man who did it.)

With the Constitution still 150 miles away and precious moments lost, I consider that I, too, may already have failed in my mission. Could it be? As I board the Megabus for my journey, now extended, I push aside thoughts of defeat and instead find inspiration in Lincoln's resolve to rally, to do something profound on behalf of America. And to get credit for having done it.

After all, that man is now on the squished penny.

The National Constitution Center's idea of a joke

Seriously, is this their idea of a joke? This has got to be their idea of a joke.

THE EXECUTIVE BRANCH

We Pledge Allegiance to That Guy Who Wanted to Be President So Damn Badly

☆ ☆ ☆

Some men look at constitutions with sanctimonious reverence,
and deem them like the ark of the covenant,
too sacred to be touched.

THOMAS JEFFERSON

Do not touch.

SIGN NEAR THE CONSTITUTION AT THE NATIONAL ARCHIVES

THOMAS JEFFERSON MAY have declared it dead long ago, but the original, handwritten copy of the United States Constitution is well over six feet aboveground, displayed proudly on the second floor of the National Archives in Washington, D.C. (I mean, *obviously*. Where else would you keep the Constitution but in our federal city on the shores of the Potomac, our seat of government since 1800, ten years after it was officially recognized in the Compromise of 1790 as our nation's capital? You didn't know that? Really, you're embarrassing yourself.)

"Ladies and gentlemen," says the uniformed docent at the front of the line. "Welcome to the Charters of Freedom. As you wait, I'm happy to answer any questions you may have about the most valuable documents in American history." A few hands are raised—*yes, these are the original documents; no, you cannot take any pictures.* And—heavy sigh—*no, this is not where they filmed the climactic scene from* National Treasure. (Forgive me, I had to ask.)

Then she gets down to business. "When it is your turn to approach the Constitution," she says, sternly, "please keep in mind: It is for *viewing*. It is not for *reading*." She does the *I'm watching you* gesture with her two fingers—she points at her eyes, then pans them across the crowd. A few people laugh, though it is fairly clear she wasn't going for that. Her eyes focus on me, as if she knows my intentions.

"Look at it, and move along."

Duly warned, we enter the Rotunda.

As I step into this vaunted chamber, housing this beacon of enlightenment, a thought enters my mind: *Damn, it's dark in here.* In *National Treasure*—which wasn't filmed here, but which I watched on my laptop during the bus ride and which is not too bad, really—when Nicolas Cage cases the joint before slipping away into the shadows (only to break back in later that night), the replica room is quite well lit. The actual room is left dim so the fragile parchments don't fade. Also so people feel obliged to whisper reverently. And—I gotta think it also makes actual heists more likely.

Before arriving at the Constitution, the line snakes past the Declaration of Independence. It's short—a quick read, had we been allowed to read it. Even shorter and quicker than Jefferson had intended. Congress spent days making editorial changes to Jefferson's original draft, which it found wordy, too florid, and unnecessarily sentimental. Jefferson's "sacred and undeniable" became "self-evident." "Inherent and inalienable rights" became "certain inalienable rights," which—since individual syllables were fair game—became "certain *un*alienable rights." They deleted a quarter of the text. Jefferson went to his grave thinking the delegates had mangled his draft with "mutilations." He later claimed great pride of authorship—success has many (founding) fathers, as they say—but the disgruntled Jefferson of 1776 might have reveled at the current state of the document. It's faded, bad. For thirty-five years, beginning in 1941, it was hung in direct sunlight on a wall in a patent office. Only the second section, beginning with "We, therefore," is somewhat legible. If she didn't know any better, any visitor would swear the famous, larger-than-life signature belonged to "Joan Hanoook." The most discernible feature is a huge handprint on the lower left corner, as if moments before leaning down to sign, Jefferson had been eating a burger and there was no Articles of Confederation around to wipe off the grease.

Five feet away lies the Constitution. It rests center stage in the Rotunda, after a marathon journey even an Olympic torch would respect. In 1787, with its ink barely dry, the Constitution was carried by the convention secretary (the absent-minded William Jackson) to the Confederation Congress in New York's City Hall. During the two years of ratification, the original was simply filed away—until City Hall was renovated, and the

Constitution was stored at the Department of State. As the seat of government moved from New York to Philadelphia to the District of Columbia, so, too, did the Constitution. For a few years it crashed at the Treasury Department, then for a few more in the War Office. During the War of 1812, on President James Madison's orders, three clerks stuffed it into a linen sack and carried it to a Virginia grist mill. Just in time: Vellum is highly flammable, and, as the British proved in 1814, so was Washington, D.C. Its safety may have been a priority, but not its location. In 1820, when James Madison was asked where the Constitution was, he had to be honest: He had no idea. Fitting that for a time in the mid-nineteenth century, it was stowed away in an orphanage; no one claimed it as their own. In 1894, it was moved from its modest home—a tin box in the bottom of a unmarked closet in the Departments of Navy and State—to a more secure, if equally modest, location: a safe in the basement. The Constitution then hopped a ride across town, cushioned on a pile of leather mail sacks, in a Model T driven by a librarian named Herbert, and in 1924 it was put on display for the first time ever at the Library of Congress. In the forties, while American soldiers fought a world war authorized by its Article I, it was packed into an oak box and stashed at Fort Knox—hidden away, as Jefferson predicted, like the ark of the covenant. When the coast was clear, it was driven to the National Archives, this time in style, the Model T replaced by two tanks and a military escort. It is now enclosed in high-impact, gold-plated titanium and aluminum cases filled with gas—at first, helium, until preservationists noticed that the cases had begun to deteriorate (and presumably feared the Constitution might just float away); now argon, the monatomic noble gas prized for its total inertness to all substances at all temperatures and all pressures, which almost makes up for the fact that it was discovered by two Brits, Lord Raleigh and Sir William Ramsay. Delicate sensors monitor the slightest change in temperature and humidity.

As I step closer, I assume it can sense my approach.

Here it is before me, one of the oldest constitutions known to man. The first constitution ever to be submitted to the People for their approval. It is "of no more consequence than the paper on which it is written," admitted Madison himself, "unless it be stamped with the approbation of those to whom it is addressed . . . THE PEOPLE THEMSELVES."

Aren't I a person?

Isn't it therefore addressed to me?

And I am only to "look at it, and move along"?

Nice try.

Step aside, six-year-old boy . . .

★ ★ ★

When Jefferson pronounced that every constitution should "naturally expire at the end of nineteen years," he didn't merely call *time of death* for our Constitution; he offered a prescription to keep it alive. He had been struck by the moxie of Daniel Shays, a farmer who, in 1787, had exposed the weaknesses of the Articles of Confederation by commanding a rebel army of eight hundred against a government militia. (One can assume Jefferson had read about the man behind Shays' Rebellion in his eighth grade history textbook, like everyone else.) Jefferson was impressed. "I hold it," Jefferson wrote to Madison, "that a little rebellion, now and then, is a good thing." Coming from such a statesman, it was a surprisingly easy-breezy endorsement of a violent uprising: It's "a good thing." Thomas Jefferson felt the same way about rebellion that Martha Stewart feels about homemade gingerbread biscotti.

Among those weaknesses, ultimately, was the lack of a strong executive, perhaps even a single executive—a President of the United States, say—who could, when required, knock heads and squelch rebellions. They spent four months debating what—and who—that might be.

I don't have that kind of time.

As I inch closer to the Founding Charter of our nation, Jefferson's phrase echoes in my mind: "a little rebellion, now and then." Practically mouthing the words, I ask myself what so many humble saviors have asked themselves: *If not me, who?* (It's a fair question; no one else around seems that concerned, especially not the junior high school choir in line behind me.) *If not now, when?* (Another fair question; the Archives close in twenty minutes.)

George Washington had demanded "radical cures" back in 1787, and here I stand, finally, positioned to administer them. But I must summon a courage unknown even to them, for even Washington, even Jefferson—and certainly the security guard at the entrance—would be alarmed to witness just how radical my cure will be. Because they don't know, they couldn't have known, that what I am about to do to this Constitution—*the* Constitution of the United States, the *only* Constitution of the United States—is not so little a rebellion.

It is an act of treason.

A CONSIDERABLE PAUSE

HISTORIANS EVEN GREATER THAN I have said the creation of the presidency was the Framers' most creative act. Their finest stroke. No argument here—the design of the Executive Branch was the most American act committed by the constitutional delegates of 1787.

But it was also their most timid.

On the issue of the Executive Branch, the men assembled that summer in Philadelphia acted not out of clear vision but out of nagging indecision, second guesses, and rising panic. According to John Yoo, the controversial former official in President George W. Bush's Department of Justice, "the only thing that made them more uncomfortable than the Philadelphia heat was the topic of the executive." Yoo also wrote the memo authorizing torture of enemy combatants, so I'd say he has a good sense of what makes people uncomfortable.

Designing the Executive Branch *should* have been easy, and the man at the front of the room was the reason why. The delegates had in their midst, sitting at the head table, the general who had won them a war and delivered them a country, "the indispensable man" on whose broad shoulders the cloak of the Executive would soon be draped. Oh, sure, the other Founders had their charms. "Franklin was wiser than Washington," wrote historian Joseph Ellis. "Hamilton was more brilliant, Jefferson was more intellectually sophisticated, Adams was more engaging, Madison was more politically astute. But Washington was still the greatest, and they would all agree to that." So as they deliberated over what the presidency might look like, no delegate present dared suggest that anyone but George Washington, "the most balanced of men," commander of the Continental Army, president of the Convention, guardian of the "rising sun" that had transfixed Benjamin Franklin, would be the first to fill its contours. It was, if you will, a slam dunk. A no-brainer. They were designing a suit of armor, and they already knew the measure of the man.

Yet, for the men in the Assembly Room that long summer, deciding the presidency was torture. So many questions had to be answered: How many executives would they need? What would he/they/she(?!) be called? How would they be picked? What exactly would they do all day? And just how powerful an office are we talking about here? They were as uncertain about the nature of the Executive Branch as they were certain that what they had wasn't working.

No surprise, then, that it was not until June 1, two weeks into the Convention—when they could procrastinate no longer—that they began the first day of substantive deliberation about the nature and function of the country's most important job. First up: How many executives are required?

Hoping to tiptoe into the subject, delegate James Wilson rose, turned the Convention's attention to the Executive Branch, and proposed a wild notion: that "the Executive consist of a single person." It might have seemed an obvious yea—after all, only a single executive, Wilson gently reminded them, would give the government the much-needed "energy, dispatch and responsibility" that the Articles of Confederation had failed to deliver. So much for power to the people. He wanted to give *power to a person*. It might have been a rousing chorus of huzzahs and yeses. Instead, according to James Madison, "a considerable pause" ensued.

Which must have been, to anyone in that room that day, considerably awkward. They had stalled before they had even gotten started.

When the silence was finally broken—by delegate Nathaniel Gorham, who merely asked if they wanted to, you know, maybe vote on it?—Benjamin Franklin quickly interrupted. He cautioned against making any hasty decisions on such "a point of great importance." Better that they should be given an opportunity to "deliver their sentiments on it before the question was put."

Um . . . can we talk about this, guys?

Over the long summer they had substantive discussions on the Executive three times, and they finished each debate with no more consensus than when they began. Even Wilson, who had designated himself as the most thoughtful on the subject of the president—who he should be, how he should be elected—admitted that it was "in truth the most difficult of all on which we have had to decide" and later confessed that "he had never made up an opinion on it entirely to his own satisfaction." James Madison, always eager for consensus, was just as perplexed. "There are," he lamented, "objections agnst. every mode that has been, or perhaps can be proposed."*

---

* Nor could they even agree on what the heck to call the Executive. All manner of titles were proposed: "His Exalted High Mightiness." "His Excellency." "The Honorable." "His Most Benign Highness." "His Elective Highness." "His Serene Highness." "His Majesty." For obvious reasons, none accurately described the man to lead America after it had just recently cast off the yoke of the British. Some of the suggestions—"His Highness, Protector of our Liberties," for example—were so imperious they would have made King George blush; few, if any, fell trippingly off the tongue. If John Adams had had his way—

With the idea of "a single person" still unresolved—to Edmund Randolph, it contained a "foetus of monarchy," and he wasn't afraid to add an extra voewel to make himself heaard—the delegates began to discuss other aspects of the Executive. Roger Sherman of Connecticut argued that the Executive should be "nothing more" than "an institution for carrying the will of the Legislature into effect"—and what's more, the Legislature should have the power to remove the Executive "at pleasure." (Sounds like *someone* had their lunch money stolen by the class president.) Benjamin Franklin overlooked the crucial questions on the table regarding the president and instead made an odd proposal: *Hey, you know that president we value so much? Let's not pay him.* (The eldest delegate in the room, he wanted a president, but asked for a senior citizen's discount.) Franklin maintained that the high office would offer quite enough temptation through man's love of power; no need to bring the corrupting influence of money into it as well.

The arguments continued, unabated and unresolved, between the delegates who saw the need to centralize power in a central figure after a disastrous decade under the Articles of Confederation, the delegates who still feared a return to a monarchy, and the delegates (well, *delegate*) who wanted the Executive, however many there might be, to work for free, like a blogger or an intern.

On June 18, sensing an opportunity in the chaos, Alexander Hamilton took the floor.

KING ME

THEY CALLED HIM the "Little Lion." Not because he was short—although, at five foot seven, he was—or because he had a reddish mane of hair—although he was our most ginger Founding Father—but because, it was said, he was deliberate in posture and aggressive in argument. But being short and red probably helped. Lions aren't known for their debating skills.

---

a man who assumed he would succeed George Washington as president—every time the first president (or, ahem, those who might have the good fortune to follow him in that office) would enter a room today, the United States Marine Band would strike up "Hail to His Highness, the President of the United States of America, and Protector of the Rights of Same." Not exactly a toe-tapper. Perhaps for its long-windedness alone, Thomas Jefferson quickly denounced that suggestion as "superlatively ridiculous." Washington was rumored to have written Adams to tell him that if such a title was even considered, he would resign.

He was also a bastard. "The bastard brat son of a Scots peddler," in the words of John Adams. Born on the island of Nevis in the Caribbean, the young Alexander lost both of his parents by age eleven—his father to abandonment, his mother to fever. After being raised by a Presbyterian minister, he was sent to the College of New Jersey at Princeton, which would one day become Princeton University, home of the Princeton Tigers. It was no place for a Little Lion—who wanted to complete his studies faster than Princeton would allow him—and Hamilton soon transferred to a place the once-and-future-king-lover would feel more comfortable: King's College. (Now known, thankfully, as Columbia University.) After graduating in three years, Hamilton joined the military, where he distinguished himself quickly. His skill at drilling caught the eye of American military commanders; his skill with a pen caught the eye of General Washington, who promoted the Little Lion to the rank of lieutenant colonel and enlisted him as his personal aide-de-camp in 1777. For four years, Hamilton handled the busy general's correspondence.

To Suzie:
Stay in schooll
And don't die of smallpox!!
Yours,
Alexand

George

He also began to form his own political philosophies. The Declaration of Independence may have called for a government that derives its powers "from the consent of the governed," but Hamilton had no such regard for the people; he was arrogant, elitist, and openly contemptuous of the common man. So certain was he that the average citizen was not to be trusted, so adamant that a more powerful central authority was needed (later to be joined by a central bank and financial system), and so resolved that the loose confederation of states that sprung from 1776 was weak and needed reform, that Hamilton began pushing for a constitutional convention to amend or replace the Articles of Confederation in 1780—seven years *before* the Philadelphia convention. This was a man in a hurry to make his mark.

Not even George Washington, the Man Who Would Be King—not to mention *the commander-in-chief of the Continental Army* and Hamilton's boss—earned his courtesy. Once, when Hamilton kept the General waiting, Washington reprimanded him for his insubordination: "I must tell you, sir, that you treat me with disrespect." Hamilton shot back, "Since you have thought it necessary to tell me so, we part." Even then, a mere ten minutes later, it was Washington, not Hamilton, who tried to apologize, "to heal the difference which could not have happened but in a moment of passion." Hamilton refused his apology, adding of his longtime mentor, "I have felt no friendship for him and professed none."

The insults from Hamilton continued. In private correspondence, he labeled Washington impatient, temperamental, "the most horrid swearer and blasphemer." (This last criticism, while true, was hardly a demerit. At the Battle of Monmouth, one of Washington's other aides recalls a day when the great man "swore . . . till the leaves shook on the trees. Charming! Delightful! Never have I enjoyed such swearing before or since.") Despite his charming, delightful temper, Washington did not return Hamilton's aspersions, instead saying of the Little Lion, "There are few men to be found . . . whose Soul is more firmly engaged in the cause or who exceeds him in probity and Sterling virtue."

Still, in 1781, the ungrateful Hamilton resigned from Washington's staff. "Genius," perhaps. Of "Sterling virtue," perhaps. But one also gets the sense that Alexander Hamilton was a jerk.

And on June 18, when Alexander Hamilton took to the stage to define the Executive, the delegates in the room already had a hunch about just whom they were dealing with. Thomas Jefferson, who despised Hamilton even from as far away as France, may even have been grateful to be absent. He had devoted much of his Declaration of Independence to itemizing the "long train of abuses" the British king had inflicted on Americans. Surely one of those abuses would have been having to listen to the Little Lion roar.

Hamilton went all in. "The British government," he announced, "is the best in the world, and I doubt much whether anything short of it will do in America."

Traitor says what?

As the delegates sat slack-jawed, the Little Lion gnashed on the Executive. "The English model," he declared, "was the only good one on the subject." What Hamilton proposed on that June day was nothing less than an American Monarch: an individual, unaccountable to the whims of his constituents, who would serve for life. Not a *hereditary* monarch, mind you—this was America, after all, and even he knew that probably wouldn't fly—but a popularly elected executive with a life term. And a powerful one, too. Even as the Executive doddered into old age, he would have an absolute "negative"—an all-powerful veto—over any laws passed by the legislature, as well as control over financial concerns and foreign policy.

Elected, yes, but forever.

The so-called Little Lion—the king of the jungle, raised in the Caribbean—had just called for a king of America.

The bastard had just become a royal pain.

After six hours, Hamilton finally stopped talking. No one rose in protest. No one called for a vote. They simply adjourned for the day. When William Samuel Johnson of Connecticut was asked to recount the proposals put on the table thus far, he was sparing in his summary of Hamilton's plan. "The gentleman from New York," he recalled, had "been praised by everybody," but was "supported by none."

There would be no king. At least, not yet. More than a month passed before the delegates dared return to the topic of the Executive. Which, if you ask me, is not very presidential of them. Where was the singular courage, the determination, the drive, the sheer guts to charge that hill and overcome the obstacle that was the Executive Branch? I tell myself that had I been there, I would have displayed such leadership, such vision that they would have had no choice but to elect me—okay, *anoint* me, that would have been fine, too—as their leader, a walking example of the kind of single executive they needed at a time they needed it most.

But in my absence, it took George Washington to raise the touchy subject again. He never offered his own opinion on the matter—since George was in line for the gig, he didn't want to start dictating its powers, let alone be accused, as he might if he were campaigning today, of "measuring the drapes" in the Oval Office. Still, he knew it was too big a subject to ignore: the elephant in the Assembly Room.

Washington's presence, at least, made most of the delegates comfortable with the idea of a single person in the position, but they still had questions. Should the president be elected directly by the people? James Wilson thought so, but Roger Sherman shot back, "The people at large will never be sufficiently informed to make a wise choice." George Mason agreed:

One might as well "refer a trial of colors to a blind man." When Wilson called for a vote on an official proposal to elect the president directly, it was defeated 9 to 1.

Should the president be limited to one term? After hearing Hamilton's tirade recommending a king for life, a one-term presidency seemed the better alternative. But when the proposal for life tenure was made, it was defeated by the narrowest margin—6 to 4. One more vote in favor and president-for-life would have been a feature of Article II of the United States Constitution.

What if we end up with a bad president? How should the president be fired? Should he be asked politely to leave? Or would he have to commit some act of "malpractice" worthy of kicking his behind to the curb? Perhaps a high crime, or a misdemeanor?

With few answers forthcoming, Gouverneur Morris asked that the assembly get some much-needed perspective. Quit squabbling about the specifics—qualifications, process of election, term of office, separation of powers, starting pay, executive washroom key, personal parking space. "Take into one view," he asked, "all that relates to the establishment of the executive." But before someone actually did anything, everyone adjourned.

How everything would turn out was anyone's guess.

★ ★ ★

I ask you to wrap your heads around this, fellow patriots: Without having made a single binding decision on the president—or presidents, or, for all they knew, robots, or hamsters—the delegates began writing the Constitution. On July 23, the assembly elected five delegates to a so-called Committee of Detail and immediately instructed them to draft a working summary of all the important parts of their new Constitution—all parts, that is, except the Executive Branch. It was like writing a screenplay without out a main character.

Some, like North Carolina's Hugh Williamson, still suspected that we would end up with a king. He merely asked that "no precaution . . . be omitted that might postpone the event as long as possible." In other words, *We're screwed, but let's at least put up a good fight.* (One precaution he suggested? "Lodge [executive power] in three men taken from three districts." If we were going to have a king, he wondered, shouldn't we at least have three? Three kings, after all, don't tyrannize their citizens. They bear gold, frankincense, and myrrh.) He also proposed another obstacle to any aspiring royalists: that they limit the president-king to one term. His preference was seven years, but if his fellow delegates were willing to sign on to the deal, he would sweeten it by supporting a longer term of office—as much as twelve years.

He had invoked double digits.

The game was on.

Elbridge Gerry saw Williamson's proposal and raised him three: a fifteen-year term. Rufus King—whose surname, frankly, should have disqualified him from the conversation—sarcastically suggested a term of twenty years, calculating that "this is the medium life of princes." King wasn't being serious; at least, so said James Madison, who commented in his notes that "this might possibly be meant as a caricature of the previous motions in order to defeat the object of them." The frustrations of the Executive Branch discussion had driven the delegates past the point of sincere debate; now they were simply mocking one another.

The "assembly of demigods" had become a bunch of smart-asses.

So unproductive had their debates been that as the convention drew to a close, the presidency was still undefined. It seemed it might stay that way. On the last day of August the delegates even voted to "refer such parts of the Constitution as have been postponed"—embarrassingly, this included the Executive—to a so-called Committee on Postponed Parts. The convention's cleanup crew. At worst, they should have been fine-tuning some language (and perhaps mopping the floors and turning out the lights); instead, they were still inventing an entire branch of government. The American presidency, which began the summer as "a point of great importance," had become an afterthought.

There were consequences. First off, as they were preoccupied with the Executive, the delegates casually endorsed an amendment adding a couple of words—"general welfare"—to the Article I provision giving Congress the poorly defined power to "provide for the common Defence and *general Welfare*"—whatever that means—"of the United States." Half a decade later, Madison himself confessed it was a mistake, since there were so many "variations and vicissitudes" in the interpretation of the phrase, even among the delegates in the room. Nonetheless, those two words forever changed the balance of power—all because the presidency spooked them.

They also invented a means of electing our president that, to this day, confounds every political science Ph.D., historian, and armchair politico who gives it a moment's thought. And they did so merely because one man—a man who, it should be noted, refused to sign the Declaration of Independence and who had been absent for much of the Constitutional

Convention—stepped in at the eleventh hour to see what he had been missing. John Dickinson, who had been sick (or at least claimed to be so) and therefore absent for much of late August and into September, joined the committee just as they were about to endorse a proposal to give the Congress—not *we the people*—the power to elect the president. Dickinson, aghast, wondered aloud how they had come to such an antidemocratic conclusion—not that he had been around to help. He warned them that the "powers which we have agreed to vest in the President were so many and so great"—to command armies, to make treaties, to appoint ambassadors—that the people would never ratify, let alone support, a plan featuring such a scheme "unless they themselves would be more immediately concerned in [the president's] election." These are *Americans*, after all. They'll want to have a say.* Murmurs of agreement began to ripple through the committee, and soon peg-legged Gouverneur Morris insisted they all "sit down again, and converse further on the subject." It was then that James Madison "took out a Pen and Paper, and sketched out a Mode of Electing the President" that involved a complex system of representatives elected by the people for the sole purpose of casting their vote for the president. It was a ridiculous Band-Aid applied only to assuage the increasingly stubborn delegates, who couldn't complain about it largely because they couldn't understand it. It was the least bad option.

It was the Electoral College.

In fact, the presidency as we know it today—a single executive, serving a maximum of two terms, elected indirectly by the voting-age citizens of the United States—is not what most of the Framers had in mind. It's not even what they settled for that summer of failed consensus; a handful of later amendments was needed to restrict the president's term and make the choice of the president a more democratic one. In some ways, on September 17, when the delegates finally signed off on—and signed—the Constitution, the Electoral College was the most definitive aspect of their Executive Branch. After four months of debate, Section 1 announced merely that "executive power shall be vested in a president of the United States of America," without defining what "executive power" might be. Section 2 named the president the "commander in chief," but didn't give him a helpful heads-up as to what his duties might be when called to command. Section 3 told the president to "take Care that the Laws be faithfully executed" but didn't take care to explain how. And despite their focus on

---

* And then a burger. And then, perhaps, a nap.

Section 4—what acts were worthy of impeaching the president—the delegates only settled on the words "high crimes and misdemeanors"; they never agreed on what those words actually meant.

The questions were just too complex for fifty-five of the nation's most learned men to agree on the answers.

From his vantage at the front of the hall, George Washington witnessed every moment of the chaos; worse, he had presided over it. He was also quite aware—as was everyone in the room—that he would inherit the fruits of their labors. So it is perhaps no surprise that when he finally accepted the honor of being the first man to inhabit the presidency—which had rankled the delegates with its complexity—he chose the least complex of all proposed titles. He knew exactly what he wanted to be called, a choice eventually endorsed by the House of Representatives:

Mr. President.

★ ★ ★

I'll say it: I'm impressed by George Washington. This is a man whose humility almost eclipses my own. To his credit, he refused to be called "Your Excellency" or "Your Highness" or anything remotely regal. He balked at "Sir Washington." According to Madison's notes, Washington never even considered "Kingfish" or "King Kong" or "Alaskan King Salmon" or "Rodgers and Hammerstein's *The King and I*" or "Don King" or "Martin Luther King." To his ears, still ringing from the Revolutionary War, such titles smacked of monarchy. If he was about to be the first to captain the ship of state out of rocky waters, he wanted it known:

"I'm Not King of the World!!!"

It would be tempting for lesser patriots to suspect that Washington was feigning humility. Some of his fellow revolutionaries certainly did; when the new government convened, Washington's choice of the spare "Mr. President" rankled some senators, who dismissed the appellation as more appropriate to the leader of a fire company or a cricket club. And true, Washington had only an occasional relationship with humility; though he had hesitated in coming, he'd made his way from Mount Vernon with all the pomp and circumstance befitting King George: Cheering crowds lined the streets as he passed, attended by so many horsemen kicking up so much dust that he complained he couldn't see the very countryside he would soon survey.

Yet to suggest that Washington's reluctance to wear the ornaments of power on his sleeve (or business card) was more affectation than principle is to suggest that George Washington, the genius of America, was being disingenuous. That he was somehow less than honest. Dishonest even.

Nonsense. George Washington, we should remember, was *always* honest. Always always always. "Honest Abe" Lincoln may have branded the nickname, but you'll recall that it was Washington, the father of America, the namesake of its capital city and (by the latest count) at least one of its fifty states, who taught us about honesty in the first place. Absolute honesty was a virtue he promoted to his children, his aides-de-camp, and his secret mistresses. (Unless he was sneaking up on the French or spying for the British.) There is even an anecdote about George Washington told so often to the nation's schoolchildren—thousands of whom attend one of the dozens of George Washington Elementary Schools around the country—that it hardly need be repeated, but should be regurgitated here: namely, that when George was six years old, or eight years old, or twelve (George's age usually varies according to the age of the child being lectured), he chopped down a cherry tree and, when confronted about it by his own father, declared, famously, "I cannot tell a lie; I did cut it with my hatchet." It was a complete sing-like-a-canary confession befitting a future war-commander-slash-British-spy, and one presumes it inspired countless (that is to say, probably zero) American preadolescents to not cut down cherry trees. Or at least, *if* they cut down a cherry tree, to fess up.

Never mind that it never happened. That it's hogwash. That it's Authentic American Apocrypha, courtesy of author and fabulist Parson Weems, a contemporary of Washington's, who made a cottage industry writing tall tales about "the HERO, and the Demigod"—his words, and his CAPITALIZATION—and who called his account of Washington vs.

the cherry tree "too true to be doubted." Naysayers will tell you that the story, despite Weems's compelling use of UPPER CASE LETTERS, wasn't TRUE at all. They'll point out that little Georgie Washington didn't lie about cutting down the tree. Nor did he *not* lie about cutting down the tree. *There was no tree.* They'll insist that the tale so often told to teach the virtues of unremitting honesty is itself a complete fabrication.

Excuse me, what part of "too true to be doubted" are you doubting?

Fair enough. We can't handle the truth. And, as President John F. Kennedy once said, "The great enemy of truth is not the lie—deliberate, contrived, and dishonest—but the myth—persistent, persuasive and unrealistic." So we can take a moment, fellow Americans, to wrap our heads around that one: We're a country whose capital is named for a man whose reputation was fortified by not just a myth, but a myth *about* a lie.

Told to *children.*

To get them to be *honest.*

It makes one wonder if there even *was* a George Washington.

Okay, you can stop wondering. There *was* a Washington—at least, there was back in 1789—and he was about to become the first president of the United States of America. Yet despite the obvious honor, he didn't want the attention, or the title, or the corner office. What a difference a summer makes—he had arrived like a king, but after watching the Convention flounder while addressing the Executive Branch, he could barely stomach the presidency.

WHO, ME? NO, I COULDN'T POSSIBLY

Uneasy lies the head that wears a crown.

KING HENRY IV

A CLOSE READING of history reveals a startling fact: George Washington wasn't president forever. The country's first president served only two terms. He could have served longer; consensus among Philadelphia society in 1796 was that its "indispensable man" would have been the easy victor. That he refused is Established Historical Fact, known among the more knowledgeable armchair historians, and is cited as a noble gesture on Washington's part, inclined as he was to provide an example to the world's kings that the peaceful transfer of American political power wasn't merely an American pipe dream; it was an implied term limit. "Gentlemen," he announced, to anyone who would listen, "if you wish to speak to me again, it will be under my own Fig and Vine."*

Somewhat less common is the knowledge that Washington had hoped to be the nation's first *one-termer*. He was so convinced that he didn't want to be reelected in 1792—"No more years! No more years! No more years!"—that he commissioned James Madison to write a farewell address to the nation. Madison dutifully completed his assignment, but before the president could deliver it, Madison convinced "the indispensable man" that he was indeed indispensable.

But entirely forgotten is the fact that George Washington, our nation's first president, didn't want the first gig in the first place. This was a man who in 1776 declared independence, in 1781 won the Revolutionary War, in 1787 presided over the forging of our founding document ... and in 1789 got a serious case of cold feet. Less than a month before he was to take office, he was frozen in his tracks. In a letter from Mount Vernon to his friend Henry Knox, soon to be his secretary of war, Washington wrote, "My movements to the chair of Government will be accompanied by feelings not unlike those of a culprit who is going to the place of his execution." Even if the prospect of the presidency wouldn't kill him, it would certainly make him seasick. "So unwilling am I, in the evening of a life nearly consumed in public cares, to quit a peaceful abode for an Ocean of difficulties, without that competency of political skill, abilities and inclination which is necessary to manage the helm." After a decade of fighting a war, shepherding a constitution, and regaining his bearings at Mount Vernon, the notion of launching such a voyage at his age was more than daunting; it was one he was eager to forgo. There's a reason you don't hear about this particular moment in most history books. For a man remembered as "First in War, First in Peace, and First in the Hearts of His Countrymen," it's disconcerting to know how close he was to being the First to Take This Job and Shove It.

When Washington decided against a third term, it was Thomas Jefferson—a man who himself claimed "no ambition to govern men" and insisted that the presidency would mean giving up "everything I love in exchange for everything I hate"—who helped punch up Washington's

---

* Referring, of course, to the flagship franchise of his chain of Italian restaurants, "George Washington's Fig and Vine" ("I cannot tell a lie: That's good eatin'!").

speech to Congress, a testimony to the voluntary renunciation of power: "While choice and prudence invite me to quit the political scene, patriotism does not forbid it." It was a farewell address that, Christopher Hitchens writes, "straightened the shoulders and spines of every believer in republican virtue."

For Washington, it wasn't apathy. It wasn't indifference. It was, to put it plainly, a gentleman's posture. As historian Joseph Ellis points out, "Anyone who actively campaigned for political office in the late eighteenth century was considered unworthy to serve, because the act of promoting oneself was regarded as a statement of personal ambition at odds with the qualities for public service." In other words, if you want to win an election, pretend you don't; winning is for losers. Washington had mastered the Art of the Reluctant Savior—a mixture of exaggerated humility, feigned but well-practiced nonchalance, and Kabuki theater. *Little old me, run for president? Save the country? Lead my fellow man? But I couldn't possib— Oh, if you insist.*

Not that Washington invented the Reluctant Savior. That was the work of the ancient Roman dictator Cincinnatus, a paragon of virtue and modesty who resigned from his position in the fifth century B.C.—back when, you know, dictators would do that—and returned to his farm, restoring power to the Roman Senate. For quitting his job, Cincinnatus was considered a model leader, selfless and visionary. So enthralled were men like Washington with the values that Cincinnatus represented that they formed the Society of the Cincinnati, whose first meeting was naturally held in (you guessed it) Cincinna— er, sorry, Fishkill, New York.* For his commitment to the motto of the Society, *Omnia relinquit servare republicam* ("He relinquished everything to serve the Republic"), George Washington was even elected its first President General, a position he held on to until—all who notice the irony here please say "Fishkill"—his death in 1799. Years before his death, however, Washington compared the Executive Branch to his actual execution. If eighteenth-century America respected Reluctant Saviors, it doesn't get much more reluctant than that.[†]

Of course, Washington *did* serve—in his service as our first president,

---

* And they all laughed when the Society of the Fishkilli met in Cleveland.

† The twenty-first century gives Reluctant Saviors plenty of cover to imitate Cincinnatus as well. Thanks to clever online campaigns pleading with them to enter the race—DraftWesleyClark.com and DraftObama.org come to mind—candidates can enjoy a groundswell of support, without ever having to—*ewww*—seek it.

Washington was often referred to as our nation's "savior." But he had the good political sense to grouse and grumble about it. For men of a certain skill at diplomacy, it was unseemly to seek power or invite glory, especially a larger-than-life man such as the first president. Only smaller-than-life men stooped so low.

Small men such as the second president.

WITH APOLOGIES TO PAUL GIAMATTI

UNFORTUNATELY, THE CONSTITUTION didn't make reluctance a requirement. So, historically, we have had three kinds of presidents: Genuine Washingtons—who seem sincere when they claim indifference for the gig (these are rare); Disingenuous Washingtons—candidates who claim indifference but want it *badly* (these are increasingly common); and Full-on John Adamses, who crave it with every fiber of their being (these are embarrassing).

In his quest for the presidency, John Adams—who was not present at the Convention as it struggled to define the presidency—may have defeated Jefferson, and he may have succeeded Washington, but he was no Cincinnatus. Whereas Jefferson was the beloved author of the Declaration of Independence, and Washington was "the First of Men," regarded by the country as "the most beloved of her citizens," John Adams was played by the guy who played the character Pig Vomit in a movie about Howard Stern. It was the best Adams might have expected, since he was, according to a Karl Rove–type attack dog hired by Jefferson, a "repulsive pedant . . . a hideous hermaphroditical character which has neither the force nor firmness of a man, nor the gentleness and sensibility of a woman." Adams may have played a leading role in our country's founding, but he was no leading man. Rather, he was the kind of historical figure who can win a funny-looking character actor a Best Actor Emmy.

Even more hideous than Adams's repulsive character, however, was his relentless ambition. Whereas Madison praised the "considerate and cautious" Washington, the tenacious Adams was "headlong and kindled into flame by every spark that lights on his passions." His overriding passion was the presidency, so much so that it almost cost him the vice presidency. In the fall of 1788, as James Madison strategized who might be best suited to become Washington's second in command, he focused on the delegate from Massachusetts, but he could hardly overlook the fact that "J. Adams has made himself obnoxious to many." To Jefferson, Adams had already proved to be "vain, irritable, and a bad calculator of the force and probable effect of the motives which govern men." Perhaps he was a good judge of something, Jefferson surmised, but he was a bad judge "where knowledge of the world is necessary." George Washington, when considering who might eventually replace him, applauded Thomas Jefferson's vaunted "repugnance to public life & anxiety to exchange it for his farm & his philosophy," and in the same breath also alluded to Adams's "obnoxious" views and his repellent and latent "monarchical principles."

This was no Reluctant Savior. While others were claiming to have "no ambition to govern men," Adams could think of nothing else. He was not Cincinnatus fixated on the goodwill of his people; he was Gollum with the Ring of Sauron, unable to suppress or hide his greatest desire:

O my presidency, my precious
precious presidency . . .

He was a man obsessed. As might be predicted of a man with only the presidency on his mind, when Adams became George Washington's vice president, he despised the job. He called it "the most insignificant office that ever the invention of man contrived or his imagination conceived."* Never mind that his boss had a hand in contriving it; to be stuck in the position himself was, to a man of his unquenchable ambition, utterly in-

---

* Up to and including "comptroller," whatever that is.

conceivable. He wanted the number one position, and he felt like a big, steaming pile of number two.*

Just *how* Un-reluctant a Savior was John Adams?

Brace yourselves, patriots. We must consider carefully the words of James Madison himself, who not only diagnosed Adams's "extravagant self importance" and "impatient ambition" but warned just how extravagant and impatient he was willing to be. Madison saw in the first vice president a dangerous zeal for power, a zeal so treacherous that—listen closely—it "might even intrigue for a premature advancement."

You heard me.

Intrigue. Premature advancement.

Was Madison predicting that Adams might kill Washington? We have no choice but to jump to that reckless, hasty, possibly spurious conclusion; to allow any other, likelier interpretation would be irresponsible. The future of the history of America is at stake.

You heard it here first.† If it's ever revealed that John Adams murdered George Washington to take his place in history, don't say I didn't tell you so.

Adams was Gollum, after all. A "hermaphroditical character" obsessed with his precious presidency. There is no telling how far he would go to get what he wanted. Surely, on the day John Adams assumed the vice presidency, the Terror Alert Level‡ burned bright neon.§ (Mr. President, the call¶ is coming from inside the White House!)\\

★ ★ ★

Okay, deep breath.

It is conceivable that John Adams had no intention of assassinating George Washington. No matter. Washington needn't have feared that his own vice president would kill him. (You should be ashamed of yourself, Mr.

---

* He also set the standard for a grand tradition of vice presidents feeling disrespected. Despite becoming the official tenth president after the death of William Henry Harrison, John Tyler aka "His Accidency" still felt so insecure over his elevation from such a lowly position that when he received mail addressed "acting president," he returned it unopened.

† And, perhaps, nowhere else.

‡ Had there been a Terror Alert Level in 1789.

§ Had someone discovered neon by 1789.

¶ Had telephony been invented by 1789.

\\ Had the White House been built by 1789.

Madison, for suggesting such a thing.) Nor need he have claimed his "move-ments to the chair of Government" were like those to his execution. Becom-ing the first president meant that, according to Article I, Section 8 of the Constitution he had just made possible, as well as the Residence Act of 1790 that he had just helped pass, he'd be spending quite a bit of time in "a district of territory, not exceeding ten miles square, to be located . . . on the river Potowmack." Which is to say, Washington had something to dread far more terrorizing than fabricated murder plots or hypothetical executions:

Giant toads.

Washington was bound for Washington, D.C. In a deal negotiated by Alexander Hamilton, the southern states agreed to assume a share of the debt the northern states had accumulated during the Revolutionary War if the northern states would support a more southerly home for the capital: somewhere near George Town, say. (Yet another compromise involved in our nation's founding.)

As for the precise location of the "ten miles square"—a fancy way of saying *one hundred square miles*—President Washington had chosen it him-self. He had surveyed the site, would be in charge of its development, and, depending how long he stayed president, might even be forced to live there. But Washington had Potomac Fever; he claimed that "no place, either north or south of this, can be more effectually secured against the attack of an Enemy"—unless of course that Enemy is the British, who not only at-tacked quite successfully in 1814 but burned down the White House. And no amount of purple prose and lofty rhetoric, of which there was plenty— George Washington predicted D.C. would become "the grand Emporium of North America" while newspapers declared the area "without parallel on the terraqueous globe" with a Potomac River "capacious enough to contain the fleets of the universal world"—could hide the fact: It was a swamp. And not just any swamp; according to one nineteenth-century Speaker of the House, "a *godforsaken* swamp." And not just any godforsaken swamp; a godforsaken swamp which, as witnessed by a local stonemason, produced "nothing except myriads of toads and frogs." And not just any toads and frogs; "toads and frogs (of enormous size)." Also, that "capacious" river? Hardly a river at all. It was only navigable forty days out of the year. (Never mind that on the somewhat rare occasion when it *was* navigable, one had to be on the lookout for *toads and frogs of enormous size*.)

Even after it became the working capital—Congress held its first ses-sion there in 1800, at the dawn of a new American century—no one brought wives or children to the "barbarous wilderness." It was still mostly "houses with no streets and streets with no houses." At high tide, the waters of Tiber Creek rose high enough to flood Pennsylvania Avenue. Horses drowned in Rock Creek. Giant toads and frogs threw victory parties.

Why on earth would President George Washington choose such a place to station our federal government? And why would I follow him here? It was a fetid, barely inhabited, rarely navigable, mosquito-infested, giant-toad-and-frog-having swamp.

In other words: the perfect place for us Reluctant Saviors.

~~PHILADELPHIA~~ WASHINGTON, HERE I COME!

THERE'S NO QUESTION: This is a strange, frustrating city. The architecture is breathtaking—marble palaces where there were once only wet cornfields—but the streets are eyebrow-raising, a series of diagonal avenues slapped atop a basic orthogonal NSEW grid, colliding into an infuriating number of traffic circles—and not the cute European kind, the industrial Anglo-Saxon kind—all the work of an "insubordinate," "insufferable," "haughty," "petulant," "beaky," notoriously difficult, not even American, very French architect named Pierre L'Enfant, who, as his name would suggest, childishly abandoned the project halfway through, refused to hand over his blueprints, spent the rest of his life suing Congress for money he claimed to be owed, and died with forty-five dollars to his name. His plan for the federal city put the gall in Gallic: to draw avenues branching out "from every principle place, to which they will serve as do the main veins in the animal body to diffuse life through smaller vessels in quickening the active motion to the heart"—which, I'm sure, sounded even more pretentious in French. His legacy? Having designed the only city on the planet that has embraced the riding of Segways on its sidewalks. Even Charles Dickens weighed in, describing L'Enfant's vision in typically Dickensian prose: "It is sometimes called the City of Magnificent Distances, but it might with greater propriety be termed the City of Magnificent Intentions: Spacious avenues, that begin in nothing, and lead nowhere." Which raises the question: C'mon, does Dickens think *everything* is a tale of two cities? And also, were the Magnificent Intentions of this place—part swamp, part center of the universe—ever realized?

First off, any question whether the "ten miles square" is still swampland is answered the moment one checks into a D.C. hotel:

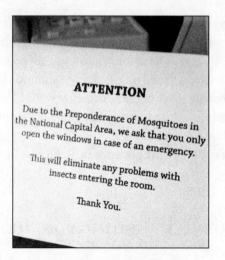

ATTENTION

Due to the Preponderance of Mosquitoes in the National Capital Area, we ask that you only open the windows in case of an emergency.

This will eliminate any problems with insects entering the room.

Thank You.

Yes, but what about the
GIANT TOADS?!

But right in the heart of the city sits a testament to the triumph of man over marsh: the National Archives, between the spacious Constitution Avenue (orthogonal!) and the spacious Pennsylvania Avenue (diagonal!). If the nation's preeminent collection of documents is housed here, they must be pretty sure it will be kept safe from both floods of swamp water and toads of enormous size.

If you think about it—or if you'll let me think about it for you—the National Archives is a museum honoring itself. That the building exists at all is only due to the power of its contents. If not for the extraordinary resilience of the documents it protects—notably the Declaration of Independence, the Constitution of the United States, and the Bill of Rights, known collectively as the Freedom Charters—the National Archives might have well been a summer home for the prime minister of England. Instead, it's the Freedom Charters' retirement home, where the documents that created America rest, unfurled and in repose, enjoying the sedentary life, the attention of reluctant high school field trippers, and the occasional interested visitor.

Of course, I am more than an interested visitor. More than two centuries after President Washington and Pierre L'Enfant set out on horseback through the misty morning of March 29, 1791, to survey and examine the "ten miles square" Washington had designated as the seat of government, I have arrived to plumb the depths of the Constitution itself—two feet wide and a little more than two feet high—not to marvel at its long shadow, but to take measure of its many shortcomings.

I have Magnificent Intentions, and I am at your Reluctant Service.

★ ★ ★

Even in a place dedicated to promoting the Constitution—located *on* Constitution Avenue—the Constitution itself is surprisingly difficult to find. It is displayed in the Rotunda, in the very heart of the Archives— accessible only by a few counterintuitive turns, a couple half-staircases, and a none-too-short wait in line.

On the day of my visit, the Articles of Confederation was also here, on temporary display. Though one might wonder why they bothered. The whole point of ratifying the Constitution in 1789 was to erase from the books the embarrassing Articles of Confederation, the first whack at our first principles, whose dangerous "defects" had failed to shepherd the new country to either international security or domestic tranquility. America's first "constitution" was not really a proper constitution at all, but merely a peace treaty among the thirteen separate states. It was nothing more than "a league of friendship"—not the League of Justice needed to save us when the country was going bankrupt, relations between the states were disinte- grating, and tensions were quickly mounting with the Legions of Doom just across the ocean. In letters from Mount Vernon, George Washington placed the blame for the country's chaos, as many Founders did, directly at the feet of the faulty Articles of Confederation, which had fostered a gov- ernment that was, in his words, but "a rope of sand."

No one likes a sandy rope. And even a casual, uninformed visitor to the Archives—looking around, I determine there are many of those here—gets the sense that the Archives, the preeminent repository devoted to the pres- ervation of all things historic, is embarrassed by the Articles of Confedera- tion. There is not much regard for its place in history, let alone its place in the building. The single thirteen-foot five-inch scroll—scrolls, of course, being the favorite format for *things that are old*—has been unfurled and laid flat, horizontally against a dimly lit wall in one of the side chambers. Aside from some cursory salesmanship on a placard above (the Articles of Con- federation is "displayed here in its entirety for the first time!"), there is no pomp, and little circumstance. Most telling, the Articles are placed just feet from—I kid you not—a replica of William Howard Taft's oversized bath- tub. If we're in Taft's washroom, it's hard not to make that leap that what

Washington deemed "a rope of sand" is deemed by the National Archives to be a thirteen-foot-long *roll of toilet paper*. I imagine President Taft, sitting on his gigantic commode next to his gigantic bathtub, having just finished his gigantic business, absentmindedly reaching for it to wipe his gigantic Rotunda.

National Archives, *shame on you*.

I *agree*, but shame on you.

Getting somewhat more respect for its place in history—even if it's merely a pit stop while waiting in line for the Constitution—is the Magna Carta, listing the rights and liberties secured by English barons from King John in 1215. It is the "Great Paper" that inspired the Framers to devote their souls to freedom and justice and "due process" of law—the radioactive spider of our Constitution's genesis story. Only four original copies of the 1215 Magna Carta remain—all hogged by the British. But only the 1297 copy displayed here (complete with the royal seal of Edward I) has a special all-American distinction on its résumé: *Once owned by Ross Perot*. What the English barons wrought, the former IBM salesman bought—for 1.5 million bucks in 1984. Two decades later, in 2007, the Texas billionaire sold it for $21 million— a Magna Profit, which he donated to help wounded soldiers—to New York billionaire David Rubenstein, who, fearing it might find its way back overseas, generously offered it as a permanent loan to the Archives, "as a gift to the American people."

It is the only copy of the Magna Carta currently residing in the United States. It is also the only copy of the Magna Carta that is currently being leaned on by a six-year-old playing a GameBoy.

But even he has to pay attention now.

"Ladies and gentlemen, when it is your turn to approach the Constitution, please kind in mind—"

★ ★ ★

Many people can say they've read the Constitution.* *Many*, but not *most*: A survey in 2009 reported that 72 percent of people had never read the whole thing. But honestly, of the 28 percent who claim to have read the Constitu-

---

* Perhaps only one person can say he has memorized it. During the Constitution's sesquicentennial celebrations in 1937, Harry F. Wilhelm recited the entire document from memory, up to and including the most recent amendment at that time, the Twenty-first, repealing Prohibition. It won him a job in the sesquicentennial administrative office mailroom.

tion, how many are lying? And of those who aren't lying, of those who *have* actually read the Constitution, how many can say they've read *the* Constitution, the actual document Madison signed? Not that many. James Madison and a few dozen Framers—if only to proofread the thing—and a handful of die-hard historians. Certainly no one visiting the Archives on this day.

It's against the rules.

But rules are for the visitors, not for the valiant. I resolve to stand here, for however long it may take, inconveniencing however many tourists I must, and read the entire Constitution. All 6,700 words. All seven Articles. All twenty-seven Amendments. All one Preambles. It's time I *know mine enemy*.

As I do, its familiar famous phrases pop up, like guideposts left by Madison so the average reader would stay interested: "the Writ of Habeas Corpus" . . . "Aid and Comfort" . . . "Full Faith and Credit" . . . "no religious Test" . . . "peaceably to assemble" . . . "to keep and bear arms" . . . "unreasonable searches and seizures" . . . "twice put in jeopardy" . . . "to be a witness against himself" . . . "speedy and public trial" . . . "trial by jury" . . . "cruel and unusual punishments" . . . "shall make no law." Unfamiliar phrases beg for attention as well, all the more unfamiliar for their fancy calligraphy: "Letters of Marque and Reprisal" . . . "Bill of Attainder" . . . "Duty of Tonnage" . . . "Corruption of Blood." But all Article II can offer is the usual well-worn fare: "natural born Citizen" . . . "He shall, from time to time" . . . "as he shall judge necessary and expedient" . . . "take Care that the Laws be faithfully executed" . . . "high Crimes and Misdemeanors."

Meh.

I can do better.

The only problem: Since September 11, 2001, security has been enhanced. Tyco/ADT X-ray machines and metal detectors are the first line of defense. A Pelco closed-circuit CCTV system monitors the perimeter. All access is controlled by a GE Interlogix/Casi security center. The Rotunda itself is under constant watch by armed guards, and each of the charters is behind thick bulletproof glass bordered by "ballistically resistant materials." Every night, each of these cases flips over hydraulically and is lowered twenty-two feet (Archive officials won't confirm the exact distance, fearing intrigue) into three Diebold-designed reinforced-concrete-and-steel Class-III-Plus vaults featuring proprietary intrusion-protection technology and five-ton doors meant to survive a nuclear explosion—a detail I thought they had invented for *National Treasure*, but which it turns out is totally true. And totally awesome.

I now realize what Nicolas Cage was up against. If you want to steal one of these documents, it helps to think quick, act fast, and be fictional.

At this moment, about to walk in his fake footsteps, I also have come to realize something else about Nicolas Cage, and to appreciate his appeal in a way I never had before. As *National Treasure*'s Ben Gates, he isn't just an amateur cryptologist out for adventure. Like Washington and Jefferson before him, he is the most heroic of American Heroes: a Reluctant Savior. He didn't *want* to steal the Declaration of Independence. He *had* to. He *must*.

George Washington would have approved. As the man who would define the Executive Branch prepared for the Convention of 1787, where he would make *his* amendments to the new charter of the country, he was convinced that he should "adopt no temporizing expedient, but probe the defects of the Constitution to the bottom, and provide radical cures, whether they are agreed to or not."

Radical cures, whether they are agreed to or not.

Now it is my turn to get radical.

But despite my Magnificent Intentions, I hesitate—if I probe *this* Constitution, won't it set off an alarm? After all, these guards are armed, a right guaranteed by the Second Amendment. The risk is real: Giving *us* liberty might give *me* death.

No, I must persevere—despite my fear, despite my misgivings. Because the fact remains: The only true saviors are the Reluctant Saviors. It is why I have traveled on my own marathon—from New York, to Greece, to Philadelphia (my bad), to a swamp next to the Potomac.

To provide *radical cures.*

Whether they are agreed to or not.

Yes, here, now, inspired by patriots Washington, Jefferson, and Cage before me, I realize I have no choice.

I am going to steal the Constitution of the United States.

FANFARE FOR THE AVERAGE JOE

AT THE CONSTITUTIONAL CONVENTION IN 1787, delegate Abraham Baldwin made a prediction about whether no-name candidates would ever have a chance in a presidential race: "The increasing intercourse among the people of the states would render important characters less and less unknown." It was a shocking forecast: that even unknown people might someday be paid attention to. (This was before our modern days of Twitter, when anyone wanting a little national attention need only announce that he or she is, in fact, #runningforpresident.) In 1942, Franklin Delano Roosevelt's vice president, Henry Wallace, went further, declaring in a speech that the twentieth century was "the century of the common man." "Everywhere the common people are on the march," he said.

The remarkable man who won the election for president in 2008—the son of a black man from Kenya and a white woman from Kansas—had spent much of the campaign trying to convince voters that his middle name could have as easily been Joe as it was Hussein. "My story," he said, at the Democratic National Convention in 2004, "is part of the larger American story. . . . In no other country on earth is my story even possible." *Please, call me Joe.* (It was a difficult sale; inexcusably, too many of his detractors questioned not only whether he should be president of this country, but whether he was even a *resident* of this country.)

The vice-presidential candidate on the opposing side was another American story. The first candidate for national office not only to invoke Joe Sixpack by name, but to offer herself as a representative of what she called *the normal Joe Sixpack Americans,* she was a woman of the people, a hardworking "hockey mom" of five attractive—though, it must be said, ridiculously named—children. A self-described "Mama Grizzly," she would no doubt have agreed with FDR's vice president, who said back in that 1942 speech, "If the rights of the common man are attacked, it unleashes the ferocity of a she-bear who has lost a cub." For Alaska's mama grizzly, it was the rights of the common *women* that concerned her, her fellow "mama grizzly bears that rise up on their hind legs when somebody's coming to attack their cubs." She was a populist of the William Jennings Bryan sort, who capitalized (and campaigned) on "the yearning for a society run by and for ordinary people who lead virtuous lives."

Two years later, after she had abruptly resigned the governorship of Alaska (because she felt she could better serve the good people of Alaska by no longer serving the good people of Alaska)—*omnia relinquit servare Eskimos?*—she made her intentions clear, singing the praises of "consummate statesman" George Washington: "He serves, he returned power to the people. . . . Then he went back to Mount Vernon, he went back to his farm. He was almost reluctant to serve as president, too. And that is who you need to find to serve in government. . . . Those who you know will serve for the right reasons because they're reluctant to get out there and seek a limelight and seek power. . . . That's exactly what we need to seek in a candidate. Someone—I'll repeat this—almost reluctant to serve." She would either run her household—willingly—or run the world—reluctantly.

Yes, uneasy lies the lapel that wears the flag pin.

That's the game now: As they race for the world's most powerful position, presidential candidates try to out-average one another, all the while implying that they would much prefer to be back tending their fields, or their families—just like regular old you or me. It's an odd feat of logic: *I'm just like you,* therefore *I should be the most powerful person on the planet.*

Which is why it was never easy to believe her protestations of reluctance. When journalists took her at her word—that she didn't want to run for president—and asked her instead who she thought would make a great candidate, she answered: "What I would look for is somebody who is, let's start off with, a woman, a mom, somebody who's administered locally, state, interstate, with energy issues, so maybe a mayor, a governor, an oil commissioner, maybe someone who's already run for vice president." There was nothing coy about her answer, even through its halting English: She was describing herself. Her sense of raw ambition and entitlement was showing through. *I may be an average Joe, but let's admit it: I'm better than anyone else.*

Alexander Hamilton would have been proud. This Mama Grizzly had a Little Lion in her.

★ ★ ★

So the question remains: What, then, makes a good president?

Is it ambition? Nah, that's ugly. Proven excellence? Sorry—these days, that reeks of elitism. What about good old rubber-meets-the-road experience? Shouldn't we seek a president who knows what he or she is doing?

No need. As history has proven, experience does not mean excellence. One of the most experienced politicians ever to live in the White House, James Buchanan, had the longest résumé: a decade as a member of the House, an ambassador to both Great Britain and Russia, two terms in the Senate, and four years as secretary of state. Yet he's generally considered one of the worst chief executives America has known.

On the other hand, the man who succeeded James Buchanan was as green as they come. Abraham Lincoln had won only a single term in the House of Representatives, and was famous only for losing to Stephen Douglas in the 1858 Illinois Senate race. Yet he's generally considered one of the best.

Our greatest presidents were a bunch of losers.

Which brings us back to James Madison. He may have fathered the

Constitution, coauthored *The Federalist Papers*, served in the first Congress, cofounded the Jeffersonian Party, and served as Jefferson's secretary of state for two terms, but as president of the United States, even he didn't have the power to stop the British from burning down Washington, D.C.

He had wanted the president to be very powerful. He was tired of the failures of a weak executive. (How weak had the executive been? Consider that after the Revolution, there had been eight men who served one-year terms as "President of the United States of America in Congress assembled," and you've never heard of any of them. That's pretty weak. Does John Hanson of Maryland ring a bell? Didn't think so.)*

Eight weakling no-names had gotten us into a fine mess—we were bankrupt, squabbling, and desperate.

Madison saw the solution: Even a country still cringing from the memories of an all-too-powerful king needed, on occasion, to speak with a single voice. And moreover, said the so-called Father of the Constitution, we shouldn't mistrust executive power.

Okay, Mr. Madison—but as the so-called Father of the new Constitution (so-called by me, the father of the new Constitution), I'm compelled to ask: If we shouldn't mistrust executive power, shouldn't we at least mistrust those who seek it? Isn't there something inherently wrong with someone who wants to be the leader of the free world? Even if coveting that much power somehow does not cast doubt on a candidate's overall psychological well-being and overdeveloped sense of entitled narcissism, perhaps doesn't it at least make them highly unusual? Would a "common man" want to run a country?

I'm almost embarrassed to mention this—if only to save a Founding Father some embarrassment—but one delegate in 1787 had a plan that attempted to address this concern. In the middle of the chaos of late July, James Wilson of Pennsylvania balked at the plan on the table—to give Congress the power to select the president—fearing that it would invite "intrigue." Scheming candidates would conspire with complicit congressmen. Wilson instead suggested that the president be elected by a small number of congressmen—"not more than fifteen"—but with a catch: The fifteen legislators would be selected not by ballot, but "by lot." They would then "retire immediately and make the election." Elbridge Gerry pointed out that such a scheme would "commit too much to chance." As if to mock him, the delegates then "indulged themselves in an ill-informed discussion

---

* Technically, George Washington wasn't our first president. He was our ninth.

of the laws of probability, expressing a wide range of opinions of varying plausibility about the extent to which chance rather than wisdom would determine" the president of the United States. Wilson himself made it clear that his idea was "liable to strong objections." And on second thought, he proposed they halt the debate and move on, since even he had to admit his idea was a silly method for choosing a president.

It sure was.

Almost random?

That's a *crazy* idea.

Foolish.

Silly.

Just not crazy, foolish, and silly for the reasons Wilson and the Framers thought it was.

Bear with me. If—as Washington showed us—being reluctant is a necessary trait of any true savior; *and*—as recent presidential candidates are quick to claim—being just an Average Joe means you're an above-average candidate: *and*—as "scholars agree"—being an utterly inexperienced politician means you might be our greatest president, choosing a president *almost* randomly is a *terrible* idea. Because it doesn't go far enough.

That's right: There's only one surefire way to pick the right man for the job:

Totally random.

Our best presidents claimed not to want the position? Fine—let's pick someone who doesn't want the gig.

Experience has no correlation to accomplishment? Swell—let's forget about résumés or college degrees.

Just anybody can succeed as president? Fair enough—let's let just anybody be president. After all, as Adlai Stevenson warned, "In America any boy may become President, and I suppose it's just one of the risks he takes."

Let's all take that risk.

Heck, it was good enough for the Greeks. In the fifth century B.C., Athenians picked their magistrates "by lot" out of "all Athenian citizens"— and let's remember: They invented Democracy.

So let's do what the Greeks did. Let's follow the Grecian Formula.*

Let's hand over the keys to a truly reluctant savior.

Not forever, mind you. As delegate George Mason wisely pointed out, "nothing is so essential to the preservation of a Republican government as

---

* Wait, that came out wrong.

periodic rotation." It is vital that a man (or, now *just as likely,* a woman) with so much responsibility "should at fixed periods return to that mass from which they were first taken." Political scientists have floated a number of different term lengths, often three to eight years, with six years being common—enough time to get the job done with no pressure of reelection. Rexford Guy Tugwell proposed a single term of—get this—*nine years.*

Nutball.

For an average American, a single term of four years is already too much to ask. But *nine* years? That's about nine years too long. Did Tugwell really think anyone could take that much time off work? And with the children, and soccer practice—Rexford, you fool. You've got to be kidding.

So then, allow me. I have a much more reasonable suggestion. We've *hailed the chief* for long enough. It's time to change our tune. It's time to cue a little fanfare for the common man.

YOUR NEW ARTICLE I

All executive power shall be vested in a President of the United States of America. No Person except a natural born and supernaturally reluctant Citizen shall be eligible to the Office of President. To that ende, He or She shall be chosen At Random from the subset of people who have never expressed interest in the job (No Purchase Necessary—odds of winning provided on request), and shall hold his or her Office from now until 11 o'clock Check-Out. (Late checkout available; courtesy fee may apply.)

*Please use towels sparingly, and beware toads
of enormous size.*

It seems almost too perfect. As I run toward the closest exit of the National Archives, four pages of hastily rolled-up parchment under my arm, no alarms go off. No well-meaning Samaritan points at me, shouting, "That's him! That's the guy!" I am not tackled by security. I am not speedily tried and found guilty of treason.

I am the D. B. Cooper of the twenty-first century. I have just pulled off the greatest heist in the history of America. And America will thank me for it.

But just as I turn the corner to see daylight outside the Archive doors, a guard steps in front of me.

"Sir!"

I no longer see daylight. I see prison bars and a date for my execution.

"Sir, please," he says again. "No running in the Archives."

Right, of course. *No running in the Archives.* I slow down to a more inconspicuous saunter, walk out of the Archives, cross the street, and disappear into the anonymity of the National Mall. Mission Impossible has become mission accomplished. The most important document in the history of America has been freed from its confines, never again to oppress the—

Oh, who am I kidding.

Try as I might, I cannot tell a lie: I did not steal the Constitution of the United States. I just bought one at the gift shop.

It's quite convincing, actually.

★ ★ ★

THE JUDICIAL BRANCH

The Whole System's Out of Order,
and Other Perfectly Valid Clichés

★ ★ ★

NTONIN SCALIA IS MAD.

Let me rephrase that: Antonin Scalia is mad at *me*.

At this very moment, in fact, so angry is the Associate Justice of the Supreme Court of the United States—at *me*, I remind you—that he has picked up a fork from the dining table we currently share and is jabbing it in my direction.

"Don't. You. Dare," he says, poking at me with each word. "You're a fool to even consider such a thing."

There are few men more intimidating than Supreme Court Associate Justice Scalia—even when experienced, as I had previously experienced him, from the relative safety of a television screen, YouTube video, or newspaper article. But his barrel chest, his cultivated jowls, his imposing forehead, his gravelly voice take on a whole new gulp-inducing resonance when experienced up close, across a lunch table, through the tines of a salad fork.

Even without a sharp utensil, the mere presence of the justice behind the bench has made the nation's preeminent constitutional scholars quake in their briefs. Surely if I were asked to think of the one man on the face of the earth who would take offense to my current mission—not merely debating the meaning of the Constitution before the Court, but rewriting it wholesale for the good of the country—it would be "Nino" Scalia. It would be the rabidly conservative, most senior, and longest-serving Associate Justice of the Supreme Court of the United States—appointed by President Reagan in 1986 with the express directive of safeguarding the original meaning of the Constitution. "Nino" is a nickname—honoring his grandfather Antonino—but it may as well be his *nom de mafia*. It's not too hard to imagine he could have a man killed and then somehow prove the murder was constitutional.

And he's got a fork. Pointed at me.

Other men might cower. Not I. I welcome this turn of events, and what it implies: I've ruffled him, and now he's returning the favor.

"But Your Honor," I say, "wouldn't you agree that—"

"Just *don't*," he says. "Stop right there."

It had gone like this for an hour or so. I would tell the justice what I had intended to change—retraction, *improve*—in the Constitution he had sworn to protect, and in turn he would alternately pooh-pooh my ideas, roll his eyes dismissively, or reel back in horror. Often, he managed some combination of all three.

I tried not to take it personally. He was, after all, just doing his job: protecting the Constitution of the United States. And I was just doing mine: dismantling it to its very foundations. He was Darth Vader protecting the Death Star; I was Luke Skywalker out to destroy it. Worthy adversaries, we.

Oh, there were pleasantries: *Pleasure to meet you. How are you? And who are you again?* But it wasn't long before talk turned to constitutions—one in particular—and soon enough he had suffered my suggestions—as he saw it, my foolishness—for too long. As the waiters took our empty plates—he had quite evidently enjoyed his *salade niçoise*, while I admit I had no recollection whatsoever of anything I swallowed that afternoon—it seemed I had pressed a final nerve.

Should I continue pressing?

Submit new evidence?

Declare a mistrial? (Can plaintiffs even do that?)

It was hard to know. I was out of my depth. Over the decades, hundreds of the world's most credentialed prosecutors had appeared before him, hoping the irresistible force of their arguments would convince the notoriously immovable justice that the Founding Charter he so adored didn't, or shouldn't, mean what he took it to mean; now it was my turn. Many had left shaken, certain they had failed to make their case. (Some never recovered. I heard one guy moved to Tibet and spends his days muttering unintelligibly about writs of certiorari.)

Would I be the latest? Would he prove too immovable for my irresistible argument? Or worse, would the trial of *Bleyer v. Scalia* be summarily thrown out of court before dessert was even served?

I swallowed hard. *No,* I thought, *I can't give up.* There was too much at stake.

I picked up *my* fork. "Now look here, Nino—"

PER CURIAM FOR A DREAM

WAIT A MINUTE. *Was this really happening? Was I really having lunch with Antonin Scalia? The Antonin Scalia, the Supreme Court justice? A man who almost never sits for interviews with anyone, let alone with troublemakers like me? And was I about to challenge this man to a fork duel? Or was this all just some strange fever dream, the product of too many late nights poring over Madison's notes on the composition of the judiciary? Would I suddenly wake to find I was arguing with my pillow about whether there's a right to privacy in the due process clause of the Fourteenth Amendment?*

I had to consider the facts.

I had to launch into the discovery phase of just how the hell I got here.

All I know is this: A while back, long before putting quill to paper, I decided to jump way ahead.

Eager to make a preemptive strike in my assault on history, I had decided to do what every public figure ultimately does: establish my legacy. I was rewriting the Constitution, after all; it seemed important to do whatever possible, as soon as possible, to burnish my standing in society. I resolved to find some way to short-circuit the judgment of historians and take my rightful place among the pantheon of patriots. It was a calculation as practical as it was narcissistic—this way, when I ultimately finished my work, I wouldn't have to waste energy on salesmanship. My reputation would precede me. Attention would be paid.

But how?

Few options availed themselves. At least, few of the options available to men like Washington, Madison, or Jefferson. No universities would bear my name, had I asked any to do so. Phone calls (had they been placed) to philanthropic endowments established in my honor (had they existed) asking for appointment to a prestigious chairmanship (had I been qualified) would doubtless not have been returned. Nor could I announce the groundbreaking of a library to house all my literary exploits—I hadn't yet written a single book by myself, let alone a libraryful. My vast collection would include a table of contents and approximately four chapters. One, predominantly, about my height.

How else might just some*one* become some*body*?

For answers, I looked to a complete nobody. But not just any nobody. I looked to one of the signers of the Constitution of the United States who has essentially disappeared from history: Jacob Broom, delegate from

Pennsylvania. Even though Broom came to the rescue of the Convention at a pivotal time—with an impassioned speech in mid-July, he alone persuaded the delegates to stay in session when there was rising talk of adjournment—let's be honest now, you've never heard of him.

Don't feel bad. There's a very good reason you don't know who he is: You don't know what he looks like. No one does. Not a single verified image of him has ever been discovered. In some historical accounts, his face suffers the great indignity of being represented by a question mark. He is—sucks for him—"the invisible signer." Which is why, in his famous mural featuring all the delegates at the Constitutional Convention, Howard Chandler Christy had to get creative. He obscured Broom's mug behind fellow signer John Dickinson's head.

Scene at the Signing of the Constitution of the United States,
Featuring the Very Top of Jacob Broom's Head,
by Howard Chandler Christy

I also looked to James Madison. I had downloaded a two-inch-high image of Madison (not actual size, but close) as wallpaper on my cellphone, so that every time I answered the phone I would be inspired by his pixilated solemnity—and would be reminded to make the call a short one: I had a Constitution to write. Frankly, it was a gambit that hadn't worked until that very moment. Because right then, his steely gaze—and Broom's complete lack of one—told me exactly what I needed to secure my legacy.

A portrait.

I needed a portrait. Something to cement my position in the annals of history and, in time, the hallways of the National Portrait Gallery. Something so austere and authoritative it would grace decades of future high school textbooks and bore countless future high school students. Something that would never be eclipsed by John Dickinson's head. (If I don't want to be obscure, I mustn't be obscured.)

James Madison had posed for portraits, many larger than two inches high. So, too, had Hamilton, Adams, Franklin. Washington had practically cornered the market.* Jefferson had posed so often that, on Madison's advice, he branched out, sitting instead for a three-dimensional plaster "life mask"—the removal of which, he reported back to Madison, was so onerous, so "difficult & even dangerous" that "there became the real danger that the ears would separate from the head sooner than from the plaister." Only when faced with the threat of earlessness did Jefferson "bid adieu for ever to busts & even portraits . . ."

A photograph wouldn't suffice. Even Lindsay Lohan can get a photo snapped of her; all she need do is step out of a limo while not wearing underwear. No, I would need my face, in oil, on canvas. For the men of the founding generation, portraits were a must. They said: This is a man who should be remembered for more than a movie premiere, or a fashion faux pas, or a nip slip. This is a man who has done great things. A man who matters. A man who can afford to sit in one place for twenty hours while his slaves tend to the plantation.

That's what I needed, minus the slaves. All the greatest patriots had portraits; so must I.

The only problem: I didn't know any portrait artists. Frankly, in the twenty-first century, I wasn't sure there *were* any portrait artists. Caricaturists in Times Square, sure. Stuffy paintings of company CEOs in executive boardrooms? I'd seen plenty. But ceremonial portraits are—rather, were—an eighteenth-century thing.

A quick Google search disabused me of my ignorance once again—not only were there portrait artists in the twenty-first century, there were a few

---

* The most famous, of Washington with clenched jaw, was merely the product of a painful dental procedure. Another Washington portrait, by John Trumbull, almost derailed a peace treaty with the Creek Indians: They had never seen a picture that conveyed three dimensions on a flat surface, and they shrieked in disbelief, accusing Trumbull of practicing "magic."

who had between them an impressive list of subjects: presidents, senators, Nobel Prize winners, popes, princes and princesses. They were the Gilbert Stuarts and John Vanderlyns of our day. They were the best. And I needed the best.

★ ★ ★

The best of the best, I soon learned, is a seventy-two-year-old fiend with a brush who had painted the pope, Pavarotti, and Princess Diana. He is a joke-telling, opera-loving, vodka-swilling, cigarette-huffing Zen master named Nelson Shanks. I know this because for the five consecutive Tuesdays I arrived at his studio overlooking Gramercy Park—he had agreed by email to hear my pitch in person—we told jokes (he even more than I), we drank vodka (both he and I), and we smoked cigarettes (he, not I). Not once, to my surprise, did we discuss the reason I had knocked on his door in the first place—hoping to persuade him to let me be his next subject.

The pattern set itself on the first day: I would arrive at 6:00 P.M., expecting to talk of portraits. And I would leave at 1:00 A.M., having not talked of portraits. Any discussion would have been drowned out by the clinking of ice in vodka glasses and the constant stream of colorful and charismatic visitors—fellow artists, writers, musicians, and socialites of every stripe. "Rabble rousers," Shanks called them, happy to include himself among the ranks. At one point, a world-famous violinist and opera star "just stopped by" for an impromptu concert. At another, I walked in on a seminude woman posing on a couch. Another, a seminude man wearing swimming goggles. It seemed I had stumbled into a recurring salon—"soirees," he called these sessions—and although I was making no progress on my legacy, I was enjoying every minute. By the fifth week, even I had forgotten why I was there.

Finally, nearing the end of another night and another bottle of vodka—sometime around dawn in Paris—Nelson made a suggestion: "You know, if you're truly serious about rewriting the Constitution—"

Am I? At this point, I barely remembered mentioning it.

"—you should consider talking to Scalia."

Perhaps, Nelson said, Justice Scalia would want to help me. I laughed. *Nelson, you're such a jokester.* Justice Scalia? *Antonin* Scalia? Surely he knows that if there's one person on the face of the planet who would *not* approve of a complete rewrite of the Constitution, it's the man most identified with the defense of its every passage. You think he'd want to help? If the paint fumes weren't getting to Nelson, the vodka was.

Antonin Scalia would never meet with me.

Why would he? So that I can tinker with the genius of his beloved dead white men?

Over his dead body.

A few nights later, my phone rings. It's Shanks. "You working tomorrow?"

"No."

"Good. Get on the 8:47 Amtrak to D.C. tomorrow morning," he says. "You're having lunch with Justice Scalia."

I don't understand. How did—?

"I didn't tell you?" he says. "I painted his portrait. He's a friend."

No, sir, you *didn't* tell me. Or at least, I couldn't hear you over the mezzo-soprano.

So while it sounds like a setup to an odd joke—"A Supreme Court justice and a guy who is rewriting the Constitution walk into the café of the National Gallery"—it is all very real. The Secret Service, the portrait artist, the *salade niçoise*, and the fork.

Antonin Scalia, Associate Justice of the Supreme Court, seen here without fork. Portrait by Nelson Shanks (2007).

THE FOOD COURT IS IN SESSION

"THE CONSTITUTION IS DEAD."

I had heard him say it before in one of his rare interviews, but now he is saying it *to me,* not long after we sit down. His way of saying hello, perhaps. *The Constitution is dead. And what do* you *do?*

Nelson had briefed him on what it is I do—I'm single-handedly fixing the Constitution—so I had expected such a bold Supreme Court justice to have a bold opening argument. This is a man, after all, who owes his career to a dead Constitution. In fact, if not for Article III, which establishes our system of courts as one of the three branches of national government, there would be no Supreme Court Justice Antonin Scalia. There would merely be Antonin Scalia. Or perhaps Antonin Scalia, D.D.S.

I'm not alarmed, or intimidated. On the contrary, I had spent the entire Amtrak ride not only refining my surefire improvement to Article III, but also convincing myself that I could win him over. That we're not too different, he and I. That even if he disagreed with my remedy, he might at least support my efforts to breathe new life into the document he has pronounced dead. (I can be very Pollyannaish on trains.)

But then, why *shouldn't* he support me? His predecessor, Chief Justice John Marshall, the man who made the Court what it is today, would have applauded my efforts; he would have even given me the green light to apply my red pen. "The people made the Constitution," he wrote, in 1821, "and the people can unmake it. It is a creature of their will, and lives only by their will." And who among us will grapple with this creature?

I will.

I am, after all, merely hoping to do what Associate Justice Oliver Wendell Holmes prescribed for any new law—that we should "wash it with cynical acid" and see what remains. What is the Constitution, anyhow, but our most important set of laws? Surely Scalia would offer a concurring opinion. This thing is overdue for an acid bath.

At least he'd agree we're kindred spirits.

"Exactly!" I say, with gusto. "The Constitution has been dead for centuries. That's why I'm trying to revive it. Because if I don't—"

"You're not understanding me," he interrupts. "The Constitution is dead, and that's a *good* thing."

★ ★ ★

No surprise—Antonin Scalia is not a man who suffers fools. And from where he sits—to the right of Chief Justice John Roberts, both literally and ideologically—there are plenty of fools to suffer. Much of the country—those who still moan about the outcome of Bush/Gore in 2000, for starters—might fall into such a category. Once, when asked about the pivotal ruling in *Bush v. Gore*—in which nine unelected judges deliberated for a mere sixteen hours and determined, by a score of five to four, nothing less than who would be the leader of the free world—my lunch date offered but three words of advice to anyone who might have preferred the decision go the other way:

"Get over it."

Spoken like one of the five.

No, Antonin Scalia is not a man who suffers fools. This applies even to the fools who have shared his bench. Of his fellow justices, he has said former justice Sandra Day O'Connor's views on abortion "cannot be taken seriously." He deemed former justice John Paul Stevens's position on the death penalty the "purest form of rule by judicial fiat"—even though, it would turn out, Stevens agreed with Scalia on the matter. Other arguments? "Beyond the absurd," "nothing short of preposterous," "sheer applesauce." He has even accused his own Chief Justice, fellow conservative John Roberts, of "faux judicial restraint."

If they are fools, anyone would qualify. I'm certain he thinks I do. After all, I'm no legal scholar. I'm certainly not a judge. The only time I wear a robe is at the spa.

"You're too late," he tells me, barely looking up.

I've explained my plans for a rewrite of the very document he's devoted his career to protect, and, as might have reasonably been expected, he's dismissive of the enterprise.

"Sorry to tell you, but you're too late."

"Why? Because our problems are too far gone to—?"

"No," he says. "You're too late, because *this* Court"—he bangs the table with his fist, more aggressively than one would expect over lunch in the café of the National Gallery—"this Court is *already* rewriting the Constitution. We've beaten you to the punch."

Despite his best efforts—his lifetime of judicial service, his forceful and elegant writing, his two decades on the Supreme Court—Justice Scalia has not been able to shield the Constitution from its foes. Not when, as he sees it, even his fellow Supreme justices sworn to protect the Constitution are judicial activists out to rewrite it. Twenty-seven Amendments and a tradition of liberal judicial interpretation have forever altered what the Constitution means, and he's not happy about it. "If it were up to me," he says, "we'd change the changes."

Due respect, Your Honor. But isn't at least one-ninth up to you? You may not have a veto, but you have a vote.

The resignation in his voice betrays the truth: Scalia would rather have a vote in the Constitutional Convention than in the Supreme Court. One suspects he'd gladly trade his robe for some buckled shoes and a periwig. If it were up to him, in the case of *2012 v. 1787,* he'd find in favor of 1787.

"I want to go back to the good old dead Constitution."

Scalia is a throwback, that's for sure; but he's more than that. As he has put it, "People always ask me, 'Justice Scalia, when did you first become an *originalist?*' as though it is some kind of weird affliction. You know: 'When did you first start eating human flesh?'" In my defense, I hadn't personally asked him any such question, but now, as he picks away at what looks like an anchovy, I have to look away.

It's true: Scalia is an *originalist.* He believes that the Constitution should mean the same today as it did when it was originally drafted. In that sense, *if it were up to him,* his job would be easy. We'd have a simple test to determine the constitutionality of every law. If the death penalty was permissible in 1789, it should be permissible today. (It was.) If abortion was made legal by the Constitution in 1789, it should be legal today. (It wasn't.) Any forms of torture that were acceptable to the signers of the Constitution should be acceptable to our modern sensibilities.

Here, Scalia is on record. On capital punishment, he approves of the view of "the believing Christian"—namely, that "death is no big deal." Of abortion, Scalia has pointed out that "the Constitution doesn't address the subject at all." Regarding torture—specifically, whether we should be allowed to put our prisoners in stocks—he shows little mercy. Such a medieval punishment "may be very stupid," he has said, "but it's not unconstitutional."

No big deal.

Get over it.

As he sips from his water glass, I point out that only a few blocks from the Pennsylvania State House where the Founders were busy chiseling in stone (which is to say, writing on parchment) the Constitution of 1787, an angry Philadelphia mob was busy stoning to death an elderly woman they suspected of being a witch.

"So?" he asks.

It's a fair point—I haven't made my case. He's not being callous. He's being a judge, or at least a lawyer—*Objection: relevance?* So I stammer though a explanation that perhaps what passed as acceptable behavior in Philadelphia in 1789 was closer to Salem in 1692 than to Anytown U.S.A. in the twenty-first century, and that—

"So?" he asks again.

—and, um, perhaps a rigid devotion to the Constitution of 1789 just handcuffs us to a time when, well, you know, I mean—

The truth is, I'm not exactly sure what I said. He had thrown me off my train of thought with a single word. With two measly letters—*so?* I vaguely recall trying to climb back on, attempting to explain why I believed (or, more meekly, why "some people might suggest") he could be wrong.

He stops me. "Look, society may have changed, but the Constitution hasn't. The Constitution is the Constitution. It doesn't change in order to meet the assumed needs of changing society."

I recall he once said that the Constitution doesn't morph. I remind him of that. (Wow—now he's got me arguing his side. He's *good.*)

"Exactly. The Constitution doesn't morph."

I wonder if Oliver Wendell Holmes ever used the word *morph.*

"Besides," he adds, "you haven't considered another possibility."

What's that?

"Maybe she *was* a witch."

He laughs.

As do I. It is not the first time that afternoon, nor will it be the last. As much as it may pain his political foes to hear it, Justice Scalia is downright funny, and more than a few times over the afternoon will he temper my hard-hitting questions with an inviting soft giggle, which turns into a hearty chuckle, which morphs into an honest-to-goodness howl. (Only once will he and I—and hand to God, this actually happened—only once will the Associate Justice of the Supreme Court and I together sing the first few measures of "O Sole Mio.")

A few gawkers, having detected the justice in their midst, take photographs from the wings. (Don't they know this man merits a *portrait?*) For his part, Scalia either does not notice or does not mind, or does not mind enough to notice. He's a celebrity, after all—comfortable with an audience even when he's not in a robe. He speaks and jokes loud enough to be heard tables away, and just because he is sitting in plain clothes in the National Gallery doesn't mean he can't hold court.

That the most conservative justice is so liberal with a laugh isn't just a claim heard by his detractors with shock and amazement; it is an established fact. In 2005, a Boston University professor studied the transcripts of Supreme Court sessions and counted the number of times "*[laughter]*" was recorded by the official court reporter. Scalia was the biggest cutup, at almost 2 to 1. He's a reliable clown; in one nine-month term, Scalia was responsible for seventy-seven "laughing episodes"—an average of more than one such outburst per argument. Let the record show he is twice as funny as Stephen Breyer, nineteen times funnier than Ruth Bader Ginsburg, and, mathematically speaking, infinitely more amusing than Clarence Thomas.*

Nino Scalia, it seems, is the Patch Adams of the Supreme Court.

Antonin Scalia, Associate Justice of the Supreme Court, seen here ruling on a case involving, we must assume, a young leukemia patient

Naturally, not everyone finds Justice Scalia amusing. It is an understatement to say he has his critics. (And an overstatement to say it bothers him. "That's why we have life tenure," he says. "Precisely so that we can, you know, let this roll off our back.") His detractors include those who found

---

* In the five years between 2006 and 2011, Clarence Thomas elicited precisely zero laughs, a feat accomplished primarily by speaking precisely zero times. His unbroken five-year silence on the bench is not exactly a headlining act at the Comedy Stop, although—and this is a possibility we should carefully consider—it may be a phenomenal piece of performance art.

his 2005 duck-hunting trip with then Vice President Dick Cheney unseemly—when Scalia was about to rule on a case to determine if the vice president could keep secret the names of those attending his secret task force on energy policy. Or the *Boston Herald* reporter who, after asking whether Scalia's Catholic beliefs had caused him conflicts of interest while on the bench, received what he deemed the Italian version of "the finger."

Or, more recently, those who were troubled by his closed-door meeting with fifty members of the Tea Party caucus in January 2010. The meeting was an ad hoc, off-the-record seminar, ostensibly to teach an appreciative, and apparently naïve, group of perfectly grown adults rudimentary civics such as, according to *Politico*, "the relationship between Congress, the Supreme Court and the presidency." It was an unusual lecture—a remedial civics lesson taught to a partisan group by a sitting Supreme Court Justice, which a University of Maryland law professor found "grossly inappropriate," but which, I have no doubt, the University of Scalia tea partiers found thoroughly illuminating and, with Scalia at the podium, wildly entertaining. Even if there was no stenographer present to record the *[laughter]*.

When I first learned that Scalia is a laugh riot, it came as a relief; as for matching him joke for joke over lunch, however, I don't even try. The official guidebook made available to lawyers preparing to argue before the Supreme Court offers a stern warning: "Attempts at humor usually fall flat." I need no such guidance. Intuitively, I know the right course of action when it comes to engaging with Justice Scalia: Be the straight man. And not just because he wrote the dissent in *Lawrence v. Texas!**

[No laughter]

Instead, I want to ask him about Woodrow Wilson. To a conservative such as Scalia, there can be few figures less amusing than the man so identified with the progressive movement in America. (In the words of Glenn Beck, "Woodrow Wilson?! Aaaggh! I hate him! I hate him I hate him I hate him.") One thing Wilson said bothers conservatives more than any other: "All that progressives ask or desire is permission," Wilson said in 1913, "to interpret the Constitution according to the Darwinian principle; all they ask is recognition of the fact that a nation is a living thing." Along with Justices Holmes and Brandeis, it was Woodrow Wilson who popularized the idea that our Constitution is not dead, but is in fact a "living constitution," designed by the Framers to accommodate our changing nation.

---

* See? *Lawrence v. Texas* is the 2003 Supreme Court case striking down the antisodomy law in Texas, and so a "straight man," in this context, would— Oh, never mind.

A Wilsonian might ask an originalist: Our needs adapt, so shouldn't our governing principles? They may not *morph,* but shouldn't they evolve?

I do not ask this directly. I already know what he would say. He's said it before. On the same weekend in 2006 that his hunting buddy Vice President Cheney shot a man in the face, Scalia took aim at the advocates of living constitutionalism. "The Constitution is not a living organism," he said, to a group of lawyers in Puerto Rico. "You would have to be an idiot to believe that."

So naturally, I'd have to be an idiot to ask him that.

Instead, I ask, "What about 'the evolving standards of decency that mark—'"

"—the progress of a maturing society?" he asks, preempting me. He looks up from his salad. "You've been reading the Constitution."

I can't tell if he means that as a compliment—as in, *Have you been working out?*—or an accusation—*You've been drinking again, haven't you.*

"A little," I say.

He knows I'm quoting the so-called *evolving standards test,* which isn't technically in the Constitution, but which proposes that the definition of "cruel and unusual" punishment in the Eighth Amendment—which *is* in the Constitution—depends on the current mores of contemporary society. It was a theory posed by Chief Justice Earl Warren, and it invites the question, if our interpretation of "cruel and unusual" can evolve over time, then couldn't our interpretation of the rest of the Constitution—

He rolls his eyes. *Please*—he's heard it all before.

"If the standards of decency are what's important," he asks, "then why in the world would you have it interpreted by nine lawyers? What do we know about the evolving standards of decency of American society?" He laughs at the thought. "I certainly don't. Heck, I'm afraid to ask."

It's another fair point. Scalia doesn't claim to pay close attention to evolving standards. This is a man who eats lunch at the National Gallery of Art. Who sings arias with strangers. Whose idea of a good time on New Year's Eve is going to the opera with a soft-spoken seventy-eight-year-old Jewish grandmother. (That she happens to be Ruth Bader Ginsburg, his fellow justice and co-worker, only affirms the point: Scalia isn't your Average Joe.)

"But," I ask, "if you, of all people, don't have the authority to interpret the Constitution, wouldn't that mean you have no power to—"

"Power to what?"

"Power to—"

"Power to make law? It means *exactly* that."

I can't help but think I've fallen into a trap.

"Look," he says, starting a lecture he seems to have practiced, "we don't sit here to make the law. That's not the business judges are in. It's 'garbage in, garbage out.' If it's a foolish law, I'm bound by oath to produce a foolish result. It's not my job to decide what is foolish and what isn't."

As Scalia sees it, the obligation to do as he's told is precisely the virtue of an originalist interpretation. It bends to the will of the people, not to the whims of judges. "My Constitution is a very flexible Constitution," he insists. Though it may seem like a paradox, to Scalia there is nothing more accommodating to popular desires than the strict adherence to the rule of law laid out by the Founders.

"You want to get an abortion?" he asks—I'm hoping rhetorically. "Be my guest. Create the right to an abortion the way all rights are created in a democracy: Pass a law. You want the death penalty? Pass a law. Just don't expect me to do it for you. Making good law is not my job. It's the job of the five hundred and thirty-five people across the street from me every day."

He means Congress. (I don't dare tell him that when this new Constitution is enacted, there will be far more than 535 people across the street from him every day.) His point stands: It's not his job to make or enforce the laws. It's his job to watch over the Constitution. And the Constitution is dead.

Get over it.

"The worst thing about the *living constitution*," Scalia once said in a speech given—one assumes ironically—at the Woodrow Wilson International Center, "is that it will *destroy* the Constitution." Not violate—*destroy*. By that logic, those who subscribe to the concept of a *living constitution* aren't just fools; they are accomplices.

The living constitution may be destroying the (dead) Constitution, but is has created quite a livelihood for Justice Scalia. It defines his judicial philosophy. It is his White Whale; he and the living constitution are in this together. And if his fate matches that of Ahab, dragged to the depths of the sea by his obstinacy, so be it; he won't let go. "Even if I don't succeed," he says, "I'm determined to keep fighting, because that's a thing worth doing." He grins as he says it. "One of my favorite Chestertonian paradoxes is, 'A thing worth doing is a thing worth doing badly.'"

Frankly, I am surprised Scalia is so fatalistic about his chances. We are, after all, a country overrun with originalists, not just those who wear tricorn hats at Tea Party rallies. More than any other Western democracy, the United States is home to a far greater proportion of citizens who believe in the literal truth of the Bible. Surely, if we can believe Lot's wife turned into a pillar of salt, it doesn't take much of a leap to think that Madison & Co. meant what they wrote, the way they wrote it, when they wrote it.*

Sitting with Scalia, I assume I am in the presence of false modesty, because for all his protestations of pessimism, the man is entirely committed to the cause. He believes the Constitution is dead. And should *stay* dead. And as a Supreme Court justice of the United States, he'll do what he can to make sure it stays dead until the day he dies, because that's a thing worth doing.

What he doesn't know is: That's why I'm here.

To stop him.

MORAL ARGUMENTS

THERE ARE PLENTY of revisions I could propose regarding Article III. Take, for example, the size of the Supreme Court. There is nothing sacred about the number nine, as President Franklin Roosevelt famously tried to prove by packing the court with judges favorable to his New Deal. A case could be made for a larger court, or a smaller court, or at least an even number of judges, which would help prevent a barrage of new precedents (tie goes to the defendant).

Nor is there anything magical about the method of picking judges— even Alexander Hamilton considered some alternate method of appointment, some way to guard against "the ordinary depravity of human nature" for candidates to the Supreme Court. A morals test, perhaps? Some kind of ethics obstacle course featuring pubic hairs and Coke cans?

Even how the justices are paid isn't perfect; as it stands, they must beg Congress for a raise, making them beholden to 535 people, some of whom may be defendants someday. Certainly, James Madison's solution seems very 1789: peg judges' salaries to a standard of "wheat or some other thing of permanent value." (If we're looking for a more contemporary standard of value, I might suggest gold, or iPads, or videos of cute kittens.)

But it was Scalia's own claim—that he, as a justice of the Supreme

---

* Then again, almost half of all Americans believe in ghosts, according to a CBS News poll conducted in October 2011 and containing a margin of error of plus or minus *boogety-boogety-boogety!*

Court, should be allowed to "keep fighting" for as long as he so chooses, even to the point of fighting "badly"—that begs for my red pen.

As the waiter refills our water glasses, I make my first move. I draw Scalia's attention to the passage I plan to amend, but I do so casually, delicately. I had, after all, spent the last ten minutes of the Amtrak ride rehearsing this moment, so that I could coolly recite it from memory: "The judicial Power of the United States shall be vested in one supreme Court." Scalia tilts his profound head the slightest bit, like a puppy that has sensed the bark of a distant dog. He can tell what I'm aiming at. "The Judges shall hold their Offices during good Behaviour, and shall—"

Out comes the fork.

"Stop," he scowls at me.

Oh *fork*.

"Don't you dare. Don't you dare mess with lifetime tenure for Supreme Court justices."

With that, he freezes in place, his fork raised high, as if posing for a portrait: *Antonin Scalia, Associate Justice of the Supreme Court, seen here intimidating his foe.* He had me pegged: I *was*, in fact, going to mess with lifetime tenure for Supreme Court justices.

Slowly, though, his scowl morphs into a grin.

"But if you do," he says, finally, "at least grandfather me in."

He laughs again. His laughter—which would resonate just fine on its own—gets an assist from the marble halls of the National Gallery. I suspect that in some other wing, a portrait rattles almost imperceptibly against a wall.

Another waiter puts down dessert. And the fork that throughout this lunch had so successfully intimidated his guest, this fool he had been suffering, is instead mercifully redeployed on his chocolate torte.

I look around to see if anyone had witnessed the Associate Justice of the Supreme Court threaten me. Would the Secret Service come to *my* defense? I suspect not. I'm on my own.

It's my turn for rebuttal.

I pick up *my* fork. "Now look here, Nino—" I say. (Okay, I did not say *Nino*.)

But Nino looks up.

"Look here," I say. "They brought us a torte," I say.

A vigorous defense of my proposed changes will have to wait until coffee is served. I need to reconsider my strategy. And with that, the Supreme Court justice and I, armed with our forks, set to work on enacting torte reform.

Antonin Scalia, Associate Justice of the Supreme Court, seen here intimidating his foe

Here's the thing: There *is* no lifetime tenure for Supreme Court justices. Article III of Scalia's precious original Constitution merely says that judges "shall hold their Offices during good Behaviour." It says nothing about "forever" or "for life" or "until death do us part." According to the original Constitution that Scalia swears by, there *is* no lifetime tenure for guys like him.

So what gives? Why do we give Supreme Court justices a lifetime pass? One theory goes that when the Constitution was adopted, the Founders had a compelling reason to pursue a liberal interpretation of "good Behaviour"—that is, good behavior was anything short of truly impeachable offenses. After kings worldwide had removed judges, willy-nilly, upon the ascension to the throne, the Founders thought it best to leave judges alone as much as possible—in part because if kings did it, that meant it was bad, but also as a check on executive power.

Another possibility: They just didn't care. Very little the Founders did, said, or wrote indicated they considered the Judicial Branch a priority. They listed it third. They kept it short. According to Madison's notes, while the delegates in Philadelphia were preoccupied with the composition of the Legislative and Executive, they discussed the Judiciary for more than ten minutes a whopping *twice* during the entire convention—once to consider Madison's request that the Judiciary be folded into the Executive (in some sort of Nancy Grace meets Judge Dredd situation, I imagine) and once on August 27, the day when the smallest number of delegates was present all summer, and only the slightest majority bothered to show up. (*What's that? We're discussing the Judiciary this morning? Okay, let me just put on my slippers and <snooze bar>*.) And although the final version of Article III prescribed "one supreme Court," it didn't require that there be any federal trial courts at all, only courts that Congress "may" from "time to time," ordain and establish—you know, if they *felt* like it. In fact, when James Madison went home to Virginia to persuade his state to ratify the Constitution, he promised he would try to get along without federal trial courts altogether. With a dismissive attitude like that—from the Father of the Constitution himself—it is little surprise that early judges honestly worried if anyone would honor their decisions. They were the unwanted children of the marriage of powers.

No less than Alexander Hamilton called the Judiciary the "least dangerous" branch of government since, as anyone could see, the Executive and the Legislative had been awarded far more power in their new system. What was the harm if judges stuck around too long? If the Judicial Branch wasn't powerful, really, how much trouble could they get into?

A lot, in fact. The Court has since become very powerful, the Judiciary is (at the least) an equal branch of government, and justices of the Supreme Court are now big men (and women) on campus—all undeniable, and all because a man named William Marbury wanted a job.

★ ★ ★

In 1803, the night before President John Adams was to leave office, he appointed Marbury, a Maryland financier, to be a justice of the peace in the District of Columbia. It was a low-paying, minor position, yet Secretary of State James Madison, as much out of spite as out of principle (he thought the obnoxious Adams was "obnoxious," mainly because Adams was obnoxious) refused to complete the commission. Marbury, like any good American, sued—for a *writ of mandamus,* to require Madison to hand it over, *mandammit.* When Chief Justice John Marshall denied Marbury's petition, ruling that the statute on which Marbury based his claim violated the Constitution, it marked the first time that a court had invalidated a law by ruling it "unconstitutional." It also introduced the idea of "judicial review," which forever promoted the Judicial Branch to be the superior authority, and the last word, on the constitutionality of laws. (If you vaguely remember *Marbury v. Madison* as one of the important cases you should have learned about in high school, that's why.)

So in the end, the Supreme Court owes its power to a job listing. We might as well get our presidents through a classified ad. (Not a bad idea, necessarily.)

After *Marbury v. Madison,* the Court quickly graduated from an after-thought to a powerhouse. Justices became rock stars. By the time John Marshall passed away after thirty-four years on the bench, so central had his Court become that his death was announced by the pealing of the bell atop the Pennsylvania State House. Perhaps the bell could sense the occasion (or, more likely, the bell ringer just pulled extra hard), but that was the moment—or so goes one story—that the bell, soon to be known as the Liberty Bell, earned its distinctive crack.

Since then, the Court has steadily trumped the other two branches. Not that it had a choice. As Seventh Circuit judge Richard Posner has argued in the *Harvard Law Review,* cases that make it to the Supreme Court are, by definition, unclear enough that justices have the obligation to impose their own political preferences on the country. The result: The Supreme Court is essentially "a Constitutional Convention in continuous session," in the words of Woodrow Wilson. So there: We have gone from Madison's promise to experiment with no federal courts at all to a country where "unelected judges" can set aside the rule of law if five of them say so; that is, to a country run by—ugh—*lawyers.*

Though it affects everyone, it pleases few. A 2010 Gallup survey found that only 14 percent of Americans had "a great deal of trust and confidence" in the Court. *Fourteen* percent—more Americans place their trust in Punxsutawney Phil than in Clarence Thomas. Liberals, conservatives, and moderates all object. Liberals view the courts as dominated by right-wing "activist judges" whose idea of a good time is overturning *Roe v. Wade.* Conservatives believe that a history of liberal judicial decisions has emboldened an unelected "super-legislature" prone to inventing new rights such as "privacy" that are not found in the Constitution. Even moderates take issue with a Supreme Court that gives local governments the right to seize their homes merely to build a MegaStore if, based on a hunch as much as on an economic study, such a seizure might help the economy (resulting in what can only be the saddest Walmart greeter ever: "Welcome to Walmart. This used to be my house").

So that's where we are now: The Court *does* matter. Judges *do* have power. And a lifetime appointment to the bench, assumed to be a harm-less perk of "the least political branch" by the Framers in 1789, now makes an already too-powerful position even more formidable—by making it *forever.*

★ ★ ★

On the issue of lifetime tenure, it would be easy to accuse me of not knowing what the heck I'm talking about. After all, I can't think of a single job I've ever had during which I died. But to claim that the Founders *did* know what they were doing is to overlook that their Article III, as written, results in a Supreme Court that behaves in many ways Madison and the Framers couldn't have planned, and would have resented.

First off, it turns Supreme Court justices into top-notch schemers. Partisan judges time their exit from the bench until a president who shares their politics can name their replacement—hardly a virtuous reason to stick around.

What's more, presidents are rewarded for appointing baby justices—the younger the appointee, the longer they'll have on the bench. So much for respecting our elders; there's more bang for young bucks. When John Roberts was appointed by President George W. Bush to be the youngest chief justice since John Marshall was confirmed in 1801, he was younger than *all eight* of the associate justices that served under him. That hardly seems fair.

Lifetime tenure also ignores the inevitable: burnout. Robe wearing may look like easy living, but law deciding is hard labor. "Most Supreme Court justices do their best work," according to law professor Lewis H. LaRue, "during the period of their fifth to tenth years." Like rock stars, they are relegated to writing their greatest hits in their first two albums. As he sees it, it takes five years to get used to the gig, five years to do solid work, and a lifetime to "defend what they did in their early careers." Even Justice Stephen Breyer admits the danger of what he calls "the self-protective psychology of human nature"—simply, the longer a judge sticks around, the more his or her decisions are made to be consistent rather than to be right. Not to mention that rock stars get old, and letting them stick around for decades virtually guarantees that they'll be out of touch with "kids today" at some point. Their formative years were decades earlier—what gives them the right to judge?

Being out of touch is one thing. Being out of one's mind is quite another. And although Supreme Court justices are very powerful, let's be honest, they are not immune to the worst side effect of aging: getting old. Losing a step. Diminished capacity looks good on no one, least of all people who already wear robes all day.

Judges, for whom hyper-rationality is a job requirement, should be the first to recognize this, through their unique powers of perception. One would assume they'd step aside when they felt they could no longer perform their duties with the same gusto and dexterity they had in their rookie years. Once upon a time—namely, the early eighteenth century—they did. John Jay, the first chief justice, stayed a mere five years; he heard only four cases before retiring to become governor of New York. His successor, John Rutledge, called it quits after four months. On average, the first ten justices donned their robes for less than eight years—scarcely long enough to get rid of that new-robe smell.

I'm sorry to say, this is no longer the case. Today's justices are in it for the long haul. I highly doubt their reluctance is because they can't figure out where to retire. My theory, which no one can possibly disprove? They've gone mad with power.

No proof is more telling—and more distressing—than this: Over 90 percent of district and circuit judges die within a year after putting in for retirement. Which means one of two things—either justices stay on the job too long, or there's a very strange serial killer on the loose.

Is a Court filled with the nation's grandpas and grandmas automatically something to worry about? Not necessarily. Some remarkably old Supreme Court justices have remained remarkably sharp. It is said that when Oliver Wendell Holmes, Jr., was ninety and had almost three decades on the Court under his belt, he glimpsed a pretty girl and exclaimed, "Oh, to be seventy again!"—the sign of a dirty old man, perhaps, but not a senile one. But for every Oliver Wendell Holmes—sharp as a tack in private, if embarrassing as a grandfather in public—there is a William O. Douglas. There is a judge who should have hung up his robe long before he did. Even after conceding, *in his seventies,* that he was too old for the job—"My ideas are way out of line with current trends, and I see no particular point in staying around and being obnoxious"—Douglas *did* stay around, and *was* obnoxious. He became known as "Wild Bill" for his unpredictable behavior. Serving for more than a third of a century, Douglas earned more than a few distinctions—he had the most wives (four), the most divorces (three), and the most opinions of any Supreme Court justice in history—including a famous dissenting opinion in which he argued, not altogether facetiously, that "inanimate objects" such as "trees, swampland, even air" should have standing to sue in court.

Even after suffering a debilitating stroke, Douglas refused to leave the bench. He may have believed he still had the goods, but his stubbornness is more commonly explained by two other, pettier motivations: his fear that a Republican would take his place, and his own hatred of President Gerald

Ford, who, as House minority leader, had tried to impeach Douglas four years earlier. A stroke, it seems, is no match for spite. (That his condition might have been ultimately harmless, if one believes it to be so, is less a product of luck than of a conspiracy fit for a John Grisham novel; his colleagues resolved among themselves not to count his vote in any case where it might be decisive, as in 5–4 decisions.) Douglas retired only after being persuaded by his trusted friend and fellow justice Abe Fortas to finally step down. Even then he did not go gently. Indeed, he did not go at all; as Bob Woodward tells it, after Douglas's seat had been taken by Ford appointee John Paul Stevens (who, not for nothing, also stayed on the bench into his nineties), Douglas kept showing up, expecting to be allowed to hear arguments in cases before the Court. He is said to have been outraged when he arrived at Court to learn that his locker had been reassigned to the new guy. (One imagines Douglas pleading with the locker room attendant: "This whole system's out of order!") Only when Chief Justice Warren Burger ordered law clerks not to assist Douglas, and when all nine sitting justices wrote a formal letter reminding Douglas he had retired, did Douglas finally stop showing up. It would be funny if it weren't so sad.

Douglas's delusional behavior was largely attributed to stroke-related anosognosia, a neuropsychological condition that prompted him, a man of reason and judgment, to invite reporters on a hike even though he was confined to a wheelchair, and despite being paralyzed on one side, to claim—sincerely, according to eyewitnesses—that he was going to try out for the Washington Redskins.

And then there is William Rehnquist, the man who succeeded Warren Burger as Chief Justice, who behaved in a way that walked the line between somewhat quirky and truly suspicious. He had been appointed in 1972 by Richard Nixon, who, ironically, once moaned about the "senile old bastards" that made up the Supreme Court. From the start, Rehnquist raised eyebrows. He wore four gold stripes on the sleeves of his robe because he had seen a character in a Gilbert and Sullivan operetta so adorned. He once skipped a State of the Union address because it conflicted with an evening art class. But it was what Rehnquist did at the end of his career, when, like Douglas, he, too, was in failing health, that pulls alarms. Simply: He stayed at his post long past his ability to perform his duties. Ironic for a man who, according to one close friend and tennis partner, was "obsessed" with punctuality. He showed up late to his own retirement.

Truth be told, he was a no-show. Rehnquist never stepped down. Like all justices, Rehnquist believed he didn't have to—in a 1990 interview he taped on the condition that it not be aired until his death, he, too, argued that "during good Behaviour" meant, "for all practical purposes, for life." But at the end, he suffered from thyroid cancer and endured unremitting back pain, for which he took painkillers that presumably dulled his judgment. He slept in the basement of his Arlington townhouse, too weak to climb the stairs. In the 2004 term—the final term before his death—he wrote only nine opinions out of more than two hundred. He died while still presiding over the Court. Either he loved his job too much to leave it, or he couldn't bear to see it go—or, as some have suggested, he was consciously trying to break Douglas's record of thirty-six years on the bench.

Not exactly an honorable motivation.

Not exactly *good Behaviour*.

Douglas stayed out of spite, Rehnquist out of pride—but neither is a sufficient excuse. Clearly, letting justices determine their own expiration date doesn't work. By the time they admit to themselves that things are slipping—if they ever do—it's too late. They've dug in, they've screwed up, and they dishonored their honorable service. All because—though schooled in Latin and legalese—they don't know the meaning of the word "quit."

TILL DEATH DO US EX PARTE

I DON'T BOTHER LECTURING Justice Scalia on any of this; after decades of legal study and twenty-five years of service as one of America's Top Judges, he's been fully briefed.

Instead, I begin my cross-examination.

"How about you?" I ask.

"How about me what?" he counters.

"Can *you* imagine just walking away?" I ask.

"Of course I can," he scoffs, with a couldn't-care-less tone that implies he'd just as soon leave today if only he hadn't signed a two-year lease on his Supreme Court locker.

"When?" I ask.

"Like I've said before, as soon as I'm not firing on all eight cylinders, when I'm not doing the job as well as I used to, it'll be time to go."

"How will you know when that is?"

He looks me straight in the eye.

"I'll know."

You're treading on thin ice, counselor.

"So you don't need some outside authority limiting the term of your serv—"

"I'm fairly aware of the requirements of the position," he says. "I'll know when I can no longer fulfill them."

Thin ice.

And yet:

"What if I told you, Your Honor, that someone even more powerful than you says you're wrong about that."

Very thin ice.

"And who is that?"

"Someone you know quite well."

He looks at me, wondering if he should ask.

"Who?"

If this were a case in some courtroom drama, this is the moment when I would stand slowly, scan the jury, look back at the judge, and call on my surprise witness:

May it please the court, I now call to the stand . . . [dramatic pause] *. . . the current Chief Justice of the Supreme Court of the United States.*

If this were indeed a courtroom drama, the double doors in the back of the courtroom would fly open, the stenographer would record the reaction of the gallery—

[Audible gasps]

—and Chief Justice John G. Roberts, Junior, would saunter up the aisle, hesitating only long enough to lock eyes with fellow justice Scalia and feel his glare: *Et tu, Roberte?*

Roberts would then explain to the ladies and gentlemen of the jury that no matter what he says, or how he pleads for mercy, Justice Antonin Scalia should have been kicked off the Court exactly ten years ago.

Back in real life, I explain what the hell I'm talking about. When he was a lawyer in the Reagan White House, twenty-two years before he joined the Supremes, John Roberts argued on behalf of a fifteen-year term limit for Supreme Court justices. It was a both a pragmatic proposal—as he saw it, the Founders "adopted life tenure at a time when people simply did not live as long as they do now"—and a principled one, for many of the same reasons I've trotted out: "A judge insulated from the normal currents of life for twenty-five or thirty years was a rarity then but is becoming common-place today," he wrote, in a White House memo. "Setting a term of, say, fifteen years would ensure that federal judges would not lose all touch with reality through decades of ivory tower existence." It is an indictment of lifetime tenure too compelling to ignore.

As I finish explaining, one thing is clear: Scalia knew nothing of this.

"Is that so?" he asks. "Roberts thought that?"

I have outlawyered the longest-serving associate justice of the Supreme Court.

"Really—he thought that?" he asks again.

"Yes," I say, pausing a beat for dramatic effect. "Yes, he did."

For a moment, Scalia seems speechless. He can muster no defense. Even though we're sitting in the National Gallery, not the Supreme Court—and eating lunch, not arguing case law—I am tempted to shout "the prosecution rests!," slam an imaginary briefcase, and march out triumphantly.

But I don't. I stay. And Scalia's grin returns.

"Well," he says, "I doubt he does anymore."

[Laughter]

He has a good point. Roberts *doesn't* think that anymore. When Roberts himself was asked about his previous comments at his confirmation hearings in 2005, he flip-flopped; predictably, his perspective on the issue had . . . evolved. As the law professor Larry Sabato has eloquently put it, on the issue of lifetime tenure, "Where one stands depends on where one sits." For Roberts, having a lifetime seat in the ivory tower, once he got inside and looked around, didn't sound so bad after all. He had a deathbed conversion in reverse—with the deathbed replaced by a Supreme Court bench.

Scalia's joke seems to put him back on offense.

"*So?*" he asks.

"*So?*"—it was an argument that had stymied me before.

So . . . what?

"*So* . . . are you going to make me retire? With your new Constitution? I mean, I've been here longer than fifteen years."

Oh. He's not on the attack. He's throwing himself on the mercy of my court.

"No, sir."

I'm not here to fire Justice Scalia—though I appreciate his acknowledgment of my authority to do so—nor am I advocating mandatory retirement ages in general. I see no reason to put Justice Scalia on an ice floe and push him out to sea just because, chronologically, he's past his prime.

"So? What exactly do you propose?"

I thought he'd never ask.

"Simple," I say.

YOUR NEW ARTICLE III

The judicial Power of the United States shall be vested in one supreme Court [I'm doing my best to speak in cursive] and the Judges shall hold their Offices during good Behavior.

Scalia seems confused. "But that's what Article III already says."

"Not exactly," I clarify. "I dropped the *u* from 'Behaviour.' To make it more American."

"But otherwise, that's Article III of the Constitution."

Indeed it is, Your Honor, indeed it is.

It was, I was certain, a remedy for Article III that an originalist like Justice Scalia could not help but support: We *take it literally*. We revive the original Article, and we honor its original language. "Judges shall hold their Offices *during good Behavior*." But instead of presuming that means *for life*, we take it to mean what it actually means: As long as justices behave, as long as they don't act crazy or prompt their law clerks to whisper about their sanity, the gig is theirs.

Surely a dyed-in-the-parchment originalist wouldn't mind a stricter adherence to the text of the original, virgin Article—the genuine Article—before it was corrupted over decades of convenient interpretations by self-serving and self-preserving justices of all political stripes who stayed too long on the Court merely to spite a president, or will away a stroke, or stave off a retirement of pinochle and shuffleboard—not exactly "good Behavior." The Founders never declared explicitly that "good Behaviour" necessarily meant "for life"; so why, on this occasion only, would an originalist throw his lot in with—ugh—*living constitutionalists*, eager to bend the Constitution to their will? Wouldn't a dyed-in-the-parchment originalist want to—be compelled to—honor the Constitution's original language? To play it as it lays?

I had him dead to rights. Surely he, a man who swore by the letter of the law, would swear by the letter of *this* law—that is, save one letter—to which he owed his entire career.

I was proud of my judicial jujitsu.

"But who determines 'good Behaviour'?" he asks.

"Good *Behavior*," I correct him. (He was pronouncing the *u*.)

"That's what I said. Who gets to decide?"

I've anticipated this question.

Scalia listens closely as I propose a judging body composed of three people, appointed by the president, whose sole responsibility is to determine whether the justices are passing the *good Behavior test* as revived by my new Constitution.

He gets what I'm aiming at.

"A Supreme Supreme Court," he says, with a laugh.

Scalia is evidently amused by the idea. I can tell he's not ruling it out.

"Just one question," he says.

I raise my chin and allow it: *Yes, Your Honor?*

"How long do *they* serve?"

I hadn't thought of that.

Fork!

[Laughter]

AND IN THE BLUE CORNER . . .

ALTHOUGH HE'S A PRIVATE MAN, there is one public indulgence for which Justice Scalia is quite well known: a recurring, highly entertaining, surprisingly candid open debate with his philosophical counterweight on the bench, Justice Stephen Breyer. It is C-SPAN's version of a Foreman-Ali fight.

The Originalist vs. the Living Constitutionalist.

The Aggression in the Session.

The Rough Sport in the High Court.

I have seen it in action and have been wowed by their candor and their charisma. So in the spirit of equal time, I reached out to Justice Breyer to see if he, too, was willing to meet and discuss things constitutional in his chambers—which, by the way, were very nice (even if he keeps the thermostat a tad warm for my taste). I gave him the obvious incentive: He'd best get in on the ground floor of this new Constitution; depending on how long he stuck around, he'd have to interpret it someday.

To my surprise, he said yes. He'd be happy to meet and discuss my proposed changes to the Constitution, with one catch: We must do so privately and off the record. And since he is one of the few who can interpret the First Amendment—and thereby my right to ever publish another book knocking the Constitution of the United States—I was happy to comply.

So forget what I said about the thermostat. I mean, how would *I* know?

DO I HAVE TO PAINT YOU A PICTURE?

I HAD GONE TOE-TO-TOE with Justice Scalia and survived. I needed to commemorate the occasion. Luckily, Nelson Shanks, portrait artist nonpareil, eventually managed to tear himself away from his heavy workload and his drive-by sopranos and his vodka-fueled, rabble-rouser-filled soirees.

I knew he would paint a masterpiece. I just didn't know how he'd turn that masterpiece into a painting.

It is a noble portrait befitting a man of my rare breeding, a man who will mount any challenge, tame any beast, and charge ahead on even the most daunting journey—such as rewriting the Constitution of the United States.

Nelson gave the portrait a title I have no interest in rewriting.

Stallion on a White Horse, *by Nelson Shanks*

ARTICLE IV
THE STATES

What's the Matter with Kansas?
Also, What's the Point of Nebraska?

ONCE DROVE THROUGH NEBRASKA, via I-80, days after my girlfriend broke up with me, on a self-imposed road trip from Los Angeles to Cedar Rapids to find my brother's shoulder and cry on it. It is a long, straight, hypnotically boring drive that not only gave me ample time to think about the loss, but also put my recent heartbreak in much-needed perspective.

It could be worse, I realized. *I could live here.*

Cold comfort, perhaps, but comfort nonetheless. And so, for providing the enforced monotony that only a dull road trip can provide, and the bleak void to which to compare my own relatively full life, I am grateful to the state of Nebraska. Nebraska has a special place in my heart.

It has no place, however, on a map of the United States.

Let me explain: California is a state. New York is a state. Texas, for the time being at least, is a state. And they deserve to be. They're big, they're boisterous—but most crucially, they're *populated*. Thirty-seven million people live in California, four million in Los Angeles alone. New York is home to almost twenty million people. If California were a country, it would have the eighth largest economy in the world. If New York City were its own state, it would be the twelfth largest—and in my humble New Yorker opinion, the best.

Whereas Nebraska?

There are more Americans in prison than in Nebraska. And not for nothing, but as I drove past endless rows of cornstalks, I couldn't help but think: *What's the difference?* Nebraska, whose official state motto is "Equality Before the Law," nonetheless feels like a punishment for a crime. And like a criminal, I whiled away the hours (or was it days?) thinking up mottoes that better apply: "Nebraska—a great place to serve some time." "Nebraska—if you lived here, you'd be bored by now." "Nebraska—Canada's Mexico!"

Sure, the argument could be made that Nebraska is in fact an idyllic land full of picturesque cities with enviable small towns steeped in small-town values personified by some of the loveliest Americans to grace the planet—and, I confess, in my wildest dreams I often fantasize about living among them in such a glorious place—but let's be honest: It's also a lifeblood-sucking leech on our body politic. Yes, my fellow citizens, despite what the original Constitution of the United States says about the qualifications for statehood and the guarantee of representation in Congress, by every measure that truly matters in America (bigness, crowdedness, awesomeness, Texasness), Nebraska doesn't deserve its star on the American flag.

Which is to say nothing about Montana (4th largest, 44th most populous).

Or Wyoming (10th largest, 50th most populous).

Or the largest but 47th most populous state we call Alaska.

Add it up, and more than half of all Americans live in eight states. The big ones. The *important* ones. How many live in the eight *least* populated states? Less than 3 percent. *Three percent*—also known as the margin of error. (Which raises a terrifying scenario: It's possible these states are completely empty.)

Yet what concerned me during my soul-deadening voyage toward Omaha was not whether these states deserve their claim on so much territory (they don't), or whether, as guaranteed by Article I, they should be represented by two senators as powerful as the senators in states where people actually live (they shouldn't). Rather, as my car sped past miles and miles of unharvested high-fructose corn syrup, my muscles atrophying and my eyes fluttering in and out of semiconsciousness, my mind was focused on Article IV. Because it is Article IV, the first in the Constitution to turn its full attention to the states rather than the branches of national government, that wants me to believe that Nebraska, this expanse of emptiness which so begs for my disdain, actually deserves my respect.

It reads, in part:

Section 1: Full Faith and Credit shall be given in each State to the public Acts, Records, and Judicial Proceedings of every other State.

Section 2: The Citizens of each State shall be entitled to all
Privileges and Immunities of Citizens in the several States.*

Put plainly, Article IV makes a revolutionary claim: All states are created equal. Laws made in Alaska, which is known for its lawlessness, are as
valid as laws made in Pennsylvania, which invented laws. Article IV insists
that, as a nation, we should care as much about the Carolinas as we do
about California. Montana matters as much as Massachusetts. And New
York is no better than any of its forty-nine neighbors—not even Nebraska.
Which is, put even more plainly, ridiculous.

I should know. I've driven through Nebraska. I *live* in New York.

★ ★ ★

Which brings me, mercifully, to Washington, D.C. I'm not going to make
the claim—as least not until I fix the Tenth Amendment—that all states
pale in comparison to our nation's capital. It would be easy to presume all
this interstate refereeing hardly matters, to believe that D.C. is where the
real action is—bills made into laws, pleasant walks made into Million Man
Marches, Washingtons made into monuments. The federal city—and the
Constitution that stipulated it—embodied, after all, a necessary and overdue consolidation of colonial power and a rebuke to those who thought a
loose assembly of autonomous states—quarrelsome, troublemaking, *stop-
it-really-you're-embarrassing-me* states—would see America flourish into
the nineteenth century.

But I will point out the often overlooked, embarrassing fact about the
capital: It is also a monument to the Founders' weak-kneed unwillingness
to play favorites among the states. So eager were the Founders to please all

---

* On another road trip, I might as easily have been obsessed with Section 3, which de-
scribes how new states might be created. It dictates that "no new State shall be formed or
erected within the Jurisdiction of any other state; nor any State be formed by the Junction
of two or more States . . . without the Consent of the Legislatures of the States concerned
as well as of Congress." To be sure, it offers its own absurdities; namely, whether the entire
state of West Virginia is unconstitutional—since it was created from the Unionist parts
of Virginia that refused to secede (its state legislature essentially voted itself into existence); or whether New York City will ever have the *cojones* to pursue statehood itself, as
even CIA director Leon Panetta once championed when he was an aide to NYC mayor
John Lindsay; or whether Texas will ever claim its unique and perfectly legal right to
break up into five states—an escape clause it stipulated when it agreed to be annexed into
the United States. Cool, right? It's as if Section 3 was designed to give us something to
talk about at cocktail parties.

their colonial constituents that when they debated where to locate the federal city, they considered a phone book's worth of places to plop it: Northerners suggested it be located as far north as possible, since it was inevitable that Canada would be subsumed into their new nation (and who knows, still might); less optimistic easterners, who predicted that the West would secede someday, proposed any lovely spot near the Atlantic; those with an eye to expansion toward the Pacific nominated an outpost on the trans-Appalachian frontier, speculating that *if you build it, they will come*—the country would catch up with the capital. No regional whim was neglected. In fact, so long did they take to make their final decision on location that the original plan for the Washington Monument (albeit a much shorter version) called for it to be put on wheels—an undignified solution but one that would have allowed it to be rolled from state to state, wherever Congress happened to be in session.

Like I said: ridiculous. Washington, D.C., for all its merits, is a living testament to the Founders' congenital inability, as they gambled the long odds on independence from Britain, to pick a horse.

One place rarely mentioned as a potential spot for our federal city? Its current home: the southern valley of the Potomac. Only Virginians argued on its behalf, with Congressman Richard Bland Lee of Alexandria insisting that if Congress failed to deliver a more southerly capital, "one part of the Union would be depressed and trampled on, to benefit and exalt the other." Placing the capital elsewhere, he warned, would be "an alarming circumstance to the people of the southern states." Only a capital near the Potomac guaranteed "perpetual union and domestic tranquility." It was clever gambit on Lee's part: By wrapping his compromise in the language of the Constitution, he was using their own words against them, but it was also the kind of demand for attention that today gives wimpy states like Delaware or Idaho grand ideas that they can play with the big dogs. Like a Chihuahua barking at a Great Dane.

That's the promise of Article IV: No part of the Union shall be trampled on, merely to exalt the other. Even if it means turning the Washington Monument into a pushcart.

THERE'S SOMETHING ROTTEN IN THE
DEMARCATION OF STATES

BY THEIR WORDS, the Framers clearly thought the principles behind Article IV important; heck, it was their idea. If one is to judge actions, however, today's congressmen, no less obligated to defend the same principles, aren't so sure. Oh, they swear on it, swear by it, and insist it means the world to them, but it would be hard for any of them to explain away this fact: When the 112th Congress of the United States convened in January 2011 with a tag-team-style reading of the complete United States Constitution—a symbolic stunt intended to show to the watching world that this was a Congress that wouldn't forget its fealty to our founding document—they made a rather spectacular flub. They skipped part of Article IV.

The man behind the stunt, Virginia Republican Bob Goodlatte, said it was intended "to recommit the Congress to the text of the Constitution." He promised it would be "a very symbolic showing to the American people, and it's a powerful message to members of Congress." That message? "We are a nation of laws, not of men." Perhaps—but none of the men (nor any of the women) who gathered to read those laws on that day bothered to read Section 4 of Article IV.*

Charitable interpretations of what exactly transpired place the blame on Congressman Jerrold Nadler of New York, a prodigious man with prodigious fingers who, when it was his turn to take the podium, accidentally turned two pages at once, launching them forward into Article V prematurely. While that may explain *how* it happened, it doesn't explain a more embarrassing fact.

No one noticed.

Not the congressman next in line, not the assembled congresspersons in the House chamber, not the congressmen and congresswomen who had already completed their assigned readings of Articles I through III and had headed back to their offices, symbolism accomplished. At least, no one

---

* To be fair, the entire proceeding was cursed. Speaker John Boehner was chosen to read the Preamble to the Constitution, even though he had previously confused it with that of the Declaration of Independence; Senator Barbara Boxer tripped on the way up to the lectern; reportedly, some congressmen were so bored they simply left, slipping away to someplace they could read their BlackBerries without appearing unpatriotic.

noticed until later that day, when a chastened Representative Goodlatte was forced to return to the chamber, read the section they had skipped, and provide everyone an unexpected lesson in basic civics: There is a Section 4 of Article IV, even if Congress itself hadn't noticed.* It had only taken two centuries, but our feelings about Article IV were revealed that morning: We have evolved from rigid overdeference to Article IV (Every state is equally worthy of the hosting the nation's capital!) to utter indifference to Article IV (There's a Section 4?).

For that evolution, we can't put the blame where we so often do: on the fat fingers of Congressman Jerrold Nadler. I say we must blame the ridiculous premise of Article IV.

Vermont is as vital as Virginia? Please.

★ ★ ★

Was I thinking about the merits of giving "Full Faith and Credit" to each state as I drove through Nebraska? Not at all. At the time, I was merely thinking: *I am soooooooo not a Nebraskan.*

I was, at the time, a Californian. I had lived in the Golden State for four years, and as such, all of the rights and benefits of California residency were mine, all mine! I could serve on California juries, vote in California state elections, and draw California unemployment checks. Had I a major case of glaucoma or a minor case of cancer, in a few years I would even be eligible for my very own California-state-sanctioned, medically warranted marijuana—if I were, you know, into that type of thing. Citizenship has its privileges.

And Article IV is cool with that. It is designed to help me be a Californian even outside California. As written, it would guarantee that if I am granted certain "Privileges and Immunities" in my home state, all other states must also grant me those rights. I can thank Article IV for the fact that when I crossed the border from Colorado into Nebraska, I wasn't immediately pulled over for not having a valid driver's license. It is why when I stopped in North Platte to fill up my gas tank, the attendant couldn't legally charge me $10 a gallon just because I wasn't "from 'round these parts." Although the Supreme Court has occasionally retreated to a more "limited interpretation" of Article IV—merely that states may not discriminate against citizens of

---

* One might assume they would have taken heed, since Section 4 does nothing less than guarantee every state in the union "a republican form of government." No small thing.

other states in favor of its own citizens—it has always returned to the basic theme of Article IV: States must play nice with others, and do unto residents from other states as they would do unto their own.

Oklahoma must say to Oregon: *Legal physician-assisted suicide? Not the way I would have done it, but I respect your choice. It looks good on you.*

Oregonians must say to South Dakotans: *Seriously? You'll only provide abortions to a woman who has been raped if her life is at stake? Seems a bit heartless, but I guess that's just another reason why we don't live there.*

This makes sense—I, for one, enjoy those regional quirks, and wouldn't want to live in a country where I couldn't tell Montana from Maine.

Yet Article IV isn't all-powerful. As a referee between the states, it has its limits. The most famous check on Article IV, in fact, involved the states of New Jersey and Delaware, a boatload of purloined oysters, and George Washington's nephew Bushrod. In 1832, Bushrod, then a federal circuit court judge, ruled on a landmark case, *Corfield v. Coryell*. The question at hand was whether the state of New Jersey should be allowed to prohibit the plaintiff, Mr. Corfield (and all other non-Jerseyans), from gathering oysters found in the pristine waters off New Jersey (keep in mind, this was back in 1832, when New Jersey waters stood the chance of being pristine) only to return back to their home states to sell them for profit. Bushrod ruled that although the "Privileges and Immunities" protected by Article IV do include "the right of a citizen of one state to pass through any other state . . . for the purposes of professional pursuits," stealing oysters isn't one of them. "We cannot accede to the proposition," he wrote, "that the citizens of several States are permitted to participate in all the rights which belong exclusively to the citizens of any particular State, merely upon the ground that they are enjoyed by those citizens."

In other words, go ahead and cruise down our New Jersey turnpike and breathe our fresh New Jersey air, but if you're not from New Jersey, hands off our New Jersey shellfish.

Article IV doesn't merely snub oystermen from Delaware. It fails to protect Mormons who might want to marry a dozen sister-wives in Utah and expect Vermont to approve of their polygamous bliss, or gun-toting Kentuckians who want to bring their semiautomatics to church while visiting gun-skittish Maryland. These, too, go too far.

But what if I'm not a Delaware oysterman or a Utahan missionary or an armed Kentuckian? What if I am, say, a gay Iowan? And instead of illegally gathering winkles in Weehawken or wives in Salt Lake City, I have gotten legally married in Iowa—which sanctioned gay marriage way back in 2009.

And what if I wanted to celebrate the nuptials with a road trip through Nebraska? (I'm not sure why I'd do that, but just roll with me.) Would Article IV compel Nebraskans to recognize my marriage?*

Congress has tried to say no. In 1996, it passed the Defense of Marriage Act, citing the broad power Article IV gives Congress—brace yourself for some gobbledygook—to "prescribe the Manner in which such Acts . . . shall be proved, and the Effect thereof." Which, if you ask me, makes about as much sense as in which such Sentences . . . shall be understood, and the Nonsense thereabouts.†

Now, such gibberish would baffle a normal human; to Congress, however, it made perfect sense. It determined, conveniently, that if could limit "the Effect" that gay marriage would have as it traveled the nation, it could also prescribe that it must have *no effect at all*—which is to say, it could give states the power to ignore gay marriages entirely. The Harvard constitutional scholar Laurence Tribe has called this linguistic tap dance "a play on words, not a legal argument," which forms in us the bad habit of creating "categorical exceptions" to Article IV, when Congress has no such power.

Neither side is happy with the arrangement. Gay couples, skeptical that the federal government will ever give them that wedding day owed to them, want to see more states legalize gay marriage; opponents of gay marriage, fearful that gays might spontaneously band together and attack their northern border brandishing Le Creuset spatulas and Rufus Wainwright CDs, want to see nothing less than a constitutional amendment defining marriage as between a man and a woman. It's all very confusing. What's a gay couple to do—other than plan their honeymoon in San Francisco?

It is this competition, between what one state might want for its citizens and what another state might demand for its own, that Article IV is supposed to referee. Yet it hasn't. It doesn't. And what's more—with all due respect to our nation's homosexual polygamist mollusk aficionados—its failure to do so has meant repercussions far greater than a marriage license, or a second wife, or cheap, tasty New Jersey seafood: Namely, Article IV,

---

* Although I am not gay myself, I can easily imagine that after hitting the road only hours after reciting my everlasting vows in Des Moines, it would be a mighty matrimonial bummer to suddenly not be married for the 361 miles between Council Bluffs, Iowa, and Julesburg, Colorado. (Not to mention the inane road trip conversation: "Are we married again? How 'bout now? How 'bout now? How 'bout now? How 'bout now?")

† You get my point.

with its schoolyard devotion to fair play and radical equality, has done something far more treacherous.

It started the Civil War.

★ ★ ★

At least, it helped. When South Carolina passed the Negro Seamen Act in 1822, authorizing the arrest of black sailors who came ashore in the Palmetto State—and threatening them with slavery if their vessel's captain refused to pay the costs of their detention—it put in motion a series of events that roused the North against the South, the Blue to take up arms against the Gray, and Ken Burns to launch countless slow pans over the handwritten letters of enlisted soldiers pronouncing their undying devotion to dearest Maggie back on the plantation. President Jackson's attorney general, Roger Taney, determined in a strange reverse logic that the black sailors weren't "citizens" as Article IV would have it, because if they were, other states would have to give them the "Privileges and Immunities" afforded to their own citizens—*and,* Taney might have added, *we can't have that, surely.* Taney would soon become the Chief Justice of the United States, and his decision on the Negro Seamen Act has been described as his "dress rehearsal" for his later opinion in the Dred Scott case, in which he wrote, infamously, "Can a negro . . . become a member of the political community formed and brought into existence by the Constitution of the United States, and as such become entitled to all the rights, and privileges, and immunities, guarantied by that instrument?" The court decided no— a despicable answer they've had to answer for ever since.

Then there's the whopper provision of Article IV: the so-called Fugitive Slave Clause, which dictates that those slaves who crossed state lines in search of their freedom "be delivered up" and returned to their home plantation. It is one of the blots in the Constitution—later rectified by the Thirteenth Amendment—and the disgusting paradox of Article IV: Citizens, constrained by the need for states to respect each other equally, were, for a time, legally prohibited from offering that same respect to their fellow man. In the name of treating everyone the same, Article IV required that an entire race be treated repugnantly. When states couldn't determine who was right on the issue—some favored the equality promised by Article IV, others favored the bigotry it sanctioned—they crept ever closer to civil war.

Luckily, braver men than I fought to rid the Constitution of this scourge long ago. We have, thankfully, moved on. And good news! We have found entirely new ways to offend each other.

Compared to the Fugitive Slave Clause, today's call-to-arms fighting words are just silly: "single-payer," "judicial activism," "creationist curriculum." But among a populace that is not confronted with the same scale of *important stuff to care about,* they seem just as potent. We scream at our congressional representatives for trying to give us health insurance. We march on Washington because schools dare teach us how the earth was formed and the human race evolved. We threaten violent "Second Amendment remedies" as a way to replace senators who are a tad too liberal for our taste. We have lost all perspective. Let's be honest—we are hardly abolitionists fighting for the equal treatment of an entire race.

But at this rate, who's to say we won't take up arms anyway? Who's to say we won't elevate our picayune concerns to the level of brother-against-brother? Who's to say that the next civil war won't be fought over gay marriage on a compound of polygamists by an army of oystermen who demand that the government keep its hands off their Medicare?

I am.

I am to say.

Because I have an "Article IV remedy" that will clear up all this confusion—and, not for nothing, would have avoided the Civil War. With Americans growing polarized and hyperpartisan based simply on where they choose to live—gun nuts flock to Arizona, hippies to San Francisco, potheads to Oregon—and with their growing certainty that the rest of the country should live as they live, the old constitutional principle that states should *simply respect each other* just won't cut it anymore. Unless we want Civil War II on our hands, it's time we separate the wheat from the chaff— the Californias from the North Dakotas, if you will—and declare once and for all just exactly who is in charge around here.

It's time we rank the states.

It's time we decide which states deserve our respect and which states do not. No longer do we need to play nice. We just need to get in line. We need to ask: What would Texas do? How would Florida handle this? We've had over two centuries to see what the lesser states can do. And frankly, Wisconsin? Maine? Nevada?

Meh. I'm not impressed.

Sound revolutionary? Hardly—at least not compared to some of the Framers' own proposals. At the Constitutional Convention, when the small states were concerned they were getting short shrift with proportional representation, New Jersey delegate David Brearley asked, "What remedy then?" and proposed "One only: that a map of the United States be spread out, and that all the existing boundaries be erased, and that a new partition of the whole be made in thirteen equal parts." Brearley was suggesting nothing less than a new redistricting of America, redrawn to make thirteen states of equal size. I'm not proposing we redraw the map; I'm proposing we respect it. I'm saying: The more map you take up, the more deference you get.

Big difference.

Are you a larger state? *More power to you.* Have you been around awhile? *Wonderful—teach us what we need to learn.* Do you have a record of awesomeness? I say: *No, please. You first. After you . . .*

In the end, mine is a much simpler solution, and it wouldn't even take much arm-twisting. States have claimed preeminent status all along, each jockeying for the top spot. Drive any interstate highway (I don't recommend the one through Nebraska) and you'll see license plates claiming "Delaware—The First State," "North Carolina—First in Flight," and "Massachusetts—The Spirit of America." You'll read bumper stickers warning "Don't Mess with Texas." You'll chuckle at novelty car window signs announcing, "Baby on Board, and By the Way, Everyone from Arkansas Can Suck Eggs."

Hard to blame them—they are all just doing what comes naturally, as even the Founders recognized. Charles Pinckney, the delegate from South Carolina who lied about his age, was regularly overruled by his fellow Framers, but there's no denying he was visionary on one point: "Each state," he proposed, "ought to have a weight in proportion to its importance." As he saw it, the federal government should recognize an overarching principle endowed by our Creator. Namely: *C'mon, seriously—Delaware?*

While the man from South Carolina (#21) makes an excellent point— *not all states are created equal*—it takes a man born in Maryland (#19) who grew up in Washington State (#13), lived in California (#2), and now makes his home in the great state of New York (#1) to make it official.

YOUR NEW ARTICLE IV

Full Faith and Credit—whereupon Credit is due—shall be given by any smaller state to any larger state that could beat it up in a Fight and/or Rumble; and the Citizens of each smaller state shall defer to the Privileges and Immunities of the Citizens of the larger states, of which there are, by Definition, more; as shall the Younger States (your Hawaiis, your Alaskas) defer to the Sage Wisdome and Greater Experience of the Older States that have been around longer and therefore know better (your South Carolinas, your Vermonts), keeping in minde the counterintuitive phenomenon that some of the states with "New" in them—e.g., York, Hampshire—are actually some of the oldest states arounde, and therefore should be listened to before Nevada or Arizona chirps in.

And don't get me started on Rhode Island.

To wit, these United States of America shall hereby be ranked, in order of Prominence, Relevance, and General Importance, accordingly,

1. New York
2. California
3. Illinois
4. Pennsylvania
5. Texas
6. Massachusetts
7. Virginia
8. Hawaii
9. Ohio
10. Colorado
11. Alabama
12. Alaska
13. Washington
14. Arizona
15. Connecticut
16. New Hampshire
17. Oregon
18. New Jersey
19. Maryland

20. Florida
21. South Carolina
22. Idaho
23. Utah
24. Michigan
25. Minnesota
26. Mississippi
27. Missouri
28. Iowa
29. North Carolina
30. Montana
31. Tennessee
32. New Mexico
33. Louisiana
34. Oklahoma
35. Indiana
36. Georgia
37. Wisconsin
38. Wyoming
39. North Dakota
40. South Dakota
41. West Virginia
42. Maine
43. Nevada
44. Kansas
45. Arkansas
46. Vermont
47. Kentucky
48. Delaware
49. Nebraska
50. Rhode Island

ARTICLE V
THE AMENDMENT PROCESS

*Honestly, We're Pretty Sure
We Screwed This Whole Thing Up*

OCTOR, I DIE HARD," George Washington said, as he lay on his deathbed, dying, preparing to take his last breath, as so many who die do. "I die hard, but I am not afraid to go."

They weren't famous last words—I, for one, had never heard them. And frankly, I might have expected a more memorable last gasp from our nation's first president, especially since he was, you know, dying, and wouldn't get another crack at it—something about Posterity, or his undying devotion to Martha, or cherry trees. But they rang true. The General was resigned to his fate: He had commanded armies, crossed the Delaware, won the Revolutionary War, founded a country, presided over the writing of its Constitution, served as its first commander-in-chief, stayed in office not one but two terms, and spent the last few years in a final exhausting campaign to establish the federal city that would bear his name. And now, on the night of December 13, 1799, on the cusp of a new millennium, he was ready to rest.

Hard to blame the guy. I'm exhausted just writing that paragraph.

Dutiful to his dying day, Washington had spent the previous morning on his usual daily rounds, five hours in the saddle, tending to his crops in a rainstorm, "no more deterred by the weather," according to the historian Fergus Bordewich, "than he had been by redcoats." On this particular day, however, the rain turned to snow, then hail, then sleet—chilling his bones, drenching his garments, slowing his progress, and making him (regrettably for a military man) late for supper. So as not to delay his dinner guests, he joined them at the dining table without changing out of his wet clothes.

The next morning, a sore throat turned into something more. Doctors were summoned. "The croup" was diagnosed, with its attendant *quinsy*, a form of tonsillitis—which, in 1799, might as well have been the plague.

George Washington, the man who brought the country to life, was dying. Here lay the indispensable man who, a decade earlier, had arrived at the Constitutional Convention in Philadelphia via what was described as a "Royal Progress," his path marked by cheering citizens five deep, his carriage attended by so many horsemen kicking up so much dirt that, it was said, he couldn't even see the countryside over which he would soon preside. Now it was his fellow Founders who couldn't see what should be done—for Washington, or for the country. For years, they could only envision the future when perched atop the General's six-foot frame. And now, their leader was being brought down by a disease that today even three-year-olds routinely overcome.*

Not that the doctors were much help. The average grasp of human physiology and pathology was, to say the least, poor. Physicians still thought bumps on a human's skull could indicate disease—when, at best, it indicated hat size. Even the most famous physician of the era, Benjamin Rush, a man indisputably ahead of his time—he signed the Constitution of the United States, for starters—showed an understanding of the human anatomy that was positively medieval. Rush administered bloodletting and sweating purges with a sadistic devotion. He bled one patient twenty-two times; bad enough, but far worse when you consider that he believed the human body contained twice as much blood as it actually does. He also believed American bodies were exceptional; he held as a medical truth that while aggressive bleeding might harm the British, who were weak from posh living, his "republican" therapy was perfectly appropriate for robust, well-fed Americans. Suffice it to say, when the yellow fever devastated Philadelphia in the fall of 1793, his methods as the city's leading physician very likely killed more victims than they saved.

The doctors at Washington's side hadn't exactly developed any miracles in the six years since. Washington had quinsy, the physicians had no idea how to cure it, and within forty-eight hours, the first president of the United States of America, the "most balanced of men," had fallen.

---

* As it happens, I was such a three-year-old. I contracted the croup as a toddler, and the tracheotomy Thornton intended for Washington was in fact administered to me in a speeding ambulance on the way to Bethesda Naval Hospital. If you're reading this, apparently I have survived. Which reminds me:

SELF-EVIDENT TRUTH #9: I'M UNBREAKABLE.
The fact that I survived the malady that felled a president proves that between the two of us, I have the better constitution. Even medically speaking.

Washington had died hard, but he insisted he was not afraid to go; the same cannot be said of those at his bedside. They were petrified to see their "indispensable man" dispensed with. So when they saw Washington's lifeless body, well, that's when things got animated. That's when the country's most accomplished medical professionals tried—true story—to bring George Washington back from the dead.

William Thornton, the architect of the Capitol Building but a physician by trade, had rushed to his good friend's bedside, determined to do *something, anything, my-God-man-get-me-a-hot-towel-and-a-set-of-pruning-shears.* He had intended to perform a life-sustaining tracheotomy, but he arrived to find that Washington had already died—"a stiffened corpse," Thornton later admitted.

But at that moment, Thornton refused to accept the truth. He began devising all manner of heroics that might cure Washington of his mortality. Within minutes, he had tossed away his crude ventilation tube and was grasping for straws, "overwhelmed with the loss of the best friend I had on earth."

Washington had died; Thornton wanted a second opinion. "The weather was very cold, and he remained in a frozen state for several days," Thornton said. He saw an opening. "I proposed to attempt his restoration, in the following manner. First to thaw him in cold water, then to lay him in blankets, and by degrees and by friction to give him warmth, and to put into activity the minute blood vessels, at the same time to open a passage to the lungs by the trachea, and to inflate them with air, to produce an artificial respiration, and to transfuse blood into him from a lamb." The other doctors present didn't deny the viability of Thornton's plan to reanimate Washington, only whether "it would be right to attempt to recall to life one who had departed full of honor and renown . . . in the full enjoyment of every faculty, and prepared for eternity." It's not that it's undoable, Doctor; it's undignified.

In the end, they let Washington go. But if William Thornton had had his way, to this day we'd still be saluting General George Washington, our first Zombie President.

★ ★ ★

It is natural to want to save something we cherish, but the Framers had another reason to cling to Washington's coattails: the haunting suspicion that he was irreplaceable. As accomplished as their biographers remind us they were, it is easy to forget that the Founders, to a man, hid behind

George Washington's leadership. Washington was the leading man. They were but colorful supporting characters.

"His Rotundity" John Adams, who would succeed Washington as president, was, according to Jefferson, a "bad calculator of the force and probable effect of the motives which govern men," whose own diary entries proved himself "a man alternately vain and insecure, constantly measuring himself against his colleagues as a way of bolstering his own self-confidence." Thomas Jefferson, who succeeded Adams, was, according to Adams's grandson, a cunning and petty hypocrite who "did not always speak exactly as he felt towards friends and enemies, [who] has left hanging of a part of his public life a vapor of duplicity"—and, worse, according to Christopher Hitchens, was "a man with very little sense of humor." James Madison, who succeeded Jefferson, was, you'll recall, a "gloomy, stiff creature"—though, I hasten to point out, perhaps not quite as stiff as the leader they had just lost.

Of course, on a deathbed, it's easy to forget the failures of a life, and Washington had plenty of his own: He had dropped out of school ("Adams had gone to Harvard and Washington had gone to war," as Joseph Ellis charitably put it), he had gone to fight as "a rank amateur who had never commanded more than a regiment in battle," and he had notoriously attacked a French scouting party during peacetime, sparking nothing less than the Seven Years' War. Washington was not a god. Still, the Founders were lost without him—dunces to his demigod—and they knew it. If they could have propped up Washington's corpse, *Weekend at Bernie's* style, they would have. Heck, they tried.

★ ★ ★

The same impulse that brought doctors rushing to Washington's bedside—to keep an irreplaceable American icon alive for the good of the country—has brought me to the midtown Manhattan office of Mr. David Rubenstein. I am no doctor, and David is not the president. Unlike Washington, David is in fine health, an avid tennis player who, I can only presume, has never suffered from quinsy. He is, however, the 182nd richest man in America.

I've considered all the remedies available to heal this Constitution. He may be my last hope.

"Hello, Kevin," he greets me, warmly. "What can I do for you?"

I am loath to correct the wealthiest man I have ever met. And yet:

"Ask not what you can do for me, Mr. Rubenstein," I tell him. "Ask what we can do for our country."

LIFE SUPPORT, LIBERTY, AND THE PURSUIT OF HAPPINESS

Article V is an admission of defeat. It is a white flag. It concedes that the Framers gave up, that their hard work in the summer in 1787 was incomplete at best—perhaps even wrong—and it punts the hard work of fixing their flubs to Congress, by giving Congress the right to propose amendments to the Constitution "whenever [it] shall deem it necessary." Article V was a tacit confession by the Framers that the Constitution they devised was not perfect and would someday need an overhaul. That's the message of Article V: *Mea culpa.*

My bad.

It is as if Michelangelo had finished the statue of David and then taped a chisel to his masterpiece, along with a sign: *Have at it.*

Naturally, it didn't take long before people started hacking away. When Thomas Jefferson—still serving as ambassador to France—received a copy of the Constitution only a few months after the Convention had adjourned, along with a long letter from his friend Madison justifying the Convention's decisions, he responded with an equally long list of changes he'd like to see made right away, including "freedom of religion, freedom of the press, protection against standing armies . . . the unremitting force of the habeas corpus laws . . . trials by jury in all matters of fact"—in other words, a bill of rights. Jefferson even went further, echoing the bold proposal set forth by Edmund Randolph and George Mason: Hold another Convention. A reboot.

It's not hard to imagine Madison's frustration when he received Jefferson's letter. *Dude, easy for you to say. You've been in France.* His actual response was far more diplomatic, and surprisingly, not laced with profanities. Still, the Father of the Constitution was clearly peeved. Getting any consensus at all, he told Jefferson, was "a task more difficult than can be well conceived by those who were not concerned in the execution of it." And as for the hard-fought, hard-won Constitution made during four months of a chaotic Convention that Jefferson had been exactly zero part of? "It is impossible to consider the degree of concord which ultimately prevailed as less than a miracle." (*So shut your trap, Frenchie.*)*

If what ultimately prevailed in Philadelphia was a miracle, it was a miracle that apologized for itself. It told Congress: We give up. You handle it.

★ ★ ★

There's at least one very good reason to avail ourselves of the amendment provision as provided by Article V; namely, Article V itself. Beyond its amendment clause, Article V lists two other provisions in its 143 words, each a proven disgrace to a country that prides itself on equality and democracy: first, that "no amendment" that would make the slave trade illegal "shall be made prior to the year one thousand eight hundred and eight"; and second, "that no state, without its consent, shall be deprived of its equal suffrage in the Senate." The first was a sop to South Carolina and Georgia, who wanted to protect their steady supply of slaves; the second was demanded by the small states that were, and still are, too big for their britches. The first has been fixed, thanks to the passage of time and the moral conscience of a nation (well, at least half of a nation); the second continues to be in force, thanks to the so-called Great Compromise, which is only great if you live in Delaware or Wyoming.

In fact, the Framers thought that they were making the Constitution easy to amend. They believed they were prescribing the newest therapies and truest methods known to government science. Thanks to Article V, no longer would Congress need *total unanimity* among the states to amend the founding charter, as had been the rule in the Articles of Confederation. Article V would provide an "easy, regular, and Constitutional way" that was, according to George Mason of Virginia, far better than "to trust to chance and violence." (Although it might be interesting to live in a country that amended its Constitution through "chance and violence." At least for a week or two.)

To that end, we the people now have two "easy, regular, and Constitutional ways" to tinker with the Constitution: Simply persuade the United States Congress to propose an amendment, or simply persuade the legisla-

---

* It was a fight Jefferson never gave up. Years later, Jefferson was still advocating constitutional changes—"Let us go on perfecting the Constitution, by adding, by way of amendment, those forms which time and trial are still wanting," he wrote in 1803—not coincidentally the same year he doubled the size of America by violating the Constitution.

tures of at least two-thirds of the states to assemble a national convention in which the amendment is proposed;* oh, and *then* simply persuade three-fourths of the states to ratify the new amendment.

See? Piece of cake.

Really, it's almost impossible *not* to amend the Constitution.

So easy is it to amend the Constitution through Congress that of the more than ten thousand proposals made since the Constitution was adopted, a whopping thirty-three have been referred to the states for ratification—a batting average of almost .0033. So easy is it to amend the Constitution through state conventions that of the more than four hundred petitions made to hold such a get-together, Congress has agreed to hold such an Article V convention exactly zero times.

Since the Bill of Rights, only seventeen amendments have been ratified. During the whole of the nineteenth century, only five were adopted, three of those springing from the aftermath of the Civil War, when, it can be safely acknowledged by both North and South, the country had some minor housekeeping to do. The pace picked up a bit in the twentieth century, with twelve amendments, but according to the constitutional scholar Jack Rakove, even many of those "tinker at the margins." Some hard-won fixes concern themselves only "with matters like the dates of presidential inauguration or procedures for determining when the president may be impaired in the performance of official duties." How many amendments have we seen ratified in the twenty-first century? Zip. So much for keeping it alive; for all the claims that the Constitution of the United States is a living, breathing document, it hasn't budged a single step since the last millennium.

There are any number of excuses. Perhaps we have simply agreed with Benjamin Franklin, who, on the last day of the Convention in Philadelphia, predicted, "I doubt . . . whether any other Convention we can obtain may be able to make a better Constitution." Perhaps few of the amendments were worthwhile. Or perhaps there's a different explanation: It's just too damn hard to amend the Constitution.†

---

* Something of a third method—persuade Congress to require ratification by special convention—has been invoked only once, to repeal Prohibition, and only because even Congress wanted its booze back.

† It all amounts to a short document, relatively speaking. Other constitutions are long enough to give us a serious case of constitution envy. Even California, merely one of the fifty states (albeit the second most important), has a state constitution that, thanks to its amendments, is 350 pages long. The draft of the constitution of the European Union is

Take it from me. Or take it from Thomas Jefferson, who, upon retiring in 1833, blamed the failure of Article V on, counterintuitively, the success of the country he helped found: "The states are now so numerous that I despair of ever seeing another amendment to the constitution, although the innovations of time will certainly call, and now already call, for some." Or take it from Justice Antonin Scalia, who, upon lunching with a constitutional authority who shall remain nameless (but is me), said that it's "too damn hard" to make amendments through Article V—"If it were easier to amend the Constitution, the courts wouldn't spend so much time trying to rewrite it." When Thomas Jefferson agrees with Antonin Scalia, and when both of the prescribed avenues for reviving the Constitution have proven no more successful than bloodletting and sweating purges—and when Zombie George Washington isn't around to rescue us—it's time for a new remedy. It's time to follow the lead of James Madison when he arrived in Philadelphia, hoping not to nurse the Articles of Confederation back to health, but to drive a stake into its heart.

It's time to put Article V out of our misery.

THE MEANS JUSTIFY THE ENDS

So I sit across from David Rubenstein, multibillionaire. I have failed, thus far, to get my hands on the Constitution—although I would have gotten away with it, if it weren't for the impractical plan suggested by *National Treasure* (thanks a lot, Nicolas Cage) and those meddling security guards at the National Archives. Now, having learned the sad truth that my last resort for amendment—availing myself of the convoluted mechanisms provided by Article V—have a shockingly limited track record of success, I have come to realize that there has to be an easier way to fix this thing. My hunch is that the easier way leads past the David Rubenstein Atrium in Lincoln Center, the David M. Rubenstein Child Health Building at Johns Hopkins, the David Rubenstein Building at the Harvard Kennedy School,

---

already 855 pages and counting. Are we willing to let West Coast hippies and Eurotrash leave us in the dust like that? If the amendments to the Constitution of the United States were written in the same hand as the rest of the Articles—that of assistant clerk/scapegoat Jacob Shallus—it would top out at seven pages. So while the muffler of Article V makes the Constitution a quick read—"one of the most concise written constitutions in the world," according to historian Richard Beeman—it also makes it a dead letter.

a few other assorted buildings Rubenstein has endowed with his largesse around the country, and straight into David Rubenstein's midtown Manhattan office.

I'll be frank. There are 2.6 billion good reasons why I think Rubenstein, a man worth 2.6 billion dollars, might be able to help me. I've got big plans—plans that require an equally big bankroll. Revising the original Constitution, it appears, can't be done on the cheap. What I need isn't a congressional resolution, or a majority of state legislatures. Nor do I need a William Thornton to my George Washington—a partnership that, let's be honest, would end in my dead body.

No, what I need is a John Hancock to my Samuel Adams. What I need is a sidekick with a slush fund.

And if that makes little sense, what you need is a quick history lesson.

★ ★ ★

Long before John Hancock and Sam Adams were, respectively, an insurance company and a brand of beer, they were, respectfully, Massachusetts' richest man and Boston's most outspoken politician. They were revolutionaries, Founding Fathers, and good friends. It was a relationship that changed history.

Sam Adams, then the clerk of the Massachusetts House of Representatives, had recruited Hancock to the cause of the Whigs in the 1760s, and they became political allies, despite being an odd couple; Adams, according to historian Pauline Maier, was "a man utterly uninterested in making or possessing money," who trolled the sidewalks in his threadbare red suit—the only suit he owned—trying to stir up revolution, while Hancock was an unabashed moneyman, the dashing merchant and shipping magnate with a smuggling business on the side. But they clicked. They had a groove. When they were the target of capture by British troops, they even made a daring escape together—with the help of Paul Revere's midnight warning, "The Regulars are coming out!"—on the very night of the Shot Heard Round the World. Over time, Hancock gave so much money to Adams's cause that Bostonians joked, "Sam Adams writes the letters to the newspapers, and John Hancock pays the postage." With Hancock's patronage, Adams flourished as a politician and ultimately helped revive the revolution; after the defeat at the battle of Brandywine in 1777, when the Continental Army had been reduced to just 2,500 troops and even General Washington himself was fearing defeat, it was Adams who took the floor of the Continental Congress and said, *Dudes, keep it together.* "If we despond," he cried, "American liberty is no more!"

Hancock and Adams were tied together, and to the cause of liberty; both signed the Declaration of Independence and ultimately supported the Constitution of the United States, and although Hancock had the Benjamins and Adams only the bright red suit, both men rose to serve as governor of Massachusetts.

So yeah, that's what I need. I need Rubenstein to be the Hancock to my Adams: the richest man around, acting as benefactor to the most visionary subversive around, working in concert to save the country. A man of means meets a man who means well.

I can see it now:

Sam Adams, in a portrait commissioned—and paid for— by John Hancock. By John Singleton Copley.

Kevin Bleyer, in a portrait commissioned—and paid for— by David Rubenstein, had he known what was good for him. By David Pettibone.

Rubenstein greets me and seats me, and we exchange pleasantries. If time is money, we spend a few million on small talk. Until:

"So, what can I do for you?" he asks.

As I said, there are 2.6 billion good reasons why a man worth 2.6 billion dollars can help me, but there's only one truly great one: David Rubenstein is as patriotic as he is rich. After a quick rise in politics—at twenty-seven, he was the domestic deputy policy adviser for President Jimmy Carter; at thirty, he admitted to being "surprised" when Carter didn't win reelection; and at thirty-four, he was disillusioned when Walter Mondale found so little support—he joined the private sector and founded the Carlyle Group, a hedge fund that specializes in the fashionable financial tool of the late 1980s: leveraged buyouts. He had already earned his stars and stripes; at Carlyle, he earned his billions. And with them, he ultimately did what no one who stayed in public service could ever do. On December 18, 2007, at a cost of $21.3 million, David Rubenstein bought the Magna Carta.

Yes, *that* Magna Carta.

The one at the National Archives.

In fact, it was his idea to put it there, so that at least one copy would be displayed on American shores, be seen by American citizens, and be kept in good shape by an American institution. (In recent years, he has done the same with a copy of the Emancipation Proclamation—now in the White House—and a copy of the Declaration of Independence—now at the State Department.)

Anyway, that's why—and how—an American kid from Baltimore purchased the founding charter of English law.*

"Well, sir," I say, "you know how Congress is broken?"

"Sure."

"And our system of choosing the president is corrupt?"

"Perhaps."

"And the Supreme Court can serve forever, and the states are all treated equally, and the Preamble doesn't rhyme?"

"Uh, okay."

I get the sense he's just humoring me now. So I skip ahead.

"And the Amendment Clause of Article V makes it nearly impossible to make the changes to our Founding Charter that the continued exceptionalism of our nation so desperately requires?"

"I suppose."

---

* Rubenstein's philanthropy didn't end there. In the years since, he has given $7.5 million to the National Park Service to fix the cracked Washington Monument, $4.5 million to the pandas at the National Zoo (well, not *to* the pandas, but you get the point), and $10 million to the White House Historical Association to establish a research institute on the history of the White House and the Executive Branch. Part of me feels bad that I'm about to change it so drastically.

"Well," I say, "I think I know how to fix it."

"Meaning?"

"Meaning," I say, "I am rewriting the Constitution of the United States."

He looks at me quizzically. Then he smiles.

"That's quite a coincidence," he tells me. "Because *I've* rewritten the Gettysburg Address."

I laugh, and laugh heartily, as one should when a billionaire tells a joke.

Only it's not a joke. He's entirely serious. It seems that in his spare time, Rubenstein has developed a hobby that, considering my own task at hand, I can't help but admire: rewriting history. At least, rewriting one particular speech in history. He entertains at dinner parties with his own rendition of Lincoln's Address at Gettysburg, reconceived as Rubenstein's Address at the Upper East Side home of Chairman So-and-So and His Lovely Wife Such-and-Such.

It's not a joke, but Rubenstein clearly has a sense of humor. I had been warned that Scalia was a jokester. That Mr. Rubenstein is too comes as a surprise. He tells me a ribald story about George Washington that shouldn't be repeated here—and, I confess, cannot be, since I was focusing less on the details and more on the fact that I was sitting across from the 182nd-richest man in America—who, understandably, is wondering why he has let me into his office.

"So, *you're* rewriting the Constitution," he repeats. "What can *I* do for you?"

And I want to tell him.

I want to tell him how he can be the John Hancock of the twenty-first century.

I want to tell him I'm about to offer him the biggest leveraged buyout of his career: For the cost of a single piece of paper, he can save a country.

I want to tell him he can help me successfully pull off what Nicolas Cage could not, even in the movies: protect a sacred document from a terrible fate without having to steal it.

I want to tell him that just as he rescued the Magna Carta from expatriation, contamination, and possible mummification, together we can achieve another miraculous feat: We can rescue the Constitution of the United States.

All he has to do is buy me the Constitution of the United States.

Then I can rewrite all over the darn thing.

Just think of it, I want to tell him, *Kevin Bleyer rewrites the Constitution, and David Rubenstein pays the postage.*

The problem is: I realize how silly it sounds.* Sillier even than when Rubenstein called his accountant and said, "free up twenty-one million so I can purchase the Magna Carta." And besides, I've never been good at asking for money. It doesn't come naturally to me. Even at the ATM, I feel guilty when it spits out a few twenties.

And what if I offend him? Moments ago, he was regaling me with dirty stories about George Washington, and now I'm ruining the fraternal mood by begging him for cash, like a common mendicant? This is a man who could kick me out of his office, or more likely, have me kicked out, or, if he so chose, simply walk out of his office and build another office building without me in it. Worse—the thought enters my mind—he could decide to purchase the Constitution for himself, so that I can't ever get my hands on it! Perhaps as he sees it, *he's* Nicolas Cage, and I'm the villain in this particular sequel.

National Treasure 3: Book of Money.

I can't risk it. So instead of telling him what I really need from him, I balk.

Instead, I say: "Moral support."

And as soon as I say it, it sounds even sillier than the truth.

Moral support?

"Oh," he says. "That's easy. You have it."

And with that, this meeting is over.

"I'll be interested to read it," he says, as he rises to his feet and reaches out to shake my hand. "Let me know if there's anything I can do to help."

To his credit, I think he means it.

But that's not all I'm thinking. I'm thinking, *Bleyer, you're blowing it. You've* blown *it. This was your chance.* As I shake his hand, I feel myself wanting to grasp it and not let go, not until he agrees to use it to write me a fat check. (Or phone his accountant and put me on the line. Or wire a billion or so to the National Archives on my behalf. I don't know—he's the money guy, he'll figure out the details.)

Anything you can do to help, sir? There's *everything* you can do to help. You can buy me the Constitution of the United States. Didn't you hear what I was thinking? Together we can make history. Together we can secure the future. Together we can outfox Nicolas Cage.

With your money, and my willingness to accept your money, there's no limit to what we can achieve together.

---

* I also recognize there's no postage involved in rewriting the Constitution, unless I was going to send out delivery announcements about it. ("It's a Constitution!")

Kevin Bleyer rewrites the Constitution, David Rubenstein pays the postage, and Nicolas Cage can go suck it.

But I let go of his hand. I turn and walk out, and his secretary ushers me to the elevator. The moment I press *down*, I wonder how I can possibly go any lower: I have just missed the opportunity of a lifetime.

Once I step inside and begin to descend, I put my hand in my pocket and finger the piece of paper—the contract I had so confidently drawn up, but had failed to deliver:

Your New Article V

Mr. David Rubenstein, billionaire Owner of the Magna Carta, will you please buy the Constitution of the United States for Me? (I'd like to amend it.)

Check yes [ ] or no [ ]

As I step out onto the street—David Rubenstein Avenue, for all I know— I try to muster the courage to persevere. Perhaps all is not lost. Heck, he didn't check "yes," but neither did he check "no." I didn't give him a chance. All he said is that he'd be interested in reading my rewritten version. And if John Hancock is interested in reading it, Sam Adams had better finish writing it.

ARTICLE VI
NO RELIGIOUS TEST?
*Thank God, Because We Totally
Didn't Study for This*

JOHN HANCOCK WON'T RETURN MY PHONE CALLS.

Having realized that no Founding Document is worth the goat-skin it's printed on unless it features an honest-to-goodness *John Hancock*, I have tracked down an actual "John Hancock" in the New York metropolitan area—the Lower East Side, in fact—and I have explained via a series of increasingly detailed entreaties that although he runs what, according to the online White Pages, is apparently called "The What Hut," and as a proprietor of such an establishment must be quite busy (I have no idea *what* "The What Hut" is), he must, for a time, attend to a greater cause: His country needs him.

More to the point: *I* need him. His John Hancock is the only thing that will give my new Declaration of Independence—which shall free us, at long last, from the shackles of the original Constitution—the authenticity such a declaration deserves.

The What Hut, whatever that is, can wait.

I've already left three messages on his voice mail. Two on his work phone and one on the mobile number he gave "if this is an emergency." This *is* an emergency, and he still hasn't called me back. It's a double indignity. First David Rubenstein refused to buy me the Constitution (granted, not that I asked), and now—adding insult to self-imposed injury—John Hancock won't call me back.

It's really starting to piss me off. I doubt James Madison had this problem.

I shouldn't be surprised. John Hancocks, as a rule, are a notoriously tardy bunch, especially when the fate of the world is in their hands. In the Revolutionary War, when General George Washington needed to shore up his reeling Continental Army and made the bold executive decision to enlist black troops in the cause—it was to John Hancock that he appealed for help. He sent Hancock, then president of the Continental Congress, a request for an emergency waiver from the Council of War decree which had prohibited Negroes from enlisting. Hancock apparently never responded. (Yet again—I know exactly how Washington must have felt.) In other words, the Continental Army was racially integrated and won the Revolutionary War—thanks to the brave efforts of blacks, many of them slaves—because John Hancock couldn't get his act together. (That is *so* John Hancock.)

A happy accident for the country. A bad precedent for me.

I go online and find a couple more John Hancocks who don't live quite so nearby but who, like good patriots, are also listed in the White Pages. I leave messages for them as well.

Just then the phone rings.

"Hello, Kevin?"

"Yes?" I say.

"It's John Hancock."

Finally.

But wait a minute—*which* John Hancock is this? Is it John Hancock #1—the proprietor of "The What Hut"? Is it John Hancock #2, who, according to the Internet, works as an audio engineer of some sort? Or is he behind Door #3, the third John Hancock, who didn't list his profession and therefore is a complete mystery? Or could it be the most unlikely scenario: that despite my calling three John Hancocks in the last few days, this is *yet another* John Hancock who is merely calling *me*, unsolicited, on another matter entirely? A fourth John Hancock! Perhaps *he* wants *me* to sign something.

I panic for a moment, and then realize: *Does it matter?*

"Hey, John," I say.

That feels weird. *Hey, John.*

"So," John asks, "what is it you *want* exactly?"

I take a breath. I may have only one shot at this—at least, one shot with this particular John Hancock.

"Mr. Hancock, if I may," I say, already imagining a soundtrack—something John Williams might compose, that enters almost imperceptibly, with a few strings and the faintest hint of a snare drum, but crescendos with French horn, trumpet blasts, and the unapologetic rumble of tympani. "When the great General George Washington defeated the British in the

Revolutionary War, he did not pause. No, he looked out upon this vast continent and asked of his fellow citizens that they not rest a moment, but rather join him on an even greater mission, to become 'Actors on a most conspicuous Theatre, designed by Providence for the display of human greatness and felicity, and—' "

"Look, that's great," he interrupts. "But I'm late for brunch."

I quickly rattle off the specifics of what I'm up to, and why I need his signature. He agrees to read my Declaration, although I detect a slight hesitation. As if he's been burned before, by previous would-be revolutionaries who have exploited him for his famous moniker. Nonetheless, I lay my case before him, and it is then that John Hancock gives me his email address: *johnhancock@independence-audio.com*.

Aha. John Hancock #2.

Huh. My money was on Door #3.

SWM SEEKS "SUMMER SOLDIERS AND SUNSHINE PATRIOTS" FOR IMPENDING REVOLUTION

IF THERE'S A REASON you've heard of John Hancock, beyond his notorious habit of wasting perfectly good iron gall ink, it may be the details surrounding that moment he stepped up to the Declaration of Independence on July 4, 1776, surrounded by his fellow revolutionaries, and, as they say, put his John Hancock to the measure.

As anecdotes go, they don't get much better. Hancock had by then gambled much of his vast personal fortune on the long-shot struggle for American liberty, financing the Whig Party, covering the bills of its leader, Sam Adams, and lending wildly to the revolutionary cause. Yet he was still eager to go *all in*—with his fortune and his fate—on total independence with no guarantee of success (the irony that John Hancock is now one of the nation's best-known *insurance* companies should be lost on no one, not least its policyholders). At the moment he put his quill to parchment, he had an outrageous message to go along with his oversized signature.

"There!" he proclaimed, as he put down his quill. "Fat King George should be able to read *that* without his spectacles!"

It was a tagline Arnold Schwarzenegger would envy—*hasta la vista, Georgie*—and with so much at stake, it proved to be a perfectly timed pep talk to help the rebels muster their courage. They weren't just affixing their names; they were thumbing their noses. They were rattling their sabers. They may have been signing their own death warrants.

At such a fraught, portentous moment, someone had to rally the troops; Hancock was happy to lead the charge. And to provoke King George in the same breath? Well, there couldn't have been a more appropriately defiant, perfectly American war cry to convince the colonists they were in this together.

If only it were true.

Hancock never taunted the king. At least, not officially. The Declaration of Independence he signed wasn't addressed to King George, nor was a copy sent to him; the intended audience, after all, was stateside, the American colonists who deserved an explanation for the bold rebellion being planned in Philadelphia. Not to mention that had Hancock made those comments on July 4, 1776—*the day that shall live in fireworks*—he would have done so to an empty room; after Congress adjourned that day, only the secretary of Congress was present when Hancock, as a matter of course, signed the copy of the revised declaration to authenticate it as president of the Second Continental Congress. The famous copy with all the frilly signatures wasn't begun until August 1776, and even then took years to complete.

The tale of Hancock's defiance is, if you will, a Hancock-and-bull story, designed after the fact to burnish the reputation of a group of courageous Founders, and, more metaphorically, to make explicit the whole point of American independence: We're doing our own thing over on this side of the Atlantic. We no longer care what you think of us. Hell, we'll even call you fat.

YES, VIRGINIA, THERE IS
A SUPREMACY CLAUSE

BUT AS JOHN HANCOCK ONCE ASKED ME, "What does any of this have to do with Article VI?"

Well, John, I'm glad you asked. Or rather, I'm glad I pretended you asked. (Hey, if history can make believe you challenged the king, I can claim you asked me a question.)

We already know that on the general point of independence—we're not your grandfather's England—what the Declaration set in motion, the Constitution kicked in the arse. We were going to do things differently in America. (For starters, we'd write *our* rules *down*.) But it's Article VI, and its two main provisions—the Supremacy Clause and the No Religious Test Clause—that most acutely illustrate just how we're like England, and how we're not.

To begin with, Article VI contains the so-called Supremacy Clause— "This Constitution, and the Laws of the United States which shall be made in Pursuance thereof . . . shall be the supreme Law of the Land"— which, even a patriot must admit, would seem to be a not-so-minor step back toward centralized (some might say monarchist) power after a decade-long experiment of letting the states party it up under the Articles of Confederation.

In plain American English: When in doubt, a tie goes to the federal government.

This power structure remains in force today, even though it is often challenged—as in 2011, when a number of states tried to "opt out" of national health care reform. But many individual states soon learned that the Constitution means what it says in Article VI: The Constitution of the United States is "supreme" over the constitution of any one state. No, Florida, it's not your prerogative to opt out. Sorry, Texas, as long as you're (still) in America you have to play by America's rules. Yes, Virginia, there is a Supremacy Clause.

The Supremacy Clause does *feel* English. It returns power to a central authority, as any king would want. The key difference, however, is that instead of a king, we have a constitution.

And Article VI, Section 3, of that constitution is what truly separates the rebels from the royals: "No religious Test shall ever be required as a Qualification to any Office or public Trust under the United States." Hallelujah. It is the only time religion is mentioned in the body of the Constitution, and as the author Seth Lipsky points out, it is the most emphatic statement in the entire document: "No . . . ever . . . any." It announces that unlike our forebears across the sea, whose king (or, for the last fifty years, queen) is also the Supreme Governor of the official Church of England— subtly titled "the Church of England"—we won't have a sanctioned religion, and we certainly won't have a religious test for any American who hopes to join the government. For the colonists who fled England, religious freedom was a reason they came to America in the first place; would they really require a religious test to hold office here?

Like hell.

Still, it was an extraordinary declaration at a time when, at the state level, we were lousy with religious tests. The Massachusetts constitution of 1780 extended the right to hold office only to Christians. Delaware restricted officeholders only to those who swore a belief in the Trinity. The Maryland constitution of 1776 afforded full equality to Catholics and Protestants, but not to Jews. The New York constitution of 1777 allowed Jews to hold office, but not Catholics. Many states had no qualms about restricting political office to people who believed in God in a very specific way. In some colonies, citizens could lead the masses only if they followed the Messiah; in others, Catholicism was a curse—they required religious Test Oaths in which Catholics were forced to renounce tenets of their faith. Even a signer of the Constitution, Pennsylvania's Thomas FitzSimons, had to overcome anti-Catholic sentiment to become the first-ever Roman Catholic elected to a public office in the colonies, although he never quite dispelled fears that he was a secret agent of the pope.

But not all states felt it necessary to test a citizen's faith. In fact, it was Virginia's statute for religious freedom—subtly titled "the Virginia Statute for Religious Freedom"—that inspired the Framers to write in the United States Constitution no mention of God. Its author, Thomas Jefferson, required no proof of religion, since he believed that the private faith of a neighbor "neither picks my pocket nor breaks my leg,"* and that a man's civil rights should depend no more on his religious beliefs than on his belief in "physics or geometry."

In the end, the "assembly of demigods" made it official: God would not be required. So, per Article VI of the Constitution, there is no religious test for any American hoping to become a public servant. Should you want to submit yourself to a higher office, you needn't submit yourself to a higher power.

And yet: Of the forty-four God-fearing mortals who have lived in the White House, none has ever declared a suspicion that God might not exist. Of the rest—which is to say, all of them—God is mandatory. There have been Episcopalians, Presbyterians, Methodists, Baptists, Unitarians, Disciples of Christ, Dutch Reformers, Quakers, Congregationalists, a Catholic, even a Jehovah's Witness. Some faiths have been overrepresented (Episcopalians, though less than 2 percent of the population, seem remarkably good at running for president, having been successful 25 percent of

---

* Except perhaps, Our Lady of the Leg-Breaking Pickpocketers.

the time); others are underrepresented (only one in forty-four presidents has been Catholic, even though one in four Americans pledge allegiance to the Holy Father). Some haven't been lucky enough to be represented at all; there have been no Lutheran presidents, no Pentecostal presidents, no Buddhist presidents, no Hindu presidents, no Eastern Orthodox presidents, no Sikhs. Despite a number of candidates, we've had just as many Mormon presidents as we've had Wiccan presidents—which is to say, none. No president has ever sold encyclopedias in an airport. No Jewish mother has ever crowed about "my son, the president." As of this printing, only one president has been a secret Muslim.

Although the Constitution says "no religious Test," it says nothing about there being no religious *litmus* test. We definitely have one of those, and we have from the very beginning. It was even something Thomas Jefferson had to worry about—since, as Christopher Hitchens points out, "even in his time, there was a politically lethal charge of atheism." *His time*, it's worth noting, was when the ink on the "no religious Test" clause of the Constitution was barely dry.

In *our* time, religion may not matter constitutionally, but practically, some faiths Need Not Apply. I remember learning in junior high social studies class about the struggle John F. Kennedy had in selling his Catholicism during the 1960 election. I was shocked, for two reasons: First, from my unlimited perspective as a twelve-year-old, everyone *I* met in church or Sunday school was Catholic, so the concept that Catholics might be unwelcome anywhere was strange to me—if you were welcome in the Lord's House, why not the White House? And second, I thought, *Whoa, whoa, whoa—wait a minute, I'm Catholic. Does this mean* I *would have a difficult time becoming president?* Because frankly, after astronaut and marine biologist, becoming president someday was definitely on my list. I was incensed to think that the particular church to which I happened to get driven by my mother on occasional Sunday mornings would brand me unelectable. I may have been only in junior high, but I could sense the injustice. I was indignant, disconcerted, perturbed, and plenty of other words I probably didn't know and couldn't spell back then.

Kennedy's Catholicism wasn't the asset I would have assumed: a way to bond with the 40 million Americans who shared his faith. Rather, it was an obstacle to overcome. It was something he had to explain, and to explain away. In a speech less than two months before the election, he tackled it head-on, declaring that he was "not the Catholic candidate for President"; rather, he was the Democratic candidate "who happens also to be a Catholic." He tried to portray his Catholicism as incidental—*Nothing to see here, move along*. And even though he addressed "those who would work to subvert Article VI of the Constitution by requiring a religious test, even by indirection," and although he challenged them that "if they disagree with that safeguard, they should be openly working to repeal it," he nonetheless had to promise that he would make presidential decisions only "in the national interest, and without regard to outside religious pressure" on any Catholic-sensitive issue that might come before him as president. Like Thomas FitzSimons in 1787, John Kennedy still had to promise not to be a sleeper agent of the papacy.* What's more, Kennedy even guaranteed that if "the time should ever come . . . when my office would require me to either violate my conscience or violate the national interest," then he would "resign the office" right then and there.

In *our* time, even lowly congressmen have their particular crosses to bear. With so many more representatives than presidents over the years, one might naturally ask, certainly there has been room for a rep from every religion on God's (or even not God's) green earth, hasn't there?

Not quite.

If there had been, Congressman Keith Ellison of Minnesota wouldn't have caused such a stir. Ellison, the first Muslim ever elected to the House of Representatives, had taken the "no religious Test" and passed it— winning almost 56 percent of the vote in a four-candidate race in 2006. Although when he announced that he wanted to take the oath of office on a Qur'an, all hell broke loose, especially among those who believed in Hell. Op-eds were written. Tongues were clucked. It got silly. One outspoken columnist suggested that Ellison swear on both a Qur'an *and* a Bible, like a double-decker Holy Book Sandwich—just as, he insisted, "one Muslim ambassador did about ten years ago, I think it was the ambassador to the Fiji Islands, I don't recall exactly."

While the columnist was busy not recalling exactly, Ellison thought of a better solution—a solution that proved, in one fell swoop, that the columnist was being foolish and that the people of Minnesota had sent the right man to Congress. He simply chose a very specific book on which he would take his oath: not a Bible, but not just any Qur'an either. The Qur'an owned

---

* What were the Catholic issues Kennedy mentioned specifically? "Birth control, divorce, censorship, gambling"—which, to a twelve-year-old, made Catholicism seem cooler in one speech than a hundred sermons had managed to do, even if I didn't know which side Catholicism was on.

by Thomas Jefferson himself, the very man who wrote the very statute that inspired the "assembly of demigods" to write in their Constitution language emphatically protecting Ellison's very right to do so. When he finally was sworn in, it must have been difficult not to add a final thought at the end of his oath:

"Well *that* oughta shut 'em up."

THE CONFOUNDING FATHERS

THAT'S THE RUB. The Founders gave mixed messages when it came to religion; well, not *mixed* exactly, but complex. Most believed in God, but thought the Bible shouldn't be required reading for a politician. They professed a devotion to Christianity, but owned Qur'ans. They pointedly didn't mention God in their Constitution, but when the Convention starting disintegrating, even Benjamin Franklin, arguably the least religious among them, proposed "that henceforth prayers imploring the assistance of Heaven, and its blessings on our deliberations, be held in the Assembly every morning." There is enough chapter and verse from Madison's notes on the Convention—heck, from Bartlett's Quotations of the Founding Fathers—to feed the appetites and prejudices of both the godless and the faithful.

But by the beginning of September, even as they appealed to God in Heaven that the Convention adjourn already (because the State House was hotter than Hell), they made a decision: There would be no religious test to be elected to the offices they had just invented.

There, it's settled.

And yet, on October 12, 2008, only sixteen days before the election of the forty-fourth president of the United States, a retired four-star general, former secretary of state, and chairman of the Joint Chiefs of Staff felt the need to spend his valuable time not commanding an army or engaging in international diplomacy, but reassuring the world that the Democratic nominee for the presidency wasn't a Muslim. "The correct answer is: He is not a Muslim," General Colin Powell said, emphatically. "He is a Christian. He has always been a Christian." The general could have left it there, but he went one step further: "But the really right answer is: *What if he is?* Is there something wrong with being a Muslim in this country?" His was more than a fair question: What is it about being among the 2.5 million of

Americans who *are* Muslims that would somehow put him any more at odds with the rest of the country than, say, being a Jehovah's Witness?

Sadly, neither the retired general's reminder that the Founders required no religious test, nor his rhetorical question—*And what if he* was *a Muslim?*—appeased the ignorant. And when the forty-fourth president was—despite lingering rumors about his faith—ultimately elected and inaugurated to the nation's highest office, no amount of swearing on any number of Bibles would convince them that he wouldn't have preferred to swear on a Qur'an.

The right answer to the general's question is, of course, *There is nothing wrong with being a Muslim in this country.* The wrong answer: *Well, obviously he might be a terrorist.* What troubles the troubled about our candidates' faith—Kennedy's Catholicism, Ellison's Islam—isn't ultimately how they pray in private, but how they'll serve in public. What matters to most voters is not whether a certain candidate believes in God, or even *how* he believes in God. We just want to rest assured that how a candidate believes in God won't affect how *we* choose to believe in God, or choose not to. Have your heartfelt theories of sin and salvation; we'll thank you not to tell us how to spend our sinful Friday nights and our repentant Sunday mornings. Pray five times a day, once a week, or not at all; as long as your religion doesn't "pick our pocket" or "break our leg" by claiming all our money or denying us health care—or birth control, or divorce, or gambling—hey, we're happy.

Now I realize I'm getting a little preachy here. But I ask you, what better subject to get preachy about? You gotta fight fire with brimstone, I say. I happen to agree with John Hancock, who once told Jesus Christ (moments before signing the Ten Commandments),* there's a difference between a fan of religion and a religious fanatic. And as rule, only the most fanatical versions of the faiths of others threaten our way of life. Voters were worried that FitzSimons and Kennedy would be agents of the papacy, sworn to deprive us of gambling, divorce, and birth control; to get elected, both reassured the country they would not. Now some worry about Muslims, because they can't discern between the Muslims that would do us harm and the Muslims that, say, do our taxes, or teach our children, or treat our cancer; they worry that "no religious Test" might let a terrorist slip into government in Muslim clothing.

---

* John Hancock never spoke to Jesus Christ, nor did he sign the Ten Commandments. Really, you should know better by now!

It's a ludicrous concern—I don't foresee anyone getting elected president from the Terrorist Party anytime soon*—but heck, since we're making ludicrous modifications, we can address it. So while I'll agree with the Framers in principle—there shall be no general "religious Test" for office—there shall be a new, more honest, pass-or-fail, naughty-or-nice, Abel-or-Cain, Isaac-or-Esau religious *litmus test:*

Be religious, but for heaven's sake, don't be ridiculous.

Your New Article VI

First off, this Constitution shall be the supreme Law of the Land—so sucke on that, Kings. The Senators and Representatives before mentioned, and all executive and judicial Officers, both of the United States and of the several States, shall be bound by Oath or Affirmation on whatever Holye Booke they darne welle please; and no religious Test shall ever be required as a Qualification to any Office. There will, however be a religious Pop Quiz: (1) Do you belong to an extremist version of your religion? (2) If so, do you swear to whatever god you believe in that you'll Chill Out for a while? You will? Cool.

SIGNATURE MOVES

John Hancock #2, a.k.a. Lower East Side John Hancock, is a pleasant, agreeable man with round cheeks, a wispy beard, and an endearing aversion to looking at any part of me other than my shoes. Only his spectacles—both in their style and in their very presence on his face—would indicate he wasn't Amish. (Well, that and his recording studio filled with towers of high-tech audio equipment the Amish also might not condone.)

Eager to help, Hancock has agreed to meet me at his studio, has poured me a cup of tea, and has signed my declaration without so much as a question wherefore.

I thank him.

"My pleasure," he says. "I get a kick out of it."

After a little small talk (there has been no large talk) and a confirmation

---

* Governor, maybe.

that he signed on the dotted line (there is no dotted line), we begin to walk back to the door. That's when I glance at the paper and notice something unsettling: His signature looks strange. Or rather, scratch that. It looks *familiar*. As if I've seen it somewhere before. The rigid top of the *J*, the oversized mouldings of the final *k*, the subset double hash mark below, neatly tying up a thatch of swirls—it's a practiced, refined, purposeful throwback of an autograph that a contemporary audio engineer wouldn't— *shouldn't*—have time to perfect *just so*. And—oh *God*—it looks exactly like the signature on the original Declaration of Independence.

His John Hancock is John Hancock's John Hancock.

Or rather, John Hancock's John Hancock is John Hancock's John Hancock.

I'm afraid to ask. "Hey, um, did you know that your signature looks an awful lot like—"

"The original?" he interrupts. "Oh yeah. People have asked me to sign things like this before."

"They have?" I ask. "Who?"

If he says Rexford Guy Tugwell, I might just punch him in the spectacles.

"I was a witness at a wedding once. Perfect strangers. They just wanted to have something to show their kids, I guess. I don't know. But, like I said, I get a kick out it."

Yeah, I heard you.

"Some people do impressions, I do signatures."

He admires his own signature again. "Not bad, right?"

No, *very* bad. Of all the John Hancocks I could have recruited within the range of a prepaid Manhattan subway pass, I've hooked up with the one who has dedicated time learning to mimic the signature of his namesake because he gets a kick out of it. No wonder he called me back. He's a revolutionary fetishist. He gets off on this kind of thing.

Don't get me wrong. I'm grateful to have John Hancock #2 on board, fetishist or no. But after all the effort to get him, I leave his apartment certain that I'll have to recruit a second John Hancock. Because as it stands, no one will believe that I didn't forge this myself, or, worse, crib it from the original Declaration.

Not even if I swore on a stack of Bibles.

ARTICLE VII
RATIFICATION

*Hang Together or Hang Separately, but Don't
Hang Out in Rhode Island*

I
T HAD BEEN AN EMBARRASSMENT from the very beginning. A shameful reminder of a less enlightened past. It was also—let's be honest—a truly godawful name for a state: Rhode Island and Providence Plantations.

Little wonder so many Rhode Islanders—pardon me, *Rhode Island and Providence Plantation-ers*—wanted it gone. Serviceable though it may have been, alliterative though it may be, the official name of the thirteenth state to join the Union didn't exactly roll trippingly off the tongue. More critically, it was the turn of the century—a bold new era had dawned—and with it came a renewed hope among its citizens that they might cast off the albatross that had hung around their neck since the birth of their state and enter the new century with a more modern, less retrograde moniker. Something shorter, sweeter, and perhaps devoid of unpleasant references to a time, not all that long ago, when humans sold humans to other humans.

How about just: *Rhode Island.*

Yeah, that should do nicely.

Rhode Island was everything you'd look for in a state name, and a sufficient number of citizens of Rhode Island and Providence Plantations were looking for it that they proposed the change in an official, one might say long overdue, amendment to the state constitution. Some islanders even ventured that the referendum would be the most compelling item on the ballot that year, easily eclipsing the second-most-talked-about provision: a $4.7 million bond issue to purchase a fleet of new hi-tech buses.

Yes, hi-tech *buses.*

What, did I confuse you?

Were you assuming I was talking about the turn of the *nineteenth* century?

I should have clarified: The new century in question was the twenty-first century, and this moment of overdue reckoning didn't come in 1789, or 1865, or even 1964. It came in 2010. The citizens of Rhode Island (sorry, the citizens of Rhode Island and Providence Plantations—you see the problem here) didn't officially consider dropping the "Providence Plantations" part of their state's name until the second year of the administration of the nation's first black president.

Hope? *Sure.*

Change? *When we get around to it.*

I told you not to get me started on Rhode Island. I warned you, chapters ago. Sure, I may have badmouthed Nebraska and Wyoming way back in Article IV, but it is Rhode Island that invites my purest, most white-hot disdain. For it is Rhode Island, officially the tiniest state in the union, that has been the nation's biggest pain in the butt.

It's quite a feat, really: It ranks 50th in both population *and* total acreage, but it is #1 on my shit list.

If it were up to me, Rhode Island would be Rhode Seafloor.

Let's see: What's the best way to put this? Have you ever seen the Rhode Island state seal? So have I:

Booooooooooooo

Seriously—tiny Rhode Island can bite me. Not that I'd notice. There are bedbugs in New York City that have done more damage.

★ ★ ★

Do not feel sorry for Rhode Island. *Poor little state, can't be expected to stand up for itself.* Hogwash. Strike that—*quahog*wash. The historical record will show that for more than four hundred years now, tiny Rhode Island has had it coming. Through a relentless obsession with having its own way, tiny Rhode Island has slowed American progress during the entire progress of America. It is a colony of heel-draggers. It is no state; it is, I say to you, a speedbump.

Oh, I'll say it again.*

Tiny Rhode Island deserves no pity. It warrants no sympathy. It has long earned its reputation as the country's crybaby; truth be told, America's tiniest state has been America's biggest troublemaker from long before the United States were even united states. Punsters of the seventeenth century knew to call it "Rogue's Island," for its relentlessly contrarian disposition, and after the malcontented mischief-makers who have lived there, making mischief malcontentedly. Anarchists. Dissidents. Freethinkers. Magician/actor Harry Anderson. *Survivor* winner Richard Hatch.† Ruth Buzzi. Rogue's Island was God's attempt to quarantine them somewhere they could do little damage.

Unfortunately, it failed. Rhode Island infects us all, and a long line of agitators and rabble-rousers have spread its disease‡—beginning with its founder, Roger Williams. Williams, a long-haired, long-winded theologian, had been invited by a church in Boston to fill one the few paid openings in all of 1630s New England—as a preacher within the Massachusetts Bay Colony. The tryout didn't go well. The colony may have welcomed Williams with open arms, but in return, Williams thought the colonists far too closed-minded. He found Bostonians to be "an unseparated people" still beholden to King Charles, and he "durst not officiate" to such loyalists. It didn't take long before the distaste was mutual, and Williams was banished from the colony, supposedly for his religious views and his "strange opinions," but one suspects also for, I durst say, being an insufferable blowhard.

---

* Rhode Island is a speedbump.

† Richard Hatch, who won the first season of the reality show *Survivor* by spending most of it naked, later reinforced his freethinking Rogue Islander bona fides by failing to pay taxes on the million dollars he had just won on the most popular show on television. For some reason, he assumed no one noticed he had just won a million dollars *on the most popular show on television.* He spent a year in jail—presumably naked.

‡ If commentators spread commentary, one might naturally assume that dissidents spread dysentery.

Williams went south and found a new home among the Indians—beating Kevin Costner to the punch by more than four centuries. The Narragansett tribe offered Williams sanctuary on the tip of Narragansett Bay, a favor he repaid by renaming their land *Providence*. No doubt the foolish Narragansett thanked him for calling their land as he saw fit—since, for more than two centuries, the tribe had merely called it "home." Providence quickly became a beachhead for a rogue's gallery of religious and social outcasts, and when the city didn't suffice, they seeped outward, blanketing the entire state that would come to be known as Rhode Island—sorry, Rhode Island and Providence Plantations. (Seriously, it's a terrible name, and I shall speak it no more.)

History is a great matchmaker; Williams deserved Rhode Island, and Rhode Island deserved Williams. After all, the Massachusetts that Williams had found so inhospitable was the Massachusetts that believed—as John Adams would write in the commonwealth's constitution—that "the body politic is formed by a voluntary association of individuals: it is a social compact, by which the whole people covenants with each citizen, and each citizen with the whole people, that all shall be governed by certain laws for the common good." As the Framers wrote their Constitution—composing Article VII in the hope that the hard work of preserving the common good was almost done—one thing became abundantly clear: If America is in fact a body politic, Rhode Island is an asshole.

HIT THE RHODE, JACK

IT WAS WITH ARTICLE VII, the last in the Constitution they utterly failed to support, that Rhode Island made its position official. Article VII is where states were asked, at long last, whether each truly believed in this new blueprint for America. Article VII separates the states that wanted in from those that opted out. Article VII is where the delegates were expected to sign on the dotted line* and accept "the Establishment of this Constitution between the States so ratifying the Same." But of the thirty-nine delegates who affixed their signatures to Article VII on September 17, indicating their support of the Constitution and the hard work of the

---

* Had the Constitution featured a dotted line, that is.

delegates that long summer, none were from Rhode Island. The rubber had met the road, and the Rogues went the other direction.

For one simple reason: No delegates from Rhode Island ever attended the Constitutional Convention. Not on September 17, not ever. Its politicians had heard the rumors that the conventioneers were devising a strong central government, and like Patrick Henry of Virginia, they, too, "smelt a rat." They felt their interests at the Convention would be better served by never showing up at the Convention.

Oh sure, there were often a few empty seats here and there over the summer—most delegates were part-timers—but only RI was totally MIA. Article VII was the moment for states to either put or shut up, and Rhode Island couldn't be bothered to show up.

The Framers from other states who made the sacrifice—months away from their families, their jobs, and their homesteads, not to mention the daily torture of wearing wigs in an unventilated sauna—more than noticed Rhode Island's insubordination. In June, the Pennsylvania *Herald* reported (hyperbolically, but that's hardly the point) that the delegates inside the hall had decreed that "Rhode Island should be considered as having virtually withdrawn herself from the union," and, what's more, the Convention had declared that the Continental government should be ready and willing to use military force to punish Rhode Island for its delinquency in paying its share of the federal debt. By the Fourth of July holiday, an increasingly popular drinking toast was echoing through many of Philadelphia's taverns: "May Rhode Island be excluded from the Union until they elect *honest* men to rule them."

July, August, September—still nothing. If any delegates were secretly hoping that Rhode Island would make a heroic surprise nick-of-time entrance before the end of summer, they were sadly mistaken. Instead they were left considering the advice proffered in the Pennsylvania *Packet*— written by someone with the totally awesome pseudonym Black Beard— who arrrr-gued that the new nation should "consider Rhode Island as Europe considers the Barbary." The twelve states that managed to write a Constitution—no thanks to Rhode Island—ought to "surround her by land, and consider her in the same class as the pirates of Algiers." The message was clear: Rhode Island should walk the plank.*

---

* I recognize that the pirates of Algiers weren't pirates in the sense we have come to know pirates—pirates of, say, the Caribbean. But faaarrgh be it from me to make that distinction.

★ ★ ★

The Framers had more than a hunch that Rogue Island would live up to its nickname, which explains the arithmetic they laid out in Article VII:

> The Ratification of the Conventions of nine States, shall be sufficient for the Establishment of this Constitution between the states so ratifying the same.

Not thirteen; nine. Unlike the Articles of Confederation, the Constitution wouldn't require that everyone agree—the Framers didn't want to be hijacked by scoundrels and malcontents. As delegate Nathaniel Gorham put it, "Will any one say that all the States are to suffer themselves to be ruined, if Rho. Island should persist in her opposition?" Better to treat Rhode Island like a pirate than to let her take down the ship.

So worried were the delegates that Rhode Island's heel-dragging would infect the mood of states wobbling on whether to ratify—"other states might tread in her steps," said Gorham—that early drafts of Article VII even left the total number of states required for ratification blank—i.e., "The Ratification of the Conventions of _____ States, shall be sufficient"— just in case Rogue Island somehow infected Rogue Hampshire or Rogue York. They didn't want one bad apple to ruin the whole union.

Requiring only nine states for ratification was, of course, a blatant violation of the Articles of Confederation, under which total unanimity was required to do pretty much anything. It replaced the idea of a "perpetual union" with a mere "partial union"—which is, by my math, not technically a union at all. Granted, requiring unanimity had been the reason so little got done in the first decade of America—when the Articles were in force—and why some Framers were so willing to start over. But the need to cater to and account for the absent troublemaking Rogue's Island in the final tally reveals just how much oversized power the tiny state had: It forced the Convention to violate a founding principle—All for One, and One for All. Tiny Rhode Island forced the Constitution itself to be unconstitutional.

Not that tiny Rhode Island cared—it hadn't supported the original Articles of Confederation, either. If America between the years 1776 and 1789 was a failed experiment, and the Constitution of 1787 was a second try, Rhode Island was the pipsqueak in the corner muttering, "It'll never work."

I know what you're thinking: *What a bunch of anarchists.**

And you wouldn't be alone. According to George Washington's diary of the summer, when the Convention finally adjourned on September 17, the thirty-nine signers "adjourned to the City Tavern, dined together and took a cordial leave of each other"—a future president's way of saying *got blotto and stumbled home.* He offered few additional details of precisely what manner of ceremony was engaged in, but one can assume none of the many toasts made that evening were to the health and well-being of Rhode Island, nor to the honesty or moral standing of the "honest men" (read: unmitigated asshats) who ruled her.

HANG TOGETHER OR HANG SEPARATELY, BUT DON'T HANG OUT IN RHODE ISLAND

I PLAN TO MAKE NO SUCH TOAST. Yet here I am, in the heart of Rogue Island, having made the three-hour trek by bus from New York to Providence. That thumb in the previous picture, the one pointing down, registering its disapproval of the Rhode Island (and, ugh, Providence Plantations) state seal?

That's mine.

Don't ask me my reasons. To be honest, I've no idea why I felt it necessary to come here, as a delegate of one, to pay forward a favor to Rhode Island that the delegates of Rhode Island never bothered to pay to Philadelphia—that is, to *show up.* I doubt it was for Rhode Island's many charms: its long history of rampant corruption at all levels of state government; the recent crackdown on illicit sexual activity in Providence's massage parlors; their relentless need to call regular old clams "quahogs." And honestly, I'm violating one of my own inviolate principles: Never trust a state that has no more congressmen than it does senators. All in all, aside from its pleasant rolling hills, live-and-let-live spirit, picturesque towns, friendly people, romantic vistas, delicious quahogs—and okay, its new, $4.7 million fleet of hi-tech buses—there's absolutely zero appeal to Rhode Island.

Zero.

Yup—I hate everything about Rhode Island.

Well, except the State House. The State House is quite lovely.

---

* Don't deny it.

Booooooooooooo

For all it has done to slow the progress of America, I'm reluctant to pay Rhode Island any attention whatsoever. It doesn't deserve a chapter in such a patriotic book. It doesn't even warrant a paragraph. And so I hereby relegate the entire account of my visit to Providence to the space it truly merits: a single footnote.*

THE RUBBER MEETS THE RHODE

Rhode Island was the last state to ratify the Constitution, surprising exactly no one. Its refusal to get with the program meant it would not

---

* The Megabus drops me off close to the State House, depriving me of even the small pleasure of riding one of those nice new buses. I enter the (granted, quite lovely) State House lobby just in time to catch a tour in progress—albeit for elementary school students. I join anyway—what were they gonna do, banish me? The guide instructs us that Rhode Island ratified the Constitution in "uh . . . 1776." I know this to be untrue, though I give her the benefit of the doubt; it's very intimidating talking to schoolchildren. Mercifully, we are forced to cut the tour somewhat short—the president of Liberia is arriving to give a speech. I peel off from the tour and crash the speech, because I hear through the grapevine that Rhode Island's governor would be introducing her; frankly, I want to hear what he has to say for himself. And yet—not once does he apologize for his state dragging its feet on the whole ratification thing two hundred years ago. (Nor does the president of Liberia apologize for stealing the colors of our flag.) The injustice continues. I leave in a huff and flee this beautiful, freedom-loving, quahog-eating, heel-dragging state as quick as a nonhybrid Megabus will take me.

admit defeat—and by defeat, I mean the successful salvation of the union—for two years, long after the required nine states had ratified the Constitution, and long after the hard work of rebooting the startup country was under way. (Vermont, which wasn't yet a state during the writing of the Constitution, somehow beat them to the punch.) And even then, when forced with a decision to ratify the Constitution or be effectively banished from the Union, Rogue Island insisted on proceeding in its own recalcitrant fashion: not calling a convention, as had every other state, but holding a statewide referendum—the only state that did so. Then and only then did the state full of Roger Williamses and Richard Hatches vote in favor. *Aw, gee, thanks.*

What is surprising is why, exactly, Rhode Islanders were so adamantly against the Constitution in the first place. The Convention in Philadelphia—where, might I remind you, no delegates from Rhode Island ever bothered to appear—had already bent over backward to ensure that small, whiny states had outsized power in the new government, right off the bat: the charitable gesture in Article I of giving every state in the union two senators. Surely they'd want a piece of that. Defying the Convention would seem to be against their self-interest, much the way voters in Kansas who support social archconservative Republicans are often, counterintuitively, overlooking their own economic despair.*

So then, what gives? *What's the Matter with Rhode Island?*

Ask an eighteenth-century Rhode Islander, and he'll tell you: It's all about the Bill of Rights.

THE INEVITABLE DISCUSSION OF THE FIRST TEN AMENDMENTS TO THE CONSTITUTION, BECAUSE LET'S BE HONEST—YOU DON'T READ THE CONSTITUTION FOR THE ARTICLES

TRUTH IS, the first ten amendments to the Constitution weren't *amendments* at all. They were a package of incentives proposed during the ratification debates to persuade the remaining American states, some of whom still suspected the motives of the Federalists, to fall in line. They weren't a bill of rights; they were a signing bonus.

* Someone should write a book about that.

A bribe.

The constitutional equivalent of a set of steak knives to sweeten the deal on a new bank account.

Not even all the Framers thought them necessary. Thomas Jefferson, despite his nose buried in French *Madeleines,** led the parade in favor of a bill of rights, but his friend James Madison considered the proposed amendments to be irritating "parchment barriers" designed to flout his Constitution. They were a personal affront to Madison; his fellow Americans had taken a cold, hard look at what he had written and had immediately found ten things wrong with it. Ten things wrong with the seven things (well, eight, counting the preamble thing) that he had written.

Madison's batting average was *negative* .400.

Those Founders who took issue with the amendments took their issue from all sides. As Madison saw it, they were irrelevant. After all, it was the separation of powers—not a tacked-on list of promises—that restricted government from violating individual rights. Hamilton found them redundant; nothing in the Constitution gave the federal government the right to restrict individual rights in the first place—which, to quote his cohort Thomas Jefferson's earlier work, were already "unalienable" and "endowed by [our] Creator." So when you really think about it, Hamilton insisted, "the constitution is itself in every rational sense, and to every useful purpose, a BILL OF RIGHTS." James Wilson of Pennsylvania wondered if they might even be confusing: If an individual right *wasn't* listed, he wondered, would it be assumed it wasn't granted? "Who would be bold enough to undertake to enumerate all the rights of the people? And when the attempt to enumerate them is made, it must be remembered that if the enumeration is not complete, everything not expressly mentioned will be presumed to be purposely omitted."

In the end, a Bill of Rights was added.† Jefferson's camp won out over Madison's, Hamilton's, and Wilson's—which may be why Jefferson is on the nickel, Madison is relegated to the so-very-popular $5,000 bill, there's a move to replace Hamilton with Reagan on the $10 bill, and Wilson's name is featured on tennis balls.

When it was apparent that the Bill of Rights was an inevitable bribe to achieve the nine states required for ratification, Madison worried how it would look. Both figuratively—he worried that a list of amendments would

---

* Both the pastries and the ladies so named.

† See Appendix C, "Things You Should Already Have Known."

imply he had somehow botched the job in the first place—and literally—he suggested that the amendments not be listed at the end of the document, as they are now,* but sprinkled throughout the Articles, as if they had been there all along. That way, perhaps people wouldn't notice the obvious: that he had botched the job in the first place. Only when Connecticut delegate Roger Sherman pointed out that Congress could not go back and alter the body of the Constitution—it had been ratified by the people—did Madison rescind his request.

Madison's fear, understandably, was that the Bill of Rights would seem like an afterthought—which it was. It hadn't even been seriously proposed until a few days before the Convention adjourned, when Virginia delegate George Mason pointed out that the merits of such a bill were twofold: (a) it "might be prepared in a few hours," and (b) it "would give great quiet to the people."

It may have given them quiet, and it may have been prepared in mere hours, but the delegates were too busy packing their bags to care. Not a single delegation from any state supported the idea.

But during the ratification debates—as if on cue—Rhode Islanders not only spoke up, they wouldn't shut up. As they saw it, their state's Royal Charter—issued by King Charles II and displayed prominently to this day on the second floor of their State House—already guaranteed them far more individual freedoms than the Constitution was offering, including a written guarantee of the freedom to govern themselves. Unless a vigorous federal bill of rights was part of the bargain, they'd happily do exactly that.

Ultimately, tiny Rhode Island banded with a few other Anti-Federalist-leaning states, and together they forced the First Federal Congress to draft a Bill of Rights if it wanted their pro-ratification vote—the set of steak knives to seal the deal. But typically, it was tiny Rogue's Island that held the new nation hostage the longest, not ratifying the Constitution until January 1790, when even Rhode Islanders realized it was not in their best interest to be left out in the cold, outnumbered 12 to 1.

So blatantly did the drafters have to pander to Rogue's Island that it's no wonder one congressman complained that the amendments they ultimately agreed on—originally twelve, but whittled down to ten—were "froth and full of wind, formed only to please the palate"—no better than "syllabub," a popular eighteenth-century whipped dessert. "Or," continued the congressman, "they are like a tub thrown out to a whale . . . to secure the freight

* See Appendix D, "Seriously, You Should Already Have Known This."

of the ship and its peaceable voyage." (Apparently tub-throwing was a common antiwhale tactic.) As pleasing to the palate as it may be, we have freedom of expression because Roger Williams led a colony full of Rhode Islanders to believe they never had to shut their blowholes.

What exactly would have happened had Rhode Island never ratified the Constitution? How narrowly did we escape constitutional catastrophe? What would have happened if the United States were not united states? No one knows. Even James Madison was at a loss. "It is one of those cases which must be left to provide for itself," he could only say.

Whatever that means, I can only think.

Left to provide for itself? Huh? Yet again I don't know what Madison is talking about.

But I do know this much: *We can't afford the risk.*

We've seen what happens when tiny states get big ideas. We let the "honest men" of Rhode Island drag their heels in signing the Constitution of 1787, and, sure enough, in 2009 the honest men of Texas are threatening to secede from the union (the exact threat made by its governor, Rick Perry, which somehow didn't stop him from running for president of that very union in 2012). If we let Rhode Island hold American progress hostage, pretty soon we have to pay attention to Rhode Island's demands.

No one wants that.

But of all the injustices and inconveniences Rhode Island has wrought on Americans in the eighteenth, nineteenth, and twentieth centuries, nothing is more unjust or inconvenient than that which it imposed on one particular American in the twenty-first: I, Kevin Bleyer, have to write more chapters.

If not for Rhode Island, if not for its malcontented, freethinking, anarchistic citizens who strong-armed the First Federal Congress into proposing a Bill of Rights—albeit to protect our most fundamental and cherished individual freedoms—my rewritten Constitution would be complete, full stop. This Article VII would render the Constitution officially signed, sealed, and delivered, and we could all retire to the parlor, toast a job well done, and enjoy some delicious quahogs—not the frothy syllabub they have forced down our throats. In short: If no one lived there, we'd be home by now.

So for that indignity alone, I say this:

Let's kick 'em out.

Let's throw Article VII back in their faces. Let's treat 'em like the pirates of Algiers and make 'em walk the plank.

YOUR NEW ARTICLE VII

The Ratification of this Constitution by the States shall be sufficient for the Eradication of Rhode Island from the Union.

Now, kicking an entire state out of the union may seem harsh. It may also seem outdated—their most egregious sins are centuries old, so perhaps bygones should be bygones. (It may even seem inconvenient—removing a star from every American flag would prove prohibitive, as well as aesthetically unpleasing.) But to that I say, there remains one very good reason not to pity those who currently live in Rhode Island: Namely, no one currently lives in Rhode Island.

Remember that 2010 referendum to drop "Providence Plantations" from the official name of Rhode Island? The measure didn't pass. Not even close. Rhode Islanders voted it down, by more than three to one. In fact, 78 percent of the citizens of Rhode Island (and, ahem, *Providence Plantations*) voted against amending their constitution and shortening their name. Outdated, indeed.

So raise a glass, fellow citizens of the forty-nine other, more worthy United States: *May Rhode Island be excluded from the Union until they elect honest men to rule them.*

Or at least until they change their name.

THE UNITED
MISTAKES
OF AMERICA

---

*The New Amendments to
the New Constitution*

THE FIRST AMENDMENT

Your Right to Say, "Because There's Something Called the First Amendment in This Country, Buddy!"

☆ ☆ ☆

I WANTED TO BE A SERIAL KILLER. And it wasn't the Sixth Commandment that wouldn't let me. It was the First Amendment.

My friend Mark, a television writer, had written an episode of *Law & Order: Special Victims Unit*, and when searching for what to call its lead bad guy—a despicable killer of innocent teenagers—he had landed on what he deemed the perfect candidate: *Kevin Bleyer*. He wanted to name the show's chief villain, an evil man with no redeeming qualities whatsoever, after *me*.

As you can imagine, I was terribly offended. And completely honored.

Little old me? Immortalized on the small screen in one of the most iconic, omnipresent, and durable television shows of all time, sure to be watched by billions long into the next millennium thanks to unending syndication? Sign me up. I'm not just a narcissist; I'm a fan.

As soon as I knew it was a possibility, I immediately wanted nothing more than to be associated with such a piece of television history. I called my parents. I told my friends. I considered updating my résumé. I thought carefully about how I might drop it into everyday conversation, or mention it on dates with women, or tell my grandchildren someday.

The way I figure it, the Founding Fathers were always going on about their concern for Posterity. Their journals were filled with references to Posterity. In one speech, Washington mentioned Posterity nine times. Even the Preamble to the Constitution secures the Blessings of Liberty "to ourselves *and our Posterity*." If Posterity is so important, why shouldn't *I* get a piece of that action?

When Mark sent me the first draft, I quickly flipped through it to see my name throughout, committing all sorts of heinous, unforgivable crimes. (I know—*how cool is that?*) It now hangs, framed proudly, above my desk.

I never stood a chance. By the time the episode started production, they had picked a different first name for the character. *Jesse,* I believe. Jesse Bleyer. Which is no more Kevin Bleyer than Billy Madison is James Madison. They could have had Thomas Jefferson, and they went with George.

It was a cruel twist of fate. Jesse Bleyer, who doesn't even exist, got to be that week's coolest serial killer, but Kevin Bleyer, actual person, was a victim of an operating rule in television that is apparently far stronger than the First Amendment: You can't name a character after identifiable, real-life humans. It might upset them. Even if they (me) agree to it. Even if they (me) want to be defamed. Even if they (me) practically beg.

Hey—what about *my* Posterity?

More broadly, it's an embarrassing indictment of the Bill of Rights. Even the First Amendment—embarrassingly, the very *first* amendment, I hasten to point out, promising among other things, freedom of expression—has its limits. It isn't absolute. In this case, my friend's First Amendment right to name a fictional character anything he dang well pleased was eclipsed by my right not to be defamed, even though I wouldn't have found it the least bit defamatory. What we have here, then, is far worse than a victimless crime. It is a missed opportunity—to, at the very least, give me something cool to talk about at dinner parties.

While I had lost the role of a lifetime, I had found a flaw in the First Amendment. Not only should I get to say anything I want to say, I should also get to have anything I might want said about me, *said* about me. And the First Amendment failed me on that measure. Or, as Jerry Orbach or Sam Waterston or Ice-T or Richard Belzer or Chris Meloni* might say: *Sounds like that's one right that needs to be . . . rewritten.*

[Sfx: *Ching Ching!*]†

I recognize that my small complaint wasn't technically a First Amendment concern—any more than a verdict on *Law & Order* is a ruling from the Supreme Court. The First Amendment says "Congress shall make no law" abridging freedom of speech; it doesn't say a company can't try to avoid being sued by someone named Kevin Bleyer who thinks the "Kevin

---

* See? Told you I was a fan.

† Not "Djing Djing" or "Kong Kong" or "Chung Chung." Let the record show that "Ching Ching" is the official, correct onomatopaeic spelling of the inimitable *Law & Order* sound, according to its illustrious composer, Mike Post. (Like I said, big fan.)

Bleyer" on television is defaming him. Which is why I didn't try to make a federal case out of it—even though I was tempted, and it's a case I'm pretty sure Sam Waterston would have taken.

But its limits on our (okay, *my*) freedom of expression reveal the true dangers of a feckless First Amendment incapable of protecting harmless, not to mention well-written, superbly acted, Emmy-winning speech. It didn't just turn me from Kevin Bleyer into some anonymous dude named Jesse; it turned me from a serial killer to an innocent victim.

It wasn't the first time the First Amendment let me down, either. Over a decade ago, the failures of the First Amendment didn't just cost me a role. It cost me a job.

★ ★ ★

Now let me say: I recognize the irony. If not for the First Amendment, I wouldn't enjoy the freedom of expression to say this: I've just about had it with the First Amendment.

But to understand why—to understand just how personally disappointing I found the First Amendment just when I needed it most—I am going to have to remind you of a time we'd all rather forget, a time when the world was turned upside down. A not particularly amusing time.

Don't worry, this isn't a story about September 11. It's a story about what came after September 11. It's a story about how fear and the desire for transcendence—even the need for vengeance—can make rational people rabid, eager to find some way to feel they're taking action, promoting justice, even if that means forgetting a basic right or two. It's about how we can lose our collective minds.

Just days after nineteen men hijacked planes and crashed them into the World Trade Center, the Pentagon, and a field in Shanksville, Pennsylvania—and just hours after President George Bush called the actions of those men "cowardly"—comedian Bill Maher took a few minutes on his show *Politically Incorrect* to take exception. "*We* have been the cowards, lobbing cruise missiles from two thousand miles away," he said. "That's cowardly. Staying in the airplane when it hits the building? Say what you want about it. Not cowardly." It was an indictment of our military policy—not, it should be noted, of our military, nor of the troops—and it was a sentiment that wouldn't have raised an eyebrow had it been expressed a few days before. But in the raw days just after September 11, many found it more than just politically incorrect. To some, it was treasonous.

Personally, I wasn't surprised Bill would say such a thing. After all,

Maher wasn't just a supremely talented, often provocative smart-ass. He was also my boss. (I was therefore complicit in whatever supposed anti-American crimes he had committed by speaking his mind. Among the controversial lines I wrote for him, in a segment needling the flag-waving jingoism that quickly followed the terrible day: "Put a flag on your car—it's *literally* the least you can do.") When Bill made his "cowards" comment, I knew it was provocative. I also knew it wasn't planned. I certainly knew it fit with Bill's devil-may-care persona. What I didn't know was that soon all hell would break loose.

Within days, thanks to the craven exploitation of the controversy by a Houston radio host who called for a boycott of the show—they insisted that Bill had slandered our troops—advertisers began to withdraw. Among them Sears, Quiznos, and FedEx—"for when it absolutely, positively has to be noncontroversial." Soon, local affiliates started to drop the show, including the large ABC affiliate in Washington, D.C., which, one might assume, would have had a higher tolerance for politically charged debate.

But the most shocking reaction that week came straight from the White House, when Bush administration press secretary Ari Fleischer was asked, during an official press conference, about Bill's comments. "Americans," he said, "need to watch what they say, watch what they do. This is not a time for remarks like that." He then added a particularly unwelcome coda: "There never is."

I'd argue there is never a time for remarks like that to come from the White House. (And apparently, upon reflection, the White House agreed; when they released the official transcript of the conference, the portion urging people to "watch what they say" was not included. Fleischer's assistant later called the deletion a "transcription error.")

It took six months—anything shorter might have seemed hasty by the powers at ABC—but sure enough, in the end *Politically Incorrect* was canceled for being politically incorrect. It wasn't the cancellation of the show that scared me (perhaps a little, as I was now out of a job and had to worry about the cost of food, let alone the cost of free speech). Rather, it was the threat by a staff member of the White House, direct from a White House podium during a White House press conference, that people should "watch what they say."

I couldn't believe that the Executive Branch would point to our late-night TV show as a model of bad behavior, or use the controversy whipped up around us as a lesson that sometimes it's inappropriate to speak freely. The name of the show was *Politically Incorrect,* and it was hosted by a comedian. We were on after midnight; most of our viewers were either having sex, half asleep, or totally asleep. Even *they* weren't watching what we say.

But many of those who *were* awake *and* paying attention couldn't help but think: Hadn't we settled all this long ago? Didn't we go over all this way back in 1798, when President John Adams signed the infamous Alien and Sedition Acts into law?

With the Sedition Acts, written two centuries before I ever considered they might somehow affect *me*, Adams tinkered directly with the Bill of Rights. It was less than a decade after Adams had helped write the First Amendment—declaring that "Congress shall make no law [abridging] the freedom of speech, or of the press"—but already the Federalists, with Adams in the lead, were so sick of a relentless Anti-Federalist press that they made it a crime to publish "false, scandalous, and malicious" writing about govern- ment. (Any claim by Adams that he wasn't motivated merely to avoid per- sonal attacks is betrayed by the bill's expiration date—March 3, 1801—the day before Adams's term was to end.) Outspoken journalists were arrested. Newspaper editors and congressmen who criticized the government were fined and sent to jail. One man in Newark, Luther Baldwin, was convicted for a wise-ass comment he muttered near President Adams. (A clever one, in fact. When the president was greeted by the firing of a cannon, a by- stander said, "There goes the president. And they are firing at his ass." Bald- win cracked that he wouldn't mind "if they fired *through* his ass.")

In 1800, the Alien and Sedition Acts became a major electoral issue— the Anti-Federalists who *weren't* in jail were fed up with it, and they voted accordingly. Federalist Adams lost his reelection to Democratic-Republican Thomas Jefferson, who helped think up the First Amendment in the first place, who as vice president was conspicuously exempted from the Sedition Act's protections (as written by Adams), and who considered the Sedition Act "an experiment on the American mind to see how far it will bear an avowed violation of the Constitution." Not that far, it turned out; the peo- ple had spoken—as was their right—and they elected a man who not only let the Sedition Act expire, he pardoned everyone who had been sentenced under it.

Two years after it was enacted, it was gone.

Yet more than two hundred years after it was gone—as I counted the days to unemployment—I could not help think it was being echoed, by a White House press secretary who thought a wise-ass comedian and his dutiful employee should "watch what they say."

Oh, I recognize my complaint wasn't technically a First Amendment issue here either—our right to speak wasn't being abridged by the White House or by Congress, just by Sears and Quiznos—but at times like these it's hard not to shout to whomever will listen, *Hey, buddy—don't we have First Amendment rights in this country anymore?*

Well, no, we don't. Technically, we never did. There are no "First Amendment rights." The First Amendment offers no rights to citizens—at least, no *new* rights not already promised in the Constitution. In fact, *none* of the so-called Bill of Rights truly imbues us with any *new* superpowers as citizens. As stated in its own short Preamble (which, I hasten to point out, also *does not rhyme*), the Bill of Rights was only written when the states asked Congress that "further declaratory and restrictive clauses should be added" to the Constitution "in order to prevent misconstruction or abuse of its powers." It's less a Bill of Rights than a Bill of Keeping the Government from Doing Wrongs.

The First Amendment wasn't even the First Amendment. When Madison first drafted the Bill of Rights, he proposed twelve amendments. The original first two, which covered the sexy topics of compensation for elected officials and the apportionment of seats in Congress, didn't make the cut. So the so-called "First Amendment," which some assume was put in first in order because the Framers thought it first in importance, actually came in third. If you're betting on that horse, you're barely in the money.

So I was a fool to hope the First Amendment would leap tall buildings to help me in my times of need. It would neither stop Quiznos from choosing where to advertise nor protect me from serial killers named Jesse Bleyer; it merely restricts the power of the government to mess with some of the rights we already enjoy. "*Congress* shall make no law," it states, "respecting an establishment of religion, or prohibiting the free exercise thereof; or abridging the freedom of speech, or of the press; or of the right of the people peaceably to assemble, and to petition the Government for redress of grievances." In other words, we can pray, speak, write, and congregate however we like. And government, at least, can't stop us.

Except when it can.

FRIENDLY FIRE IN A CROWDED THEATER

ON THIS POINT—and I never thought I'd say this, but—*Geraldo Rivera is a perfect specimen.*

Not as a human. Or as a reporter. But as a test case of the limits of free expression as guaranteed by the First Amendment to the Constitution, they don't come any better. If Fox News were forced to produce an exposé on the threats to First Amendment, even Geraldo—he of the iconic mustache, the self-satisfied smirk, and the unseemly tight black muscle T-shirt—would have to admit that the best plan of attack would be to grab the nearest microphone and interview himself.

I don't think it would take much convincing.

Long before a teary-eyed Glenn Beck and smirk-faced Sean Hannity became the faces of Fox News, Rivera caused a First Amendment kerfuffle that not even Roger Ailes would have invited. In April 2003, days after the American invasion of Iraq, Rivera entered the war zone through Kuwait, having hitched a ride with the army's 101st Airborne Division near Baghdad. He was broadcasting live from the scene of his latest display of camera-friendly intrepidity when, like a child in the world's most dangerous sandbox, he began to draw a map in the sand detailing the exact location of his borrowed unit, where it had been so far, and—wait for it—*where it was headed.*

He might as well have sent the enemy an eVite.

Geraldo may have put his head up his ass, but he also put his finger on the root of the problem: There is a right to free expression, but not all free expression is right. (For example: I can say "Geraldo Rivera is blinded by his own ego"—it might even be true—but that doesn't mean I should.)

That's the crucial question: When should we?

For his part, Geraldo would say the First Amendment guarantees him the "blessings of liberty" to reveal the truth about war. And it does, right up to the moment it endangers another constitutional guarantee, "the common defence" of our country. In other words, the First Amendment grants Geraldo the freedom to be a journalist, but not a jackass. And certainly not an accidental—even unintentional—jihadist.

Geraldo may have thought his report was harmless—after all, he wasn't giving hard coordinates, latitude or longitude; he was drawing in the sand with a stick. But he had obviously never met any members of al-Qaeda. Sand *is* their Google Maps. They may not have a phalanx of Abrams tanks and Bradley Fighting Vehicles, but they could launch a coordinated assault with a kiddy trowel and a sharp stick. No, Geraldo's stunt, like his mustache, is indefensible in this day and age. He said the wrong thing, in the wrong place, at the wrong time.

We can't know if Geraldo violated the Constitution—whether he provided "aid" to the enemy ("aid and comfort to the enemy" being forbidden by Article III, Section 3); lucky for him, it didn't get that far. But Central Command did tell him he had compromised "operational security" and promptly sent him, and his muscle T's, back to Kuwait.

★ ★ ★

For the rest of us, it all comes down to fire in a crowded theater.

Back in 1917, Charles Schenck, the general secretary of the Socialist Party and all-around rabble-rouser, began distributing leaflets urging young Americans to refuse to serve in World War I if drafted. When the Woodrow Wilson administration informed him he couldn't do that, Schenck did what any self-respecting antigovernment socialist would do: He made a federal case out of it.

He took it all the way to the Supreme Court. But in *Schenck v. the United States,* the Supreme Court refused his argument that the leaflets were protected under the First Amendment. In a phrase that should ring a bell, Chief Justice Oliver Wendell Holmes held that their publication created a "clear and present danger" that would result in a "substantive evil"—namely, empty foxholes, and an unprotected country. Holmes based his ruling on the idea that the First Amendment "would not protect a man in falsely shouting 'Fire' in a theatre and causing a panic." (He didn't have to mention the "crowded" part; remember, this was back when people went to the theater.) With those five words—"fire in a crowded theatre"—free expression found its litmus test.

After all, as a society we agree that we should be allowed to *shout* in a theater. We do it all the time. But shouting "Fire!" in a theater—that triggers a constitutional commotion. The Constitution doesn't grant the freedom to incite a trampling as panicked theatergoers run for their lives, which is why, constitutionally, there is one time, and one time only, when it is perfectly acceptable to shout "Fire!" in a crowded theater: when there is, in fact, a fire. (Or maybe snakes. If there were snakes in a crowded theater, even if someone shouted "Fire!" people would still take the hint, head for the exits and, in all likelihood, be grateful for the heads-up.)

One could suggest, even, that shouting "Fire!" (or "Snakes! *Snakes!* For the love of God, *there are SNAKES!!!*") in a crowded theater is not only *defensible* speech under the First Amendment, but *required* speech under our simple obligation to protect our fellow man (even if our fellow man had the poor judgment to see *Wicked* at the Sunday matinee, when everybody knows that the show's only pyrotechnician–snake exterminator shows up drunk on Sundays, what with the 2-for-1 Saturday all-night special they've got running at McMurphy's Ale House on the corner). That is to say, the "clear and present danger" is not the panic caused by the speech, but the flames lapping at the upper mezzanine and the snakes that have taken over the orchestra pit.

Despite what you might have heard or read about Congress "making no law" restricting the freedom of speech, the First Amendment isn't a platinum "get out of jail free" card to say anything, anytime, anywhere. It merely places the "unacceptable" bar a little higher on a list of things you might acceptably shout:

"There is fire in this crowded theater!"—*acceptable* if true, *unacceptable* if not true

"There is a car show in this convention center!"—*acceptable* whether true or not true

"There is a tsunami in this library!"—*acceptable* if true, but I'm gonna go with "not true"

The freedom the First Amendment grants is complex and multifold: the *right* to speak freely, yes, but the *responsibility* to speak carefully, and the *obligation* to warn everybody about the snakes. But it's also vague. Because the First Amendment mentions none of this specifically—neither "fire" nor "snakes" are ever mentioned in the Constitution—to this day we are left with very troubling, very confusing guidelines about the ways we can express ourselves: how and where we can pray, where and what we can say, what and when we can publish, when and where we can assemble.

Can we *pray* however we like? As a rule, yes—and Hallelujah. But what if our church holds its services on the freeway during rush hour? Or believes in the Gospel According to Controlled Substances?

Can we *say* whatever we wish? Generally, we can. But what if we choose to scream obscenities during a military funeral? Or claim that, as a corporation, we should be able to contribute unlimited funds to political candidates because "money is free speech"?

Can we *publish* anything we want? Almost anything—pornography, state secrets, inane and annoying tweets—and for that we should thank the

Thomas Jeffersons of the world. But will having a *Law & Order* villain named after you ever be anything more than a pipe dream?

Can we assemble wherever we please? We can join together, to protest whatever, to our heart's delight. But does that mean we can occupy a shopping mall, or set up permanent tents in a private park?

You get the idea. The right to free expression as provided by the First Amendment isn't absolute. Nor does the First Amendment say anything about some other, louder voice drowning out ours. And while in theory we generally agree with the famous mantra of writer Evelyn Beatrice Hall*— "I disapprove of what you say, but I will defend to the death your right to say it"—in practice we grab the biggest bullhorn we can find and turn it up to 11.

And now that I have it, I'll use it to proclaim something that no one can deny: Clearly, if we're going to keep claiming to have so many inalienable "First Amendment rights," and if we're going to successfully fend off threats from the government that we "watch what we say," we're going to have to amend the First Amendment.

We're going to have to start getting a little more specific.

Your New First Amendment

Congress shall make no law respecting any established religion as long as it's a real religion and, like I said, not something I could have made up; or abridging the freedom of speech especially when there is Fire (or Snakes) involved, or of the press when they're just trying to name a Timeless Character after you; or the right of the people peaceably to assemble as long as they don't tie up traffic during rush hour; and to petition the Government for a redress of grievances vis-à-vis its apparent inability to deal with the aforementioned Fire and Snakes everywhere.

---

* A woman who felt so free to express herself that she wrote under the pen name Stephen G. Tallentyre.

THE SECOND AMENDMENT

Starring Charlton Heston's "Cold, Dead Hands!"

THE SECOND AMENDMENT BEGINS and ends with matters of life and death. It's serious business.

So let's start with a joke:

Panda walks into a café. He sits down, orders a sandwich, and devours it. When he's finished eating, he pulls out a pistol, shoots the waiter, and starts to walk out. "Hey!" shouts the manager. "Where do you think you're going? You just shot my waiter and you didn't pay for your sandwich!" Panda yells back to the manager, "Look, man, I'm a panda.*" Panda tosses the manager a badly punctuated wildlife dictionary, and on his way out the door, mutters, "Look it up." Panda leaves, and the manager quickly thumbs his way to the correct entry: "Panda: A bear. Native of China. Characterized by its distinctive black-and-white coloring. Eats, shoots and leaves."*

Okay, it's not much of a joke. Actually, it's a terrible joke. But in the context of the Second Amendment, it's a vital one. Don't worry, I'll explain.

★ ★ ★

She shot wolves from the sky—from airplanes, helicopters, perhaps hang gliders—or so she was eager to have us believe, as it played nicely into the image she had cultivated: a real-life, grown-up Annie Oakley who had single-handedly managed to tame the Great Wilderness of Alaska. Her way with a gun was part of her appeal; to her fans, she was a maverick with a musket. But for her many detractors, the more rabid her defense of our constitutional right to bear arms, the more rabid their hope that one day they'd see a constitutional right to arm bears—if only to level the playing field.

But in the summer of 2011, as she stood in line at a Boston bakery, *she* was the target of some unfriendly fire.

She had been bouncing around the country on a "family vacation," touting America's most photo-op-able and exploitable national monuments—

the Liberty Bell, Ellis Island, Fort McHenry. And, like all families, her brood traveled in a bus festooned with a giant copy of the Constitution—as if James Madison were on tour with his fife-and-drum band. (It's great to be here in Gettysburg! Are you ready to rock, Mount Vernon?!) The agenda that particular morning featured a guided tour of the home of Paul Revere, he who famously made a bold retreat to Lexington and Concord to warn the countryside of the advancing British—a bedrock American anecdote immortalized by Henry Wadsworth Longfellow and scores of fifth grade history textbooks.

Later, while on line for pastry, she took questions from a few reporters who had trailed her that day. In one of her answers, she chose to remember the man behind the Midnight Ride somewhat differently. Her Paul Revere? "He, who warned, the, the British that they weren't going to be taking away our arms, by ringing those bells, and uh, making sure, as he's riding his horse through town, to send those warning shots and bells that, uh, we were gonna be secure and we were gonna be free." One more thing: "And we were gonna be *armed*."

In her version, Paul Revere wasn't warning the colonists that the British were coming; he was firing warning shots (and ringing warning bells?) to alert the British that *we* were packing heat.

As a man rewriting the American Constitution, I respect her choice to rewrite American history. Her right to get American history so wrong is, after all, protected by the guarantee of free expression I just spent precious paragraphs reaffirming. But not everyone that day was so supportive. To many, even to some of her fans, her attempt to co-opt Revere's ride backfired. For days, she was the target of a barrage of ridicule—from the left, from the "mainstream media," and from anyone who had a stubborn allegiance to "the facts." (The facts being: Yes, the British *were* planning to seize the colonists' guns, and yes, as Paul Revere rode to Lexington to warn Samuel Adams and John Hancock, he did "alarm" the countryside. But he did not do so by firing "warning shots." Boston was filled with British patrols and loyalists to the Crown, so Revere did little more than whisper his alarm quietly, door to door. As he arrived at the house where Adams and Hancock were staying, a sentry even asked that he keep the noise to a minimum, lest they be discovered. "You'll have enough noise before long," Revere cried. "The regulars are coming out!")

That's not the way she saw it. This was not a time to cease fire, no sir; to the contrary, as she had said countless times during her rise to prominence, when confronted with a defeat on the battlefield: "Don't retreat; *reload.*" She took to the airwaves in the following days and announced that she had been the victim of a "gotcha" question designed to disgrace her and expose her ignorance to the world—in front of her children on a (ahem) family vacation, no less. (What *was* the "gotcha" question that entrapped her into getting so famous a tale so blatantly wrong? Brace yourselves: "What are you going to take away from your visit?")

A few days later, she held her line again, and shot back at her attackers. "You know what?" she asked, rhetorically. "I didn't mess up about Paul Revere."

And this time, she was absolutely right.

She *didn't* mess up. She was *incorrect, mistaken,* and flat-out *wrong,* but she didn't *mess up.* Sure, she got the basics of the revolution backward, but the point of recounting such a fake history wasn't to try to impress anyone with her knowledge of American history, even had she been able to; she was pandering to her constituents, who—she rightly surmised—much prefer their history to be pro-America than pro-reality. Jingoism trumps realism. In the history books of the Tea Party, Americans don't retreat; we take dead aim. We fire warning bells.

A week later, she released a glossy video of the highlights of her family vacation to her 600,000 Twitter followers—as any family would—and announced what she had learned from the trip: "We need a fundamental restoration of what's good about America." As she saw it, what's good about America is that Paul Revere warned *the British* that *we* were coming—whether he did or not.

HAVE GUN, WILL TRIUMPH

AMERICA IS, after all, gun country. Our nation was founded by gun owners: George Washington owned fifty guns; John Adams wrote that "arms in the hands of citizens" were a great method of "private self-defense"; Thomas Jefferson received his first firearm at age ten. (Years later, Jefferson advised his fifteen-year-old nephew, "A strong body makes the mind strong. As to the species of exercise, I advise the gun. . . . Let your gun therefore be the constant companion on your walks. Never think of taking a book with you.") Our first three presidents were gun nuts. Our forty-sixth vice president shot his best friend in the face.

Full disclosure: I, too, have enjoyed shooting guns, the few times I've done so—although I admit I don't quite see, as Thomas Jefferson does, their inherent "exercise" value. (My mom warned me about running just with *scissors*.) As a teenager, I shot tin cans with my then girlfriend's father while on vacation at their small lake cabin. (It was a blast, although I realize now he just wanted me to know he had a gun and was willing use it.) As an adult in 2007, I spent two hours at a shooting range in Iraq when I was on a USO tour traveling with the military. We "tested" all sorts of weapons—machine guns, sniper rifles, an AK-47 confiscated from an Iraqi insurgent. I understand the visceral appeal of firearms. They go boom.

They feel American. They *are* American. America was born with the Shot Heard Round the World, and we made a name for ourselves, for better or worse, by fighting wars all over the earth. The Chinese may have invented gunpowder, but Americans invented reasons to use it.

Guns in America aren't merely protected; at times, they've been mandatory. The Second Amendment to the Constitution protected the *right* to bear arms; only three years later, President Washington signed the Militia Act of 1792,* a bill requiring "every able-bodied white male citizen" between the ages of eighteen and forty-five to "provide himself with a good musket or firelock, a sufficient bayonet and belt, two spare flints, and a knapsack, a pouch with a box therein to contain not less than twenty-four cartridges, suited to the bore of his musket or firelock, each cartridge to contain a proper quantity of powder and ball; or with a good rifle, knap-

---

* A bill that was less controversial in the eighteenth century than it proved to be in the twenty-first, when the so-called gun mandate of 1792 was used to legitimize the so-called health care mandate of 2010.

sack, shot-pouch and powder horn, twenty balls suited to the bore of his rifle, and a quarter of a pound of powder"—you never know when they might come in handy.

More than two centuries later, there are 280 million guns in civilian hands in America—nearly enough for every able-bodied man, woman, and child to point, if they chose to do so, at every man, woman, and child. During her failed vice-presidential campaign of 2008, the Revere Revisionist had a handy way of summarizing this American devotion to guns, at least among her supporters: "We'll keep clinging to our Constitution, our guns, and our religion, and you can keep the change." It wasn't as catchy as it was redundant. To many Americans, our guns *are* our religion, because they're mentioned in the Second Commandment of our Constitution.

Sorry—did I say Commandment?

I meant *Amendment*. Second Amendment. The one that states,

> A well regulated Militia, being necessary to the security of a free
> State, the right of the people to keep and bear Arms, shall not be
> infringed.

We cling so dearly to our guns because we've seen what happens when we don't. At least, we've read about it.

We vaguely recall our seventeenth-century British ancestors, who enjoyed the right to bear arms until King James II, fearing that Protestants might bear arms against *him*, authorized his Catholic deputies to seize the weapons of all subjects deemed to be "dangerous to the Peace of the Kingdom"—in other words, Protestants. Only after a full-scale revolution— the Glorious Revolution, during which William and Mary* ascended to the throne and agreed to respect the rights of all Englishmen, not just non-gun-toting Catholics—was the right of individuals to own guns reestablished.

We weren't going to fall for that. No one was going to take *our* guns. When the British Crown again tried to disarm its sworn enemy—this time, the American colonists—we would have none of it. Soon enough, Paul Revere was bounding through the countryside, firing warning shots and warning bells and screaming "Go ahead, make my day!" and "Eat lead!" and "You can have my gun when you pry it from my cold, dead hands!" (Hey—as long as we're making stuff up, let's *make stuff up*.)

---

* Joint sovereigns, and namesakes of the alma mater of both Thomas Jefferson and Jon Stewart.

And today we feel the same. Three out of four Americans believe that the Second Amendment protects their right—as individuals—to bear arms.

Outside the United Nations headquarters in New York City, there stands an iconic sculpture—a giant .45-caliber revolver whose barrel has been tied into a knot, rendering it useless. It is meant to represent nonviolence and pacifism for nations around the world. For many Americans, it merely represents a waste of a perfectly good giant gun—one that could have been used to shoot a giant moose. Or a giant intruder. Or a giant friend of Dick Cheney's.

Nonviolence may be swell for the U.N.—but that's not how we do it in the U.S. of A. As a country, we're locked and loaded. We pledge allegiance to the flag, but we're a *gun nation, under Glock, with licenses and ammo for all.*

HOLD YOUR FIRE!

WELL, NOT ALL. We may be locked and loaded, but we've also taken care to keep the safety on. Guns have been a part of America from the beginning, but so has our understanding that they should be regulated. "Gun control," notes constitutional law professor Adam Winkler, "is as much a part of the history of guns in America as the Second Amendment."

Even the Founders supported shockingly severe gun control laws. They denied gun ownership outright to anyone who declined to swear loyalty to the Revolution. (The whiplash must have been something: Only a few years earlier, colonial governments denied the same right to any person unwilling to affirm his allegiance to the British Crown.) All white men, since they were considered to be part of a militia, were required to bring their guns for mandatory inspection at "musters" where the government would catalog their weapons on public rolls—essentially, required registration. And in a move that would have made King James II proud—and, let's be honest, would never fly today—gun owners had to submit to "impressment"; if the government decided it needed the guns for its own use, it could confiscate them. It wasn't an idle threat; ten of the thirteen colonies impressed private citizens' firearms during the war against England.

As America expanded, so did the struggle to hold our fire. Lawless frontier towns where (Hollywood tells us) countless scores were settled by shootouts at high noon had at least one sensible gun control measure:

Strangers had to hand over their pistols to the sheriff, or leave them with their horses on the outskirts of town. (Leaving guns with horses is not quite arming bears, but we're getting closer.) Even the National Rifle Association, in whose view no gun law is a good law, was a far more moderate force when it was established in the nineteenth century. It supported strict gun-licensing policies and lobbied state governments to adopt them. That's surprising when you consider the NRA we know today, but not so surprising when you consider the NRA's dirty, dark secret: It was founded by a former reporter for *The New York Times*.

It's inevitable that we're a country divided between "gun nuts" and "gun grabbers"—between those who read the Second Amendment as guaranteeing individuals the right to guns and those who see such a guarantee only for militias. By those who believe "the people" have an unlimited right "to keep and bear arms" and those that believe gun owners can be "well regulated." Which is precisely the problem with the Second Amendment: It is, in the words of one constitutional historian, "maddeningly ambiguous."

That alone is reason enough for me to rewrite the amendment: As written, it's ambiguous—maddeningly so. And it seems to me that the last thing we should do to someone wielding a gun—while they hastily consult whether the Constitution gives them that right—is to make them mad.

CASE IN POINT-BLANK

IN REWRITING THE SECOND AMENDMENT, I won't be the first.

Just as some have rewritten the story of the tea party patriot Paul Revere—who blazed a freedom trail by warning the British that *we* were armed—others have taken a stab at rewriting the Second Amendment. In fact, the self-appointed Tea Party patriots of the twenty-first century have their own entire *Constitution*, thank you very much. Only theirs was composed not by James Madison, but by a Christian college–educated, NRA-certified handgun instructor named Michael Holler. His Constitution, titled *The Constitution Made Easy*, is "a reference you can trust . . . a modernized version for easier reading," with the original 1787 language on the left and the simplified 2008 version on the right—the far right, some might argue. Essentially, it is a "translation" of the Constitution from English to American, deciphered by a man who sells classes in how to obtain a concealed handgun permit, and available online for only $8.95 plus $3 shipping and handling.*

Holler's version is officially endorsed by the Tea Party Express, the largest chapter of the Tea Party, which has turned it into something of a bestseller among the "taxed enough already" crowd, many of whom have fallen easy prey to its promise that they'd soon "read and understand the whole Constitution in under 30 minutes!!!"—as soon as they wait, as I did, more than three days for it to arrive. (In other words, many of the people so up in arms about their constitutional right to keep and bear arms have often not read the Constitution that supposedly gives them that right. They've read the Cliff's Notes—if Cliff were a Bible-reading gun nut.)

So be it. The Second Amendment is the perfect example of why the entire Constitution is due for a much-needed tune-up—and if the mechanic in this case happens to be a gun instructor, who am I to raise a fuss? Because if there's one thing Mr. Holler and I would agree on regarding the original Second Amendment: It is *terribly written*. It makes no sense. I defy you to follow its logic:

> A well regulated Militia, being necessary to the security of a free
> State, the right of the people to keep and bear Arms, shall not be
> infringed.

Excuse me? Did I miss something? I think I missed something.

Oh, it starts clearly enough: "A well regulated Militia"—I might not have capitalized *Militia*, but that's just me—then a *comma*, then "being necessary to the security of a free State"—fine, no hiccups yet. The sentiment so far is clear: *Some kind of local army, comma, would be nice.* But did you notice what happens next? It seems to start over with a new thought, a new sentence: "The right of the people to keep and bear Arms, shall not be infringed." What happened to the first part? Did the writer lose his train of thought? Did he step outside for a bit o' snuff, only to get shot dead in the street? Did someone else then take over, without bothering to see where his stricken predecessor had left off? In the end, what exactly does the first half have to do with the second?

---

* Although when I ordered my copy, the standard "student edition" was out of stock; they automatically upgraded me at no extra cost to the pricier "deluxe edition," which not only is printed on parchment-colored paper, but thanks to a spiral-bound feature, also "lays flat for easy reference and comparison." Top that, Madison.

Hard to say. Easy to argue.

I admit, I'm a stickler for good grammar. (Bad grammar, as Churchill might have said, is the sort of English up with which I shall not put.) So I'm tempted to fix the sentence, regardless of the consequences.*

What's certain is that if either Holler or I had composed such a sentence in elementary school, it would have been returned to us crossed out in red. It is the kind of clumsily crafted, poorly punctuated, grammatical word soup that would make any fan of the English language go off half-cocked. But it raises a more urgent warning: Thanks to its maddeningly ambiguous grammar, when it comes to opportunities to draw contrary opinions on what this amendment actually means, *this thing is loaded*.

As written, the Second Amendment could mean two things: (a) We all get to have a gun; (b) We only get to have a gun if we're part of a well-regulated militia. Holler's "modernized" version, on the other hand, is refreshingly straightforward:

> The people have a right to own and carry firearms, and it may not
> be violated because a well-equipped Militia is necessary for a State
> to remain secure and free.

In Holler's America, we get to have a gun, because we *could be* part of a militia. With a simple flip of the clauses and the clever use of the word "and," Holler leaves nothing to chance: *We get to own guns, and here's why.* It's simply not debatable.

Except that it is. The true meaning of the original isn't as obvious as Holler, the Tea Party Express, or the Alaskan Annie Oakley might wish. It is quite debatable, in fact—by no less than the Supreme Court of the United States.

★ ★ ★

If only the Judicial Branch of the United States could swear to uphold *The Constitution Made Easy*, rather than *The Constitution Left Difficult and Ambiguous*. Then we wouldn't have to question whether, as was true for most of American history, the Second Amendment was accurately understood as protecting merely the right of citizens to form militias (and, once en-

---

* It might be argued that the first half is a simple gerund phrase—as in "all things being equal." But then what's with the comma? Would we stand for "all things, being equal"? I think, being not.

listed, bear as many arms as they please), or whether, as the National Rifle Association began arguing in the 1970s and throughout the Heston administration,* the amendment in fact protects the right of ordinary individuals to bear arms willy-nilly. (Even the NRA has rewritten the Second Amendment. Outside their former offices on Rhode Island Avenue, they chose to display the only part they liked: THE RIGHT OF THE PEOPLE TO KEEP AND BEAR ARMS SHALL NOT BE INFRINGED. Perhaps there wasn't enough room to mention the part about the well-regulated militia.) The NRA saw the individual's right to arms as a restoration of the original meaning—a claim that former Chief Justice Warren Burger pooh-poohed as "one of the greatest pieces of fraud, I repeat the word 'fraud,' on the American public by special interest groups that I have ever seen in my lifetime." Whether you agree with Charlton "cold, dead hands" Heston or Warren "I repeat the word 'fraud'" Burger, whether you're pro-gun or anti-gun, just think of it: With a Constitution Made Easy, every time an individual claimed his right to pack heat, we wouldn't have to make such a federal case out of it.

Yet we do. And in 2008, the Supreme Court did. The same year Michael Holler published his own version of the Second Amendment, another version was fantasized by yet another Tea Party patron, and my fork-wielding lunch companion: Supreme Court Justice Antonin Scalia. In deciding *District of Columbia v. Heller*—at issue, whether a retired security guard should be allowed to keep an assembled handgun in his home—Scalia, who was on his shooting team in high school and often rode the Manhattan subways toting his .22-caliber rifle, wrote an opinion that relied as much on Strunk & White as it did on Blackstone's *Commentaries*. "The Second Amendment," he wrote, "is naturally divided into two parts: its prefatory clause and its operative clause. The former does not limit the latter grammatically, but rather announces a purpose." Of course, Scalia had a purpose of his own. His lesson in grammar was just preamble to his very own rewrite. "The Amendment could be rephrased, '*Because a well regulated Militia is necessary to the security of a free State, the right of the people to keep and bear Arms shall not be infringed.*'"

---

* Charlton Heston, that is. The star of *Planet of the Apes* was president of the NRA from 1998 to 2003. At an NRA convention in 2000, he raised a rifle aloft and challenged presidential candidate Al Gore to wrest his Second Amendment rights "from my cold, dead hands." No word on whether he was buried holding a gun.

★ ★ ★

For a man who complains that his own Supreme Court too often rewrites the Constitution, it's hard not to notice that he just rewrote the Constitution. He couldn't resist the temptation to join James Madison and Michael Holler in the small fraternity of presumptuous men who have claimed to know just what the Founders intended, who have parsed a sentence that utterly defies parsing, who have tried their hand at writing the Second Amendment to the Constitution.

To which I say, *How dare you, Michael Holler.*

Shame on you, Justice Scalia.

And also: *My turn.*

What "is not debatable," Scalia wrote in the *Heller* decision, "is that it is not the role of this Court to pronounce the Second Amendment extinct." Perhaps not; but it is the role of this Author to pronounce the Second Amendment poorly written.

EATS, SHOOTS AND LEAVES

WHICH BRINGS US BACK to that joke. The one about the panda who shoots the waiter and splits. As I said, it's not a good joke—it's not much of a joke at all—but it makes a good point about the dangers of bad grammar. If a panda "eats shoots and leaves," it's just a harmless panda that eats shoots and also eats leaves. If a panda "eats, shoots and leaves," it's a panda that commits cold-blooded murder. And if there's one thing both armed pandas and the Second Amendment have taught us, it's that bad grammar can kill. Punctuation, poorly placed in the wrong constitutional sentence, can result in guns, poorly placed in the hands of irresponsible individuals—most of whom have never taken Michael Holler's gun class. Rightly or wrongly, when bad grammar is left uncorrected, it's chaos. Supreme Courts decide our fates. Individuals get their paws on pistols. Wolves are shot from airplanes. Pandas go on shooting rampages.

Chaos, I tells you.

So where would I put my red pen? What would my amended amendment say?

This one isn't easy for me to answer, for one reason only: In January 2011, my friend Gabby Giffords, the Democratic congresswoman from

Arizona, was shot in the head by a lunatic. (Now you see why I began with a joke; I knew where this was heading.) On that day my thoughts on guns evolved in an instant; inevitably so. I can't simply reaffirm the right to bear arms, as Scalia and Holler have done and I was previously inclined to do; one of those arms forever changed the life of someone I care about.

And yet I take my cue from Gabby. Before the shooting, she didn't mince words: "I am a strong supporter of the Second Amendment." Gabby owns the same type of gun that was used in her attempted assassination, a Glock semiautomatic pistol*—and by her own account, she's "a pretty good shot." She was among the more than three hundred members of Congress who signed an amicus brief urging the Supreme Court to strike down the ban on handguns in D.C., and when it passed, she celebrated: "As a long-time gun owner," she said, "I believe the right to keep and bear arms should not be dependent on the city in which you live. . . . The provisions of the U.S. Constitution apply to all Americans." She happens to live in a particularly gun-loving part of America: Gabby's district is home to the O.K. Corral and Tombstone, and allows guns in bars—as long as the person carrying them is not drinking.

Gabby has never complained about the inherent violence of guns; she has, however, taken issue with the casually violent rhetoric of her fellow politicians, and how it might trigger disturbed people to do disturbing things *with or without* guns. Her experience is firsthand: The previous year, someone had shot a pellet through the window of her campaign headquarters.

Just a few days before the shooting, when Congress read the entire Constitution on the floor of the Capitol, Gabby didn't read the Second Amendment; she read the First. She was honored to do so. She would support anyone's right to speak freely. But she had also begun to feel that it had gotten out of hand. She would often email me when things were getting truly crazy—as when her window was shattered, or when a former militia leader encouraged people to throw bricks into local government offices to protest health care reform. The night before she was shot, she sent me an email that would take on new resonance only hours later: "My poor state!" she wrote. "The nut jobs have taken it over from the good people of Arizona."

---

* In an orgy of tastelessness, later that year the Republican Party in Gabby's district auctioned off that exact model gun in a "get out the vote" fundraiser. It was a disgusting tactic that barely warrants a footnote, from the mind of a political strategist who clearly warrants a foot in the groin.

★ ★ ★

I do think that gun ownership is an American right. It is the privilege of a free country. It is the cost of doing democracy. As early-nineteenth-century Chief Justice Joseph Story proclaimed in his *Commentaries on the Constitution of the United States,* the right to bear arms is "the palladium of the liberties of a republic; since it offers a strong moral check against the usurpation and arbitrary power of rulers; and will generally . . . enable the people to resist and triumph over them." It's the American way. Have Gun, Will Triumph.

Also, they go boom.

But do I think gun control measures should be so toothless that an emotionally disturbed nut could have access to one? Or that states should reinstate gun rights to nonviolent felons the moment they've served their time, as some do? I do not. (Nor do I think pandas should shoot waiters or that aircraft should be employed in the hunting of wolves.)

How do we stop that? I'm not sure. After all, guns don't kill people; people kill people, especially when the wrong people get guns. And you can't stop people from being nut jobs.

I can only use the powers that I have. Sentences. Prefatory clauses. Operative clauses. And hell, if punctuation can somehow confuse the issue enough—if more commas can make more courts consider new interpretations that might keep weapons out of the hands of wackos—then on behalf of James Madison and my friend Gabby, I'll do whatever it takes.

Period.

Your New Second Amendment

A, well; regulated! Militia—being. (necessary) to, the, security? of, a, free...State, the, right...of, the, people...to, keep! and, bear? Arms; shall, not, be, infringed?!

THE THIRD AMENDMENT

Knock Knock! Who's There? A Soldier! A Soldier Who? A Soldier Who Demands to Be Quartered During Peacetime!

PITY THE POOR THIRD AMENDMENT.

No soldier shall, in time of peace be quartered in any house, without the consent of the Owner, nor in time of war, but in a manner to be prescribed by law.

An entire amendment debated, devised, and drafted to address the pressing constitutional question: Okay, now that we have a military, *where will it sleep?*

It is no wonder, then, that the Third Amendment gets so little respect. It has never been heard by the Supreme Court. Few Americans can tell you what it says. It comes third in the Bill of Rights—a position that, fair or not, makes it the bronze medal of amendments.

While other, flashier amendments have received marquee treatment in the grand theater of American history—the First, which lets us shout almost anything we darn well please in that theater (as long as it's not too crowded), the Second, which reserves our right to bring concealed weapons into some theaters (as long as we don't shoot them at presidents), even the little-known Fourth, which gives us the right to, well, let's not spoil the surprise (I haven't gotten that far myself)—the Third Amendment, according to the historian Richard Beeman, "may be the only Amendment in . . . the Bill of Rights that doesn't come into terribly active play in our lives today."

May be?

Beeman is being charitable. He knows that the pathetic Third Amendment has felt the glare of the spotlight only once in its unsung life as a bit player, with a single starring role in a less-than-Supreme Second Circuit Court case you've never heard of: *Engblom v. Carey.* (It's safe to say even

Engblom and Carey barely remember it.) Not until 1979, almost two hundred years after it was ratified, was the Third Amendment—which forbids the government from forcing any citizen to quarter a soldier in his home during peacetime, but allows it during wartime, should lawmakers deem it necessary—first put to the test. That year, the governor of New York sent members of the National Guard to live in the on-site residences of striking New York State prison officers. The prison officers protested, citing their Third Amendment right not to be forced to let the guardsmen—who, in this case, had the additional distinction of being union scabs—crash at their place. (Don't worry, you'll learn how this movie ends.)

Except for this fleeting taste of fame, in the roster of celebrity amendments the Third Amendment has been either relegated to supporting character status in dramas concerning other amendments—in *Griswold v. Connecticut*, somehow the guarantee against quartering soldiers was used to affirm the right of a woman to use birth control, which might not be what James Madison had in mind*—or to an even worse indignity, cited in significant court decisions only as a good (bad) example of one of our freedoms that has "faded into relative inconsequentiality."

Such is the fate of the Third Amendment: a silent film star in a talkie era, demoted to third billing for a time before being moved, unwillingly, into the Old Actors' Home, whence it is occasionally yanked now and then for a bit of stunt casting.

Even then, none of its cameos have gone well. The pitiful Third Amendment has been trotted out for irrelevant prosecutions and far-fetched defenses, its mere existence proof that the litigants involved were desperate. In *Jones v. United States Secretary of Defense*, a group of Army Reservists claimed that the Third Amendment somehow gave them the right to avoid marching in a parade. Plaintiffs in *Securities Investor Protection Corp. v. Executive Securities Corp.* tried to suggest that the Third Amendment forbade the use of a subpoena. One defendant, in *United States v. Valenzuela*, relied on the Third Amendment—and an ample coat of purple prose—to allege that the 1947 House and Rent Act "is and always was the incubator and hatchery of swarms of bureaucrats to be quartered as storm troopers upon the people."[†] Most embarrassing for the poor amendment, certainly, was the case of *Marquette Cement Mining Co. v. Oglesby Coal Co.*, in which the Third Amendment at first seemed to be front and center in the proceed-

---

* Perhaps Dolley, but not James.

[†] An argument unsuccessfully repeated in the 1977 case of *Skywalker v. Vader*.

ings (a star is reborn!) until it was determined someone had just made a mistake: The Third Amendment had been confused with the Seventh Amendment.

And insult to injury, in each of these cases the courts summarily rejected the Third Amendment claims. Yet another reason to pity the poor Third Amendment. It has never—not once—enjoyed the taste of Victory, not even the bittersweet tang of Reflected Glory. Historically speaking, the Third Amendment gets Sloppy Seconds.

If you think about it, then, the Third Amendment has never been truly litigated. Since the end of the Revolutionary War, not once has a Hessian ever been heaved from a house, or a Redcoat rejected from a residence, or a Marine removed from a McMansion. Even *Engblom v. Carey* was decided in favor of the defendants. So if a case were to be decided affirmatively on Third Amendment grounds, what would be the remedy? No one knows. No one has ever developed a proven method for removing a soldier from a home. (Hard to kick someone out when, between the two of you, he's the one with a gun.)

What's more, *Engblom* was decided by the Supreme Court three years after the case was first heard in New York, long after the prison officers' strike was resolved; one assumes there were quite a few awkward dinner table conversations between the prison officers and the guardsmen still sharing their bedrooms. Dissenting judge Irving Kaufman provides one reason the Court may have dragged its heels, writing that the majority's "willingness seriously to entertain a 'quartering of troops' claim" in a prison strike "holds us up to derision."

That's how embarrassing the Third Amendment is.

Never enforced, rarely mentioned, often mocked—the Third Amendment is the vestigial tail of the Bill of Rights. It must have been important to somebody at some time for some reason, but these days, when it has more often been mistaken for the Seventh Amendment than it has been considered in a court of law, let's be honest: We could lop off the Third Amendment, and no one would notice.

HOME IS WHERE THE PURPLE HEART IS

WHOSE BRIGHT IDEA was it, anyway? Who decided that we should have two standards—one for peacetime, during which homeowners can bar their doors, and another for wartime, when homeowners can be forced to be unwilling landlords to a bunch of men with guns?

Naturally, it would be easy to blame Baron Samuel von Pufendorf. For it was Von Pufendorf, the seventeenth-century German jurist, legal theorist, and political philosopher (like I have to tell you), who informed many of the earliest Americans' philosophies about war and peace. Von Pufendorf suggested that we distinguish not between war and peace, exactly, but rather between *perfect* wars—those fought in a formal manner, with rules of engagement and copious use of *please* and *thank you*—and *imperfect* wars—intermittent skirmishes linked by intermittent outbreaks of peacetime. It was Von Pufendorf who kickstarted the idea that perhaps there are different ways for societies to behave during perfect wars and imperfect wars. The same question can have a different answer. (Such as: Where the heck will our soldiers sleep?) Thanks in large part to Von Pufendorf's influence, the Third Amendment is considered the most European amendment, dating back to a time and a place when people were named *Von Pufendorf.* (Even Rexford Guy Tugwell would have my back on this: It's a silly name.)

But really, it's James Madison's fault—for not heeding Von Pufendorf's advice. Before Madison's Convention in Philadelphia, all American constitutions already included two protections from quartering—a stringent policy during peacetime, and a more relaxed policy for times of war. Nothing for the hazy middle ground when the country is neither at war nor at peace. The 1683 New York Charter of Libertyes and Priviledges declared that "Noe Freeman shall be compelled to receive any Marriners or Souldiers into his house and there suffer them to Sojourne, against their willes provided Alwayes it be not in time of Actuall Warr."

Baron Samuel von Pufendorf developed the theories behind the Third Amendment, after he grew tired of quartering soldiers in his hair.

Von Pufendorf tried to warn Madison: It's not so simple. After all, what exactly *is* "Actuall Warr"? It's very hardd to sayy.

Madison was in a bind. He couldn't simply ignore the issue; allowing soldiers to be quartered in any random house, in peacetime and wartime, would be unacceptable to the Founders. They had already condemned the Quartering Act of 1774, which authorized the quartering of British regulars and Hessian mercenaries in private homes based on the centuries-old—and extremely annoying—practice of *royal purveyance* (by which the king or his family could drop by unannounced and claim your house for England). It became known as one of the "Intolerable Acts" that the American Founders refused to tolerate. In the Declaration of Independence, the Founders had in fact officially complained of King George's habit of keeping "among us, in times of peace, Standing Armies, without the consent of the legislatures" and of "quartering large bodies of armed troops among us."

Nor could Madison prohibit quartering, full stop, in war *and* peace, although his first draft of the Third Amendment came close: "No soldiers shall in time of peace be quartered in any house without the consent of the owner; nor *at any time,* but in manner warranted by law." The select committee rejected this version—it was far too comprehensive and comprehensible—and again Madison was forced to compromise. The compromised amendment he rewrote and resubmitted in 1787 became the Third Amendment we mock, ridicule, and totally ignore today:

> No Soldier shall, in time of peace be quartered in any house,
> without the consent of the Owner, nor in time of war, but in a
> manner to be prescribed by law.

So there it is: our official policy on quartering soldiers. It's totally illegal, except when it's really important.

It has also proven to be a recipe for disaster. Over the centuries, the Third Amendment hasn't just been mocked, it has been ignored—as in the War of 1812, when Congress officially declared war against England, but turned a blind eye to the quartering of troops in American homes. Or the Civil War, when the Supreme Court permitted quartering of Union troops not only in Confederate states (again, *awkward*), but in loyal Northern states as well—a practice that was so common that the military established a formula for compensating homeowners for the rent and damage it inflicted; army boots are the death of hardwood floors. For more than two hundred years, thanks to its lack of sensitivity to what we think of wars and warriors, Madison's amendment has gone unheeded by history.

Call it Pufendorf's Revenge.

★ ★ ★

But Pufendorf and Madison both miss the point. The problem with the Third Amendment isn't that it's incomplete. The problem with the Third Amendment is that it's upside down. It relies on a premise that may have been true once, but is true no longer: that Americans wouldn't want soldiers quartered in their homes.

On the contrary, for more than a century, we've been officially cool with it. The Framers had their reasons, but we're a lot less spooked by the military than they were. "Part of the reason why," says the constitutional expert and Yale professor Akhil Reed Amar, "is the Civil War proved that the Army could actually be a pro-liberty, pro-freedom institution, rather than something that threatened liberty and freedom." The war may have been between the states, but the soldiers (well, at least half) were on the side of liberty—which meant that, from then on, we could be on the side of the soldiers.

During World War II, civilians regularly opened up their houses to military personnel on leave. Troops were invited in, and families were more than happy to cook a meal for an enlisted man on his way to war. Other than collecting tin, it was the least they could do.

Today, it's a lovefest. In the annual Gallup ranking of the confidence we place in our Americans institutions, no one beats the military. Nothing comes close; it has ranked #1 since 1998, and in the top two for over thirty-five years. In the poll conducted in 2010, more than three in four Americans said they had a "great deal" or "quite a lot" of confidence in the exact people the Third Amendment protects us against.

In the same poll, *the church* received less than 50 percent confidence; we officially have more faith in our soldiers than our priests—and probably more room for them at the dinner table. *The president* earned only 36 percent—hardly enough to offer him the guest bedroom. *Congress* received just 11 percent approval; they'd be lucky for a vacancy at the Motel 6.

Our troops are now our rock stars. We can't fight wars without them, and politicians can't get elected without honoring them, careful to make it clear that whichever side they're on—conservative or liberal, Republican or Democrat—they are on the side of the troops. (A distinction my former boss Bill Maher made only too late, as he exercised his First Amendment right to put his foot in it.)

These days, *We the People* don't mind *They the Soldiers* knocking on our doors. In fact, as Akhil Reed Amar points out, "we think that the Army isn't *them*, but *us*."

Better than us, I'd say. The best of us. Braver, more honorable, and—after a military education and deployment perfecting practical skills we never bothered learning—handier around the house. Most homeowners would love a few good men to stop by and change a few tires, clean a few latrines, perhaps kill a few spiders. (The uniforms have their appeal as well; I've seen how my female friends in New York act during Fleet Week.) Hey, I get it—I once spent a week hopping around Iraq under the capable escort of dozens of skilled enlisted men and women, armed with heavy artillery and light, easy banter; I felt so safe that I wanted to take one home just to tuck me in at night.

As far as the country is concerned, we no longer fear a standing army. On the contrary, we'll offer it a place to sit. Quartering soldiers isn't considered a loss of freedom at all. Far from it. We have a win-win situation: The soldier gets shelter, and we get supremely skilled labor. And really, who better to have at our home standing sentry when a Hessian mercenary swings by to claim our basement on behalf of England, just for olde times' sake.

As far as I'm concerned, *mi casa es su casa.*

Your New Third Amendment

No Soldier shall, in time of peace be quartered in any house, without the consent of the Owner. But any Soldier shall be quartered in any house, at the request of the Owner, who would be lucky to have him—because hey: free Soldier.

⭐ ⭐ ⭐

THE FOURTH AMENDMENT
Hail, Seizer!

⭐ ⭐ ⭐

HE NEXT TIME a CIA agent searches your home without probable cause, or an FBI agent taps your phone, or a dog sniffs your luggage in an airport security line, or a lawyer subpoenas the photos you posted on Facebook—you know, the ones of you partying with a Mexican drug cartel while dressed up as sexy Hitler—just do what I do.

Blame Egbert.

The flawed Fourth Amendment, which keeps us safe from "unreasonable searches and seizures" and "secure in our persons, houses, papers, and effects"—but, history shows, sometimes doesn't—is the fault of Egbert Benson, the New York State attorney general from 1777 to 1788. If Egbert, who would become a member of the very House of Representatives that ratified the Constitution, had just done what he was told, the Fourth Amendment wouldn't be the utter failure it is. If I've said it once, I've said it a thousand times: Egbert Benson is the Baron Samuel von Pufendorf of the Fourth Amendment.

Egbert has no excuse. He knew what he was supposed to do; James Madison himself had given Egbert his marching orders. The Father of the Constitution had written the version of the Fourth Amendment that he intended to be sent to the states for ratification, and he had entrusted Egbert to forward it along to the U.S. Senate: "The rights of the people to be secured," Madison had written, "from all unreasonable searches and seizures, shall not be violated by warrants issued without probable cause supported by oath or affirmation." It couldn't have been more straightforward—*there shall be no searches without a warrant.* But Egbert thought it was too weak. (Not, it should be noted, that anyone had asked him.) He wanted to limit the number of warrants issued in the first place, and he thought he could do this by changing Madison's clean language—"shall not be violated by warrants issued without probable cause"—to his own—"and no warrants *shall* be issued, but upon probable cause."

It wasn't a welcome swap; the U.S. House of Representatives rejected his version "by a considerable majority." But that didn't stop Egbert, who was, conveniently, also the chairman of the committee appointed specifically to submit the amendments to the Senate. When no one was looking, he sent his wording, not Madison's. The Senate approved it. The states ratified it.

We, unfortunately, live with it.

Hard to say which is more alarming: that Egbert, the chairman of the committee in charge of assembling the amendments, would try to subvert democracy so blatantly by slipping one by his colleagues in the House; or that no one noticed. To be sure, that a Founding Father you've never heard of would pull such a fast one, and have such a lasting impact on your right to privacy, is incredible. (Indeed, it may not actually be true. The Egbert Switcheroo is but a theory posited by some historians; the Yale professor Akhil Reed Amar instead blames House stenographer Thomas Lloyd, "the Father of American Shorthand"—and a notorious drunk—for misrecording the initial vote.) But does it matter? Either way, we're stuck with the wrong Fourth Amendment.

However it happened, the language Egbert proposed ultimately became the Fourth Amendment—"no Warrants shall issue, *but* upon probable cause."

But upon probable cause.

As buts go, that's a big but. Egbert intended to strengthen the Fourth Amendment; instead, he weakened it. He opened up a big loophole—the possibility that probable cause is only required in those cases that involve warrants—which, in this day of warrant*less* wiretaps, data mining, heat mapping, and lipstick cameras, is a loophole big enough to spy through.

Egbert Benson, seen here not trying to peek into your bedroom, he swears. Portrait by John Vanderlyn.

Egbert, next time just do as you're told.

Like an embarrassing number of other amendments (three, so far, and counting), the Fourth Amendment springs from yet another Olde Englishe legal doctrine: "The house of every one is to him as his castle and fortress," wrote the Elizabethan jurist Sir Edward Coke in 1604, "as well for his defence against injury and violence as for his repose." Put less Englishy, *a home is a man's castle*—not to be violated except by fire-breathing dragons and flaming cannonballs, *if* they have a warrant. (Many years later, it was put in downright American terms when the so-called Castle Doctrine was redefined as the "Make My Day Law," an official, legal shout-out to Clint Eastwood in a provision that permitted home-owners to use lethal force against violent, warrantless attackers who in-vade their homes.)

"Go ahead, seize my effects."

Yet history shows that even in the eighteenth century, despite the con-tinued prevalence of powdered wigs and buckled shoes, America wasn't England: At the time, we had relatively few castles. (Even today, the over-whelming majority of our castles are not royal but inflatable—"bouncy," in the parlance—the preferred domicile of birthday-cake-stuffed eight-year-olds, not peacock-meat-stuffed English noblemen.) Still, the principle of "butt out" was embraced—not because *a home is a man's castle*, but because in colonial America, where the British taxed many of the products colo-nists relied on, *a home was a man's black market.*

In other words, the home is where an American could hide all the con-traband he didn't want the king to know about.

Even many of our adored Founding Fathers, fantasized as men of peer-less virtue, were in reality a band of smugglers. By day, the Framers may have been constitution writing and nation building, but at night they were bootlegging.

Or if they weren't bootlegging, they were at least coming to the rescue of those who were. Lawyer (and future president) John Adams once defended a notorious bootlegger against charges that the scofflaw had not paid taxes to the British Parliament on his smuggled goods and had therefore violated the Townshend Acts. (He had, but so had half the colony.) It was a slam-dunk case: The scofflaw could not deny the cases of illegal French burgundy that had been found on his sloop, the *Liberty*, which had been seized by British customs agents. Nor can history deny the name of the defendant:

With Adams's help, the charges against Hancock were eventually dropped. His sloop *Liberty*, however, was never returned to him; in an especially galling extreme makeover, it was refitted to serve as HMS *Liberty* in the Royal Navy and—in what had to be considered a slap in the face— used to patrol for customs violations. That is, until it was burned in 1769 by American colonists in the waters off Newport as one of the first acts of open defiance that sparked the American Revolution.

As the colonists saw it, for too long we had been the victims of a uniquely British invention: "writs of assistance," which allowed the king's men to trespass on colonists' property and confiscate "prohibited and uncustomed" merchandise—a.k.a., the good stuff. When the writs expired, a group of colonial merchants went to court to try to block them outright. They lost, but one man in the courtroom that day, John Adams, felt in that moment "the spark in which originated the American Revolution." As he recounted it, "every man . . . appeared to me to go away, as I did, ready to take up Arms against Writs of Assistance. Then and there the child of independence was born." We would become the United States of America based largely on the idea that Britain shouldn't poke its nose into our basements and attics, where we keep our contraband and black market liquor. That's really what this was about: cheap booze.

Of all the amendments in the Bill of Rights (which was written to sell the Constitution, which was ratified to fulfill the promise of the Declaration of Independence, which was signed by notorious French wine smuggler John Hancock), the Fourth Amendment has the most ironic, perhaps even inconvenient, birth story. It was devised not so we Americans could protect one of our cherished freedoms, but so we could continue breaking the law. We were tired of the British cracking down on our illegal smuggling operations and bogarting our stash.

The problem wasn't that we were onto *them*; the problem was they were onto *us*.

THERE'S AN APP FOR *THAT*?

HENCE, WE HAVE THE FOURTH AMENDMENT—a.k.a. Egbert's Amendment, insisting that no warrants shall be issued "but" upon probable cause, and securing the people against "unreasonable searches and seizures."

Egbert is long gone; his "but" lives on. True, we no longer worry about telling British redcoats they should buzz off. And granted, even letting German shepherds sniff our baggage at an airport feels like old news. But in the intervening centuries, the Fourth Amendment has found a more formidable foe: technology. Because of the marvels of modern science, the government is now capable of spying on us without knocking on our front doors or opening our suitcases. Yet, thanks to Egbert's oversight, there's no app to remind them they might need a warrant.

In the very first Supreme Court wiretapping case, 1928's *Olmstead v. United States*, the Court ruled that "the [Fourth] Amendment cannot be extended and expanded to include telephone wires reaching to the whole world." Only the home is a man's castle—not his phone.

Roy Olmstead was a man the Founders might have admired. Not only was he devoted to public service—he was a lieutenant in the Seattle Police Department—he was also one of the most successful bootleggers in the history of the Pacific Northwest. Like John Hancock, he too had run afoul of the law, and was deemed to be in violation of the National Prohibition Act by trafficking from Canada large quantities of "intoxicating liquors" (which, we can agree, are the best kind of liquors). Olmstead, who earned his nickname of "the Good Bootlegger" by not getting involved in the unseemly trades of prostitution or gunrunning, also thought he had a foolproof plan to avoid drawing attention to his business: He carefully used the word "stuff" when describing his shipments of two hundred cases of liquor per day. Somehow the authorities, who had inserted "small wires [along] ordinary telephone wires . . . without trespass upon any property," still managed to crack his undecipherable code.

Hard not to notice the obvious irony here: Like many of the Founding Fathers, Olmstead was a bootlegger. They might have rooted for him. But times had changed for bootleggers, as had the technologies used to trap them. In his opinion, Justice Brandeis predicted that someday even wiretapping would seem quaint: "Discovery and invention have made it possible for the government, by means far more effective than stretching upon the rack, to obtain disclosure in court of what is whispered in the closet. . . . Ways may some day be developed by which the government, without removing papers from secret drawers, can reproduce them in court." The amendment written in 1789 to protect John Hancock and his illicit French wine no longer applied, in 1928, to Olmstead's intoxicating Canadian liquors.

Since that moment, the long arc of history has bent toward the government getting all up in our business, and the Fourth Amendment doing very little to stop it. We allow wiretaps. We let employers peek into our workplace computers. We let cops shine flashlights into our backseats if we've been driving too fast in the front. We let the government put GPS devices on the cars of those they merely suspect may commit a crime. We let dogs sniff our carry-ons and TSA employees pat us down at will. (If you think about it, we should be the ones charging *them* a baggage handling fee.)*

And when we protest, it is often to no avail. In 2010, when a nervous flier posted a video of himself warning a TSA agent not to "touch his junk"—only to then have his junk touched—it earned him scores of YouTube hits, but no Supreme Court case.

It's worse than you thought: These days, law enforcement employs full-body scanners not just in the security line at the airport; it also uses them in traffic on Main Street USA. Vans outfitted with backscatter X-ray gizmos currently roam the avenues of America, peering into passing vehicles. It's a civil libertarian's worst nightmare: A technology ideally suited to patrol the border and crack down on drug runners—already bad enough, in civil libertarians' eyes—is instead being used to snoop into average Americans' Hyundais as they wait at a red light.

Honestly, it would appear the Fourth Amendment doesn't have all that

* Pow! Homeland Security slam!

much to say about privacy these days. So impotent has the Fourth Amendment become in protecting our privacy that the Supreme Court has had to be supremely creative to make up for its shortcomings. In *Griswold v. Connecticut*, a 1965 Supreme Court case (and my least favorite of all the *National Lampoon Vacation* movies), Justice William O. Douglas wrote that he located the right to privacy not in the amendment, but in the vague "penumbras" and "emanations" of the other constitutional protections. Yet he chose not to identify which protections those might be. (Can't help but think he emanated it right out of his penumbra.)

The Supreme Court has even carved out official exceptions to the Fourth Amendment, including the "Special Needs Doctrine," which suggests that the Fourth Amendment always applies unless the government really, really needs it not to, and the "Reasonable Person Test," which suggests that our privacy can only be considered violated during those moments when privacy would have been expected by *a reasonable person*—as if those exist anymore. So much for Egbert's concern that warrants be few and far between. It's not hard to imagine what the future might bring; as Doc Brown might say, where we're going, we don't need warrants.*

For very good reasons, the Fourth Amendment was no match for the eleventh of September, 2001. When terrorists attacked the World Trade Center, it didn't take much convincing for Americans to accept a broadening of government powers to improve their security, and with it a litany of restrictions on their Fourth Amendment rights, in the form of the "Uniting and Strengthening America by Providing Appropriate Tools Required to Intercept and Obstruct Terrorism Act of 2001," otherwise known as— and by that I mean, *only known as*—the USA PATRIOT Act. The PATRIOT Act, a coproduction of the Bush administration and a culture of sheer panic, dealt a serious punch to the gut of the Fourth Amendment. Along with a bill updating the Foreign Intelligence Surveillance Act of 1978, it offered law enforcement agencies unprecedented leeway to search email, phone, and medical records; it authorized the treasury secretary to regulate foreign financial transactions; it loosened restrictions on foreign

---

* There are rare exceptions. In 1967, the Court did rule that a criminal gambler had his Fourth Amendment rights violated when the government spied on his conversation in a telephone booth. But let's be honest, when's the last time you used a telephone booth? Even Superman has a cell phone, and, if he's being super-honest, would probably change his clothes in the bathroom of a Starbucks.

intelligence gathering within the United States, and empowered immigration authorities to deport immigrants suspected of terrorism. It gave the government the power to subpoena the books we check out at the library. (The PATRIOT Act managed to do something not previously thought possible: piss off librarians.) If I'm not mistaken, it even let the president read the diaries of the nation's twelve-year-old girls.

Thanks to the USA PATRIOT Act, when it comes to the disintegration of Fourth Amendment protections, the genie is out of the bottle—to say nothing of what we have on tape of the genie doing in the bottle.

We saw this coming. Even a hundred years ago, Woodrow Wilson, who was no great defender of civil liberties himself and even spied on people in his own administration, was nonetheless already predicting that the Fourth Amendment would need a tune-up. "When the Constitution was framed," he wrote in 1908, "there were no railways, there was no telegraph, there was no telephone." Wilson had no idea how far he had yet to come. When he was president, there were no wiretaps. There was no Internet. There were no lipstick cameras, no recording devices, no Wikileaks. There was no wi-fi. There were no T-1 lines, there was no Twitter, there was no Norton Anti-Virus software. There was no GPS navigation, there was no motion-sensor technology, there were no X-ray Specs. There were no iPads, no e-Solutions, no Oprah. There was no Red Bull, there were no hybrid cars, there was no karaoke. No polyester, no 3-D movies, no high-speed rail. There was no Pinkberry. No online pornography. No Star Trek. No Amazon-dot-com. No control-alt-delete. No Tickle-Me-Elmo.

Wait, what was I talking about?

Oh right—the Fourth Amendment.

President Obama knows what I'm talking about. In *The Audacity of Hope,* he writes, "The constitutional text provides us with the general principle that we aren't subject to unreasonable searches by the government." But, continued the man who would soon swear to defend it, "It can't tell us the Founders' specific views on the reasonableness of an NSA computer data-mining operation." Two hundred years after Madison's draft of the Constitution was replaced by Egbert's "but," and a hundred years after President Wilson marveled at the space-age promises of the telephone, future president Obama confessed that the Constitution doesn't tell us what such freedoms—expression, privacy, security—truly mean "in the context of the Internet."

Technology has made the Fourth Amendment more relevant, and more necessary, but less helpful. There are thousands of technological innovations that let us peer into one another's lives, and still only the same fifty-four words to determine how we can protect ourselves from their invasions.* So much for resting comfortably in our castle—especially now that it's been outfitted with wi-fi.

I submit to you, it's not technology's fault. It knows not what it does. Most technologies were introduced to improve our lives—to make us faster, more efficient, more expressive, more productive, more communicative—*more perfect,* if you will; it's not their fault that almost every technology has been exploited by humans for far less noble purposes. The Internet wasn't invented for online pornography, but try telling that to anyone who has disabled their cookies. Social networking should help us increase productivity and outreach, but instead it lets us rub our most recent promotion/marriage/triathlon in the avatar faces of our high school "friends." Wikipedia was designed to be a repository for all human information, not a convenient way to let students skip the assigned reading.† Every new innovation has a regrettable side effect. (Build an automobile that goes two hundred miles per hour, soon you'll have NASCAR.)‡

The cell phone, one of the tools of the war on terror that just happens to be in the hands of almost every single American, wasn't invented to track in real time the locations of would-be terrorists, or ex-girlfriends, or Mafia bosses. When he invented the telephone, Alexander Graham Bell said only, "Mr. Watson, come here. I want to see you." He didn't add, "Because I suspect you're running a drug-smuggling ring in our basement." Yet the government has determined that cell phones are fair game, warrant or no; unreasonable search or no. Fourth Amendment be damned.

ALL YOU HAD TO DO WAS ASK

THE THING IS: We're kinda okay with that. As it turns out, we've simply grown accustomed to the government spying on us in our private mo-

---

* And to think, it could have been fifty-seven. Thanks a lot, Egbert.

† For the definitive analysis of Wikipedia, see "Wikipedia and Its Effects: An Epistemology," by Herschel Strumbacher, found in the Basement South Stacks, aisle J, shelf A2 in the Walla Walla Municipal Library in Walla Walla, Washington. JetBlue offers biweekly flights on Sundays and Thursdays. (You see my point.)

‡ Pow! NASCAR slam!

ments, and in those private moments very few of us are caught complaining loudly about Big Brother violating our private moments. Mainly because many of us, it would seem, enjoy making our private moments public. We don't care about the repercussions, because we're too busy updating our status on Facebook. Or checking in on Foursquare. Or sending a TwitPic of ourselves posing naked, or fomenting armed revolution, or fomenting armed revolution naked.

Technology has become the bane of the Fourth Amendment, and since we prefer to know where the closest sushi restaurant is, we prefer the conveniences of technology to the protections of Egbert Benson.

Certainly, those who understand technology the best—anyone born after Al Gore invented the Internet, say—have no qualms about posting their otherwise embarrassing acts on EmbarrassingActs.com. Librarians may hate the constant invasions of privacy, but teenagers don't mind too much. Ask any teenager, and they'll tell you that they subscribe to the immortal words of Benjamin Franklin, who said (actually, it may have been the immortal words of Thomas Jefferson, but the tapes were erased), "Those who would give up Essential Liberty to purchase a little Temporary Safety, deserve neither Liberty nor Safety, and are totally missing out on, like, a serious haul of Friend Requests."

We still do private things; we just don't do them privately. Because if we did, no one would see us doing them. We'd be invisible. And no one wants that, even if that's the safer way to live.

So the only question is: How do we make it official? How do we amend the Fourth Amendment in order to make it reflect our newfound willingness to surrender the privacy we once demanded? It would never fly to merely say, *From here on out, the government can do all the unreasonable searches and seizures it wants, warrant or no warrant.* There are still a few places where there is a "presumption of privacy"—the home, even in a nation of underwater mortgages and bank foreclosures, is the closest thing a man has to a castle. Nor is the solution to let the government issue as many warrants as it wants to violate those private places. Egbert Benson may have been stupid and presumptuous and conniving and insubordinate, but he wasn't crazy.

What to do?

On this, I was at a loss. The answer didn't come easily. I sought counsel, but my advisers still denied the problem. Craig Newmark, the genius behind Craigslist, suggested that I at least "tell people not to post anything they'd mind seeing on a gossip site"—sage advice, but that ship has sailed.

Jimmy Wales, the genius behind Wikipedia, sent me a great idea, but it was modified by forty-two million people before I could read it. I was getting nowhere. I considered crowdsourcing the problem, but a quick scan of every Twitter account on earth turned up nothing; most were just smart-ass comments about Kim Kardashian. Or retweets of something Kim Kardashian said. About Kim Kardashian.

I feared I might not be up to the task, until I stumbled on the Supreme Court case of *Kyllo v. United States*.

In 2001, the same year the PATRIOT Act was devised, an Oregon man named Danny Lee Kyllo argued before the Supreme Court that the Department of the Interior violated his Fourth Amendment rights when it searched his home and found more than a hundred marijuana plants he had been growing there. (The sheer number would suggest he was planning to sell some to his fellow Oregonians. One imagines that bootlegger John Hancock would have been proud.) But the government hadn't stormed Kyllo's castle. Nor did it have a warrant to even peek inside. Never, in fact, did they set foot inside Kyllo's home before his arrest. Rather, the government had used hi-tech thermal imaging devices and had determined that the amount of heat emitted from his home could only come from lamps designed to grow pot. Clever, but perhaps too cunning; in a 5–4 ruling, the Supreme Court ruled that it constituted a Fourth Amendment search, and as such should have, at the very least, required a warrant.

The Court found in favor of the Fourth Amendment—as it was written back then. But it was Justice Scalia's majority opinion that just might be the precedent we need for its rewrite: "Obtaining by sense-enhancing technology any information," Scalia wrote, "that could not otherwise have been obtained without physical 'intrusion into a constitutionally protected area' . . . constitutes a search."

Scalia could have stopped there.

He didn't.

It "constitutes a search," we wrote, "at least where the technology in question is not *in general public use*." Scalia didn't add the italics. But I suspect he meant to. Because he emphasized precisely how to rescue the Fourth Amendment. He inadvertently revealed how to update the Fourth Amendment to reflect our more contemporary mores. He provided the loophole to get around the loophole.

All we need to do is get all of these invasive technologies—thermal imaging, X-ray technology, wiretaps, unmanned aerial spy drones, orbiting communications satellites—in the hands of everyday Americans. If everyone has a thermal imaging device, then no one can *reasonably* expect that what they're doing at home is private! The best part is, we're almost there already—what, after all, is a constant Twitter feed but a self-imposed wiretap? If we don't mind when our privacy is violated—and as our constantly updated Foursquare accounts, Flickr pages, and Facebook status updates would suggest, we certainly seem not to—we just need to make sure it's done constitutionally.

By changing the Constitution.

Your New Fourth Amendment
You get a wiretap! You get a wiretap! Everybody gets a wiretap!

THE FIFTH AMENDMENT

The Amendment Guilty People Use

FOUND A TYPO in the Constitution.

It's in the Fifth Amendment, and it directly affects when, and under what circumstances, the United States government can kick you out of your own house.

You have to admit: As typos go, that's a pretty powerful typo.

And *I found it.*

Take a look:

Do you see it?

Hard to believe, I know—but it's right there in black and white (well, brown and slightly lighter brown) and it's been there for more than two hundred years. The tiniest, seemingly unintentional scuff mark, just after the *e* in "use," sunken slightly below the rest of the letters, hiding as subscript, as if it didn't even *want* to be seen. But I see it.

Surely you see it, too.

Here—take a closer look:

Not quite?

How about this:

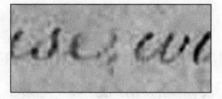

Still nothing? Well then, you'll just have to take my word for it. It's a barely perceptible scratch, a tiny smudge that for the past two centuries has masqueraded as a comma, a comma that does nothing less than change the meaning of an amendment to the Constitution of the United States of America. Specifically, it alters the Takings Clause of the Fifth Amendment establishing eminent domain—the government's right to take your private property and turn it public: a park, a subway, a new shining city hall on a hill, the hill where your family used to live but where now stands a highway exit ramp.

Admittedly, I wasn't the first to find it. Constitutional scholars have been debating its presence for a decade or so. There was even a subplot on *The West Wing* about it. But considering how faint it is, I'd say that just finding it, on a parchment full of similar-looking pockmarks, feels like an accomplishment.

And okay, it's not technically a *typo* in the modern *whoops-I-pressed-the-wrong-key* sense—typewriters weren't invented until the 1870s.* The Bill of Rights was written, by hand, long before. What is it, then? A quillo? Just an unintentional speck of ink dripped from an errant cufflink inadvertently dipped in a nearby inkwell? If we're just hypothesizing here, we should consider the most obvious explanation: that that faint dot is where the sheep, having sacrificed its skin for the cause of America, was nicked, ever so slightly, as it tried to leap over a spiked fence—when, along with its owner, it was kicked off its cherished land to make way for a new highway exit ramp. (Oh, the irony.)

The National Archives—which, let's be honest, wouldn't want to see their cherished document embroiled in any more controversy than it has already stoked, and would therefore be complicit in the obvious cover-up—wants visitors to believe it's an intentional comma. Their official transcript allows no such debate: "nor shall private property be taken for public

---

* And if you truly wanted to replicate that snazzy constitutional script, you'd have to wait until 1961, when IBM introduced the IBM Selectric I, with a "revolutionary" selection of custom fonts.

use [*comma*] without just compensation." But history isn't so sure. Over the years, the clause has been printed—in books, journals, and broadsheets—as often without the comma as with it. And if you ask me, it's suspicious, on even an aesthetic level. Spacing-wise, there doesn't seem room for a comma, especially one that might somehow make it easier for the government to seize my house.* (Surely that would warrant a more emphatic piece of punctuation—an exclamation point, perhaps. Or a double exclamation point. Or the rarely-used triple exclamation point.)

Smudge or comma—does it matter? Apparently it does! Smart people certainly think so!! Law professor Tom Merrill, who is not only a Rhodes scholar but a former clerk for the late Supreme Court justice Harry A. Blackmun,[†] believes that whether there is or is not a comma would either affirm or not affirm Madison's intention that the words "for public use" modifies the word "taken." In other words, houses taken for the public use are merely a subset of the houses the government could take if it so wished. If it wished, it could take houses because it's broke, or it's Monday, or it just feels like it.

In other words: *!!!*

Scary to think all this depends on a comma that is really just a smudge.[‡]

---

* I choose not to notice that the rest of the sentence, "without just compensation," is increasingly crammed together as well—as if it were written by a schoolchild writing a Mother's Day card without realizing he's running out of room to tell his mother he "lovesherverymuch."

† I also appreciate that he's the Charles Keller Beekman Professor of Law at Columbia Law School, which is just across New York's Central Park, where I am currently sitting under a tree writing these words, the world's best park made possible only through—you guessed it—the "public use" eminent domain power described in the Takings Clause. The one with the smudge.

‡ I confess, this captivating question of "Is there a typo in the Constitution?" distracts from a more important question regarding the Fifth Amendment and when exactly the government can take your house: Namely, "*Hold on a sec, the government can take my house?!*" Yes, it can—and no longer merely for "public use." In 2005, the Supreme Court upheld the right of the town of New London, Connecticut, to seize private homes—an entire neighborhood, in fact—but not to turn it into an off-ramp for a much-needed highway. Rather, to hand over the real estate to Pfizer, the largest pharmaceutical company in the world. The decision was applauded the very next day as "a welcome vindication of cities' ability to act in the public interest," according to *The New York Times*—a paper whose current gleaming headquarters, coincidentally enough, is also a product of the same kind of economic-based eminent domain. (A funny grace note, perhaps. But this one is funnier: Upset with the Supreme Court's decision, citizens in Plainfield, New Jersey—where Justice Stephen Breyer owned a home—launched a campaign to seize it to

And that it took two hundred years to find it. And that the National Archives is trying to cover it up. Now I appreciate why the National Archives only let me scan the original copy for a few moments before nudging me along. They were afraid I might discover a semicolon that dissolves the Executive Branch.

★ ★ ★

Whichever version of the Takings Clause you prefer—smudge or comma, accidental or intentional, small concern regarding property rights or huge conspiracy contrived by the National Archives—it is but one of many provisions guaranteed to Americans in the jam-packed Fifth Amendment: the right to due process of law; the right to a grand jury in a "capital, or otherwise infamous" crime; and the right not to be tried twice for the same crime.

They are protections inspired by language in the Magna Carta itself: "no freemen shall be taken or imprisoned or disseised or exiled or in any way destroyed"—I understand "imprisoned" and "exiled," and can decipher what "disseised" is in context, although I'm most concerned that "destruction" of freemen was on the menu back then—"nor will we go upon him nor send upon him, except by the lawful judgment of his peers or by the law of the land." We are a nation of men, but we are a land of laws.

So then: due process, grand juries, and double jeopardy. With these, I hereby take no quarrel. Should any of us "be deprived of life, liberty, or property, without due process of law"? I'd say not—rules are rules, and even the government (rather, especially the government) should have to abide by them. Should "capital, or otherwise infamous" crimes be tried before a grand jury, rather than just a regular penny-ante jury? Yes, sir. Go big or go home, I say. And the prohibition against double jeopardy makes sense to me as well: The rule of law shouldn't be "Heads you win, tails we flip again."

Anyhow, this is all beside the point. Let's be honest: None of these provisions are why we've become so familiar with this particular amendment over the past few decades. Even the question of whether there's an errant comma in the Constitution—a phantom comma, a ghost comma!—isn't

---

create a new public use area. They had already picked out a name: "Constitutional Park.") Soon, however, the backlash had gone from personal to national: Within a year, twenty-five states had passed reforms to curb abuse of eminent domain. It's hard to imagine a more divisive issue; exactly half of America had determined that eminent domain had been taken a step too far.

the most memorable feature of this amendment. No, the average American knows this particular amendment for one reason, and one reason only—because they've heard it countless times, when an accused criminal or a suspected sinner, facing a congressional committee or a suspicious girl-friend, leans into a microphone or across the dinner table and says four simple words:

"I plead the Fifth."

THE WITNESS SELF-PROTECTION PROGRAM

WHEN I WAS A CHILD, my older brother Keith and I were very competitive. In sports, in academics, in who got the lead in the school play. The competition was especially acute, and traumatic, when we played the board game Monopoly. When he'd win, he had a typically "older brother" way of celebrating his victory: After throwing his fake money in the air, he would tackle me, throw me on my back, sit on my stomach, grab my wrists with his hands, and proceed to pummel me with my own fists, all the while cautioning me against the very thing he was forcing me to do: "Stop hitting yourself! Stop hitting yourself!"

That's why I have a soft spot for the Fifth Amendment. To this day, I treasure what the Fifth Amendment's right against self-incrimination guarantees us: We can finally stop hitting ourselves.

And that's why I'm so sad to see what has become of the Fifth Amendment—even if it took five hundred years.

Back in the sixteenth and seventeenth centuries, the English Court of High Commission routinely administered "oaths ex-officio" to accused criminals about to face trial. Oath takers were bound by a sacred compact to tell the truth—the judicial equivalent of Wonder Woman's magic lasso. Anyone who refused to take the oath? Their very refusal was considered an admission of guilt. So forget innocent until proven guilty; defendants accused of a crime in England had to testify against themselves, or be presumed guilty.

It was hardly a fair fight.

Would-be immigrants to America—eager for a new life with a new set of rules in the New World—weren't so thrilled with that old arrangement. Though still bound by the oath, they were reluctant to reveal any secrets of their Puritan sect, which, they believed, could withstand persecution only through tight-lipped secrecy. When Englishman John Lilburne, a twenty-year-old Puritan also known as Freeborn John (so named because he believed there are rights bestowed on us at birth, rather than by governments—and apparently that earned you a nickname back then) was called to testify before a tribunal in 1637 under the charge of printing unlicensed books, he called the whole system out of order. Asked to dish some dirt on his fellow Puritans, he stood and insisted that he would not be "ensnared by answering things concerning other men." For his insubordination, he was flogged and pilloried and suffered other cruel and unusual punishments that the (spoiler alert) Eighth Amendment—a century and an ocean away—had yet to prohibit.

The people rallied to his defense—perhaps not in time to stop the flogging and the pillorying, but as soon as they could, they swear. They formed the Levellers, a political movement that drew up thirteen demands and presented them to Parliament as—in a typically British example of too-polite understatement—*The Humble Petition of Many Thousands*. Among their humble demands: If it's not too much trouble, if you wouldn't mind, could you be a sport and please stop making us incriminate ourselves? Let us plead the Fifth. (Although technically, in their humble petition, it was the Third.) Sure enough, when Oliver Cromwell's army not-so-humbly destroyed the vested power of the Church a few years later, one of its first actions was to declare that "no person . . . shall have power . . . to enforce any person . . . to answer any interrogation against himself." (That's a lot of ellipses, but that's how they talk. This is, after all, the country that sent us Hugh Grant.)

By the time the American Framers wrote the Fifth Amendment, they weren't keen, either, on the idea that we should be expected to help our accusers incriminate us. They believed every individual should be granted the human right to give full voice to his defense, and his defense only. They designed the Fifth Amendment, according to Professor Amar, to protect "the innocent but inarticulate defendant, who might be made to look guilty if subject to crafty questioning from a trained inquisitor." Thus: No person "shall be compelled in any criminal case to be a witness against himself." No persons, and no society, no matter how guilty, shall be forced to hit themselves.

But by my clock, the last time the Fifth Amendment did what it was supposed to do—let an innocent man refuse to answer on the grounds that it might falsely incriminate him—was sixty years ago.

"ARE YOU NOW OR HAVE YOU EVER BEEN A MEMBER OF THE COMMUNIST PARTY?"

THAT WAS THE DECADE when a group of screenwriters known as the "Hollywood 10" were brought before the House Un-American Activities Committee to be bullied and browbeaten by anticommunist crusader and all-around not-nice-guy Senator Joseph McCarthy.

It went a little something like this:

```
                     INT. HUAC HEARING ROOM—DAY
           TEN SCREENWRITERS sit at a TABLE, looking like
           COMMUNISTS, for all we know.


                          SEN. MCCARTHY
           Are you now or have you ever been a member of the
           Communist Party?


                          TEN SCREENWRITERS
           We plead the Fifth.


                          SEN. MCCARTHY
           Aha! Communists!
```

The point is: A lot of good it did them. At the exact moment they needed it most, the Fifth Amendment fell short. Although it saved their breath, it did not come to their rescue. Not only were their actions still deemed illegal, all ten were jailed for contempt. Worse, they were blacklisted, suspected of being Soviet sympathizers despite their protestations (or perhaps because of them), and they struggled to find work in the decades to come. Senator McCarthy had successfully branded them "Fifth Amendment Communists."

Besides, even if the Fifth had done its job, should we really be forced to reach so far back into history to justify any amendment? The persecution of the screenwriters is history as ancient to us as the persecution of the Puritans was to the screenwriters.*

---

* The seventeenth century may be separated from the 1950s by three hundred years, but think about it: How far removed are the 1950s from today? A whole millennium!

Since then, the Fifth Amendment has proven itself worse than weak; it has been perverted, by defendants far less worthy of its noble pedigree. Since then, Oliver North has pleaded the Fifth. Mark Fuhrman has pleaded the Fifth. The late disgraced Enron executive Ken Lay has pleaded the Fifth. The executives of oil giant BP, after polluting the ocean, pleaded the Fifth. After they crashed the White House state dinner without an invitation, and after they left the cast of the reality show *The Real House-wives of D.C.*, and after they were subpoenaed to testify to Congress on their brazen security breach, Tareq and Michaele Salahi, a.k.a. "the Salahis"—you guessed it—pleaded the Fifth.* Think about it: When was the last time a genuinely faultless person pleaded the Fifth?

The Fifth Amendment was intended to help shield the innocent, or at least those who might be innocent. Now it's the amendment guilty people use.

The Fifth Amendment was once rooted in the noble tradition of defending the innocent from being "imprisoned or disseised or exiled"; in stacking the burden of proof on the prosecution; at the very least, in letting helpless victims stop hitting themselves. Now we know the Fifth Amendment not when it's celebrated, or even when it's invoked, but when it's *pleaded*. It's what guilty people rely on to keep from having to lie in a courtroom, to avoid hearing themselves say: *Yeah, you got me.* Even Ken Lay, upon pleading the Fifth, pleaded with his interlocutors not to get the wrong impression: "I am deeply troubled about asserting these rights," he said, "because it may be perceived by some that I have something to hide." Gee, *you think*? As Justice Brandeis once said, "Silence is often evidence of the most persuasive character."

I recognize I may be outnumbered on this one. I recognize the Supreme Court ruled, 7 to 2, in *Griffin v. California* that a prosecutor could *not* ask a jury to infer guilt from a defendant's refusal to testify in his own defense.†

But isn't it time we admit the obvious? Pleading the Fifth is the action of a guilty man. Pleading the Fifth is an admission that you have no defense, that none of the other dozens of Articles or Amendments in the entire Constitution of the United States can come to your rescue; you are

---

* So frustrated was one congressman by their constant evasions and non-answers, he asked, "Are you here today, right now? You got an answer from your attorney on that?"

† Even John Grisham would have to admit—if only as a matter of legal theater in a dramatic murder trial—that the prosecutor made a compelling argument: "Essie Mae is dead. She can't tell you her side of the story. The defendant won't."

just that irredeemable. If you're pleading the Fifth, odds are you're hiding the body. Odds are you did something. At the least, someone should tackle you, grab your wrists, and make you start hitting yourself.

YOUR NEW FIFTH AMENDMENT
No person shall be held to answer for a capital crime, unless on an indictment of a Grand Jury; nor shall any person be subject for the same offense to be twice put in jeopardy of life or limb; but if any person says, "I plead the Fifth," they shall Go directly to Jail. They shall not Pass Go. They shall not Collect $200. Whereupon, they shall not be allowed to stop hitting themselves.

THE SIXTH AMENDMENT

Establishing Your Right to Be Judged by a Jury Comprised of People Exactly Like You, and Really, Congratulations on That

IT IS WITH NO LACK OF DISGUST at my own behavior that I come to this unfortunate conclusion: If ever, by some accident of fate or tear in the fabric of the cosmos, I somehow ended up serving on a jury levying ultimate judgment *on myself,* there could conceivably come a time when I would, during the course of that service, be either so righteous or so distracted or, worse, so sick of the whole system being so out of order, that I, as but a part of "We the Jury" in the case of *The People vs. Kevin Bleyer,* would, for the sake of expediency, vengeance, reparations, or just to get away from these twelve angry people (myself included) and home in time for *Law & Order,* find the defendant, Kevin Bleyer—a perfectly innocent man, mind you—guilty, guilty, guilty in the first degree.

Kevin Bleyer the juror would have no mercy on Kevin Bleyer the defendant. Because life in prison might be purgatory, but jury duty is a special kind of hell. And there's no reason we *both* have to suffer.

I say this from experience. I am in my third day of serving on a jury in the New York criminal court system. It has, I admit, been an unanticipated roadblock on my self-imposed journey to rewrite the Constitution, but it is also—as anyone who has ever found a summons in their mailbox will attest, after muttering their choicest curse word and regretting having registered to vote when they moved into the neighborhood—an unavoidable one. Even men on the most monumental missions—astronauts in the final phase of training for a moon walk, researchers a chemical reaction shy of a cure for cancer, patriots rewriting the Constitution of the United States—get called for jury duty. And while some can defer once or twice, a patriot ultimately shows up.

I showed up.

And now I'm sitting in the deliberation room, staring incredulously at my fellow jurors and praying to God that my own fate will never be in the hands of a group like this one, a jury of my peers. A jury of Me the People.

★ ★ ★

Three mornings ago, like a patriot—nay, *as* a patriot—I arrived in the lobby of the flagship courthouse of the New York State Unified Court System a full twenty minutes early. I was eager and prepared to serve.

And yet I took my seat in the jurors' holding room on the eleventh floor fifteen minutes late. My tardiness, of course, was not my fault; the intervening thirty-five minutes entailed an obstacle course of humanity—beginning with a longer-than-even-is-to-be-reasonably-expected wait at the lobby metal detectors (I triggered the alarm for no apparent reason, prompting the feckless guard standing sentry to advise me to, and I quote, "just kinda *run* through it") and continuing with the unexpected delay at the bank of eight lobby elevators, of which only three were apparently in working condition. Scores of plaintiffs, defendants, defendants' girlfriends, plaintiff's boyfriends, clerks, stenographers, the guy in charge of fixing the vending machines, and we the prospective jurors shifted our weight, stared at the numbers seemingly fixed on the high floors, and groused under our breaths variations on the same theme:

This whole system is out of order. Starting with the elevators.

It was the first piece of evidence that the fundamental right to a speedy trial, as provided by the Sixth Amendment to the United States Constitution, doesn't exactly guarantee the right to speedy jury duty.

Yet although my jury experience began with this inauspicious start—elevators delayed is justice denied, I say—the sluggishness of the court system is not my fundamental problem with the jury system. That's just a gambit to win you over to my side. That's just my opening argument. That's just my attempt to work myself into your good graces so that you'll be amenable and suggestible when I tell you: The Sixth Amendment of the United States Constitution is guilty of a far more serious charge.

THE SIXTH SENSELESS

MAY IT PLEASE THE COURT, the Sixth Amendment seems harmless enough, does it not? It is short, and straightforward, and starts out with one of the most peculiar uses of the word "enjoy" that anyone, most certainly a defendant accused of a crime, is likely to encounter. "In all criminal prosecutions," it begins, "the accused shall enjoy the right to a speedy public trial." Um, *enjoy*? As if it were possible to enjoy a trial as one would a theme park, or a delicious meal, or a trip to Spain. We can agree a bandage ripped off quickly is merciful, but enjoyable?

Then come the many clauses.

First up, the showstopper: the Right to Trial by Jury Clause, which decrees that your trial shall be decided "by an impartial jury of the State and district wherein the crime shall have been committed." Hear that, criminals? Your friends and neighbors will be your last hope or worst nightmare. Think globally, be judged locally—it's only fair.

Next, the Arraignment Clause: You, the accused, shall "be informed of the nature and cause of the accusation" against you. This way, there's no confusion. This also makes sense: You'd hate to go to jail for life because of some crazy mix-up with the defendant in the jury room next door.

Followed by the Confrontation Clause: In a trial, the accused has the right to be "confronted with the witnesses against him"—legalese for "Oh, yeah? I dare you to say that to my *face*."

And finally, the Compulsory Process and Right to Counsel Clauses. The first entitles any accused defendant to a "compulsory process for obtaining witnesses in his favor"—your right to get people to vouch for you—and the second guarantees every defendant "the Assistance of Counsel for his defence"—what's known as your right to "lawyer up."

So again, a short amendment, but packed with crucial, basic constitutional guarantees for defendants at every step of their trials. Which means a long wait at the elevators.

Should we be grateful? Absolutely—especially when we compare our American system to a drawn-out trial in private, a specialty of European legal systems and novellas by Franz Kafka. Or a verdict that hinges solely on a defendant's ability to win a battle or a duel—a specialty of Germanic legal systems of yesteryear—or to withstand a great ordeal, such as walking over hot ploughshares, or removing a rock from a pot of molten lead, or floating after being tossed into a river while tied up in a bag—a specialty of bygone European legal systems and Monty Python sketches. We should be proud that our speedy, public jury trials are speedy and public.

It's the *jury* part I'm not so sure about. Oh sure, juries are a celebrated feature of the American justice system. And true, among the "facts . . . submitted to a candid world" in the Declaration of Independence was a complaint against King George "for depriving us in many cases, of the benefits of a trial by jury." But a jury also found O. J. Simpson not guilty. And after three days serving on one, I've come to recognize that in our justice system—among all the ways that justice could be disserved—it's the jury itself that's the injustice.

I should know. As I said, I'm Juror Number 7.

And between you and me, I'm getting pretty tired of Jurors Numbers 1 through 6 and 8 through 12.

★ ★ ★

Just so we're clear: William Penn had the best of intentions. He couldn't have known that when he was a defendant, he would inspire an entire movement based on defendants' rights, leading to our current jury system. When Penn—the English philosopher who ultimately converted to Quakerism, fled to America in 1682, and purchased the settlement that became the Commonwealth of *Penn*sylvania—was a twenty-one-year-old preacher in England, he was arrested for violating the Conventicles Act of 1670, which made it illegal for any religious group (other than the Church of England, that is) to assemble. In response, he merely asked to see a copy of the charges against him. When the judge refused, Penn pressed his case publicly and loudly. And in doing so, he sparked a populist uprising, setting in motion the defendants' rights cause that ultimately led, in 1787, to the Sixth Amendment in the Bill of Rights.

A laudable act of activism, by any measure. And a principled one: When Penn found himself in the Tower of London, he refused to recant even though the Bishop of London had promised him freedom in return. "I owe my conscience to no mortal man," Penn said. "My prison shall be my grave before I budge a jot."

I know how he feels. It is, after all, Penn's personal stubbornness that appeals to me. Because four hundred years later, in Jury Room 5 of the New York State Unified Court System, I am being asked to budge a jot.

And although the jot I am being asked to budge is far less consequential, and I am being asked by eleven of my "peers" rather than a Bishop of London, I am no less upset about it.

I owe my conscience to no fellow juror.

★ ★ ★

Ours is a fairly straightforward case—a twenty-two-year-old white man is accused of selling a small amount of heroin to an undercover police officer.

A typical "buy-and-bust," they keep saying. Over the last three days, the officer has testified, the accused has invoked his Fifth Amendment right against self-incrimination (which, as we know, means he must be guilty), and a surprisingly young lab technician named Kamiko has explained in great detail how the substance in the baggie in question is, unquestionably, heroin. The court-appointed attorney assigned to defend the accused hasn't done his client any favors either; he has been flustered and confused, and at one point even forgot his client's name. His lack of skill brings to mind the words of Supreme Court Justice William Brennan: "I cannot accept the notion," he said, "that lawyers are one of the punishments a person receives merely for being accused of a crime." At the very least, it makes one question how much of a favor the Sixth Amendment does this alleged criminal in guaranteeing him a lawyer.

Frankly, I think he did it. I suspect this defendant did, in fact, commit this crime. Almost all signs—a *preponderance of the evidence,* I think they call it—point to his guilt.

Yet they don't point all the way. Beyond a *reasonable* doubt? Probably—but not all the way. The most glaring concern for my fellow jurors: There's no eyewitness other than the cop himself. The most glaring concern for me: Even the cop admits he made a mistake in protocol—he lost track of the drugs for a few moments. Which, once we finally retreat to the jurors' deliberation room number 5, is about how long it takes for my fellow jurors to move to acquit. A few moments, at most. I am inclined to debate a little while longer—though only a little, if only to make certain we're comfortable with our decision—but the rest of the jury thinks a few moments is quite long enough, thank you very much. They have jobs to get to, families to see. They are ready to acquit this man. They want me to budge a jot.

But I wonder: After three days, we can't afford ten more minutes to make sure that justice is served? Are my fellow jurors that impatient? I mean, who the heck are these people?

★ ★ ★

They are, whether I like it or not, my peers.

They are, as the Sixth Amendment guarantees, "an impartial jury of the State and district wherein the crime shall have been committed."

They are, said Thomas Jefferson in a 1789 letter to Thomas Paine, "the only anchor ever yet imagined by man, by which a government can be held to the principles of its constitution."

They are also, it must be granted, the only dozen who didn't escape being plucked from a pool of over a hundred potential candidates, a shockingly high percentage of whom claimed during jury selection—almost all successfully—that they had either a direct conflict of interest with the crime or some other good excuse to leave.*

The instructional video at the beginning of the day (for some reason, hosted by television's Diane Sawyer) explained the process of jury selection, or voir dire, which prerecorded Diane helpfully points out is "a French phrase that means, literally, 'to see them say.'" (I half expected her to ask us to use it in a sentence.) The idea behind voir dire is to give prosecuting and defense attorneys the chance to pick a jury "they feel will be most receptive to their arguments." But with so many getting excused for such paltry excuses, it's hard not to think the jurors are doing the picking. So, depending on your perspective, the twelve men and women sitting in judgment on this drug case are either the most devoted patriots in town—myself included!—or the fools too stupid to get out of jury duty.

Myself included.

The modern jury of "twelve angry men"—rather than just three, or two and a half, or more than twenty—comes courtesy of Constitutional Convention delegate David Brearley. As chief justice of New Jersey in 1780, Brearley ruled that a conviction against a smuggler should be dismissed because the jury numbered only six, thereby violating the state's constitutional right to a trial by (full) jury. Those six found the smuggler guilty; it's possible, Brearley surmised, that six more might have found him innocent. (The magic number of twelve is more tradition than calculus, dating back to the ancient Welsh king Morgan of Gla-Morgan, who established trial by jury in A.D. 725 and who declared, "For as Christ and his twelve apostles were finally to judge the world, so human tribunals should be composed of the king and twelve wise men." Which sounds even more compelling in a Welsh brogue.)

Brearley's decision not only came to the defense of juries, it is cited as one of the first to affirm the controversial power of *judicial review,* the right of a court to decide whether a law is constitutional. (Don't be impressed. Brearley is also the same delegate who, in order to allay his fear that bigger states would have too much power under the new Constitution, suggested

---

* Among the many half-baked, likely invented, and surprisingly successful reasons for dismissal: "My father was a drug dealer." "As an actor on Broadway, I once researched the role of a cop." "My religion doesn't believe in judgment." "I may do heroin someday." "I slept weird last night."

spreading out a map of the United States on the Convention floor and re-drawing it, right then and there, into thirteen states of equal size. Think about that the next time the Supreme Court decides not to commute your death sentence. Their right to do so comes from the guy who thought Rhode Island should be as big as Virginia.)

But that's ancient history. Over the last twenty minutes, not to mention the last seventy-two hours, one thing has become clear regarding the twelve angry (and frustrated, and exhausted, and impatient, and patriotic, and, let's admit it, foolish) men and women in this jury room, one thing that the Framers of the Sixth Amendment couldn't have anticipated, and surely didn't intend: namely, that no matter what had transpired over the last three days, this "impartial jury"—whether we be six men, or twelve men, or twelve hundred men—would never have found this defendant guilty, not in a million years.

LADIES AND GENTLEMEN OF THE JURY, HAVE YOU REACHED A VERDICT? GOOD, NOW LET'S BEGIN THE TRIAL

MIND YOU, there are very good reasons why some guilty men should go free. Or at least, there *were*. Back in 1735, when the newspaper editor John Peter Zenger printed seditious criticisms of the governor of New York, a jury rightly decided that the law was unjust—and that sedition ain't so se-ditious if it's true. Before the Civil War, many juries refused to return freed slaves to Southern, slave-owning states, even though the Fugitive Slave Act required them to do so. During Prohibition, three out of five juries refused to convict tipplers who merely had an illicit drink at a speakeasy—one assumes three out of five jurors were running a tab themselves.

This right of a jury to ignore a law it disagrees with—now known as *jury nullification*—even saved Dr. Spock. The famed pediatrician (not, sorry to disappoint, the famed Vulcan) had been convicted of abetting draft dodg-ers during the Vietnam War, but by jurors who had been directly instructed by the judge to *not* vote their consciences. When a U.S. court of appeals heard the case, it determined that the judge had committed a "prejudicial error" in hamstringing the jury. Spock's conviction was overturned. The right of the jury to vote its conscience trumped the judge's apparent need to stick it to Dr. Spock. When stupid laws violate natural laws, or moral laws, many juries feel obligated to, essentially, break the law, by ignoring it or pretending it doesn't exist.

As I sit in the deliberation room and feel the glare of the impatient jurors waiting for me to go along, I grant it's possible that a few of the jurors eager to acquit on this minor drug-bust case are falling into the great history of jury nullification from Zenger to Spock. Is Juror Number 2 quietly protesting a history of targeted racism by the police? Maybe, though I suspect not—the defendant is white. Is Juror Number 12 secretly, even subconsciously, making a stand against drug laws, as anti-Prohibitionists did for alcohol? Possibly, but I doubt it.

Juror Number 7 can't know for sure. And frankly, I wouldn't begrudge them if they did. Jury nullification seems unfair on its face—I believe in playing by the rules, and the rules say it's unfair—but as the English jurist William Blackstone put it in 1765, the jury's power to nullify a law is "the most transcendent privilege which any subject can enjoy"—a much better use of "enjoy," I must say. Any subject can rest assured "that he cannot be affected either in his property, his liberty, or his person, but by the unanimous consent of twelve of his neighbors and equals"—no matter how, ultimately, those twelve come to their decision. And if I know anything about Juror Number 7, it's that he would never try to revoke someone's transcendent privilege.

That's just not the kind of guy he is. He's no buzzkill.

★ ★ ★

But that's not what I'm talking about anyhow.

I'm not talking about the many very good reasons why, historically, juries have refused to send a guilty man to jail. I'm talking about the one very bad reason. The one that is happening before my eyes.

When I see an injustice unremedied, I can't just sit back and watch a guilty Constitution play the innocent. I must throw myself at the mercy of the court, and state my case against the Sixth Amendment.

Your Honor, I'm talking about the fact that for at least three of these jurors—I'm looking at you, Jurors Number 6, 9, and 10—there is no amount of solid evidence or compelling argument that the prosecutor could have submitted to a candid world (or to this sworn-to-be-impartial jury) that would have convinced them he had the right guy. From the second we walked into the deliberation room, the cynics took charge. The skeptics commanded the conversation. Where's the smoking gun? Where's the DNA match? Where's the unique, perfectly rendered fingerprint?

To put it plainly: These people have watched too much *CSI*.

They're no fools, they'll insist; they are far too informed about what kind of evidence the truly guilty are confronted with in television courtrooms—CGI reenactments, laser mapping of entry wounds, handwriting identification, bite-mark analysis, fingerprints, thumbprints, footprints, earprints, noseprints—to be convinced by simply "the facts of the case." No, sir, unless someone produces the kind of smoking gun they expect—an inimitable cross section of a hair, an incriminating angle of entry, an exhausted bullet signed "With Love, Yours in Guilt, the Defendant"—they can't be convinced. Not these experts; they've seen all the coolest episodes. They know all the tricks.

I haven't diagnosed a new problem; it's just the first time I have experienced firsthand what prosecutors like me have been complaining about for over a decade. It even has a name: "the CSI Effect." Jurors now have highly unrealistic expectations of forensic techniques and, worse, expect airtight cases with evidence so concise, convincing, and overwhelming that they can, without a sliver of doubt or a moment's hesitation, deliver a slam-dunk conviction without a second thought. They don't want to be bothered with the facts—that DNA testing takes weeks, not hours, and, despite what TV insists, is not always conclusive. That forensic evidence is often neither necessary, nor available, nor affordable for a case with such small stakes. That you don't always get absolute satisfaction just because you think you deserve it, and because they always do on TV.

Your Honor, consider your sworn duty to the Sixth Amendment. The group of eleven Manhattanites sitting at the table with me isn't "an impartial jury of the State and district *wherein the crime shall have been committed*," even though the crime shall have been committed in Manhattan. They may be locals, but this jury lives in Hollywood.

Consider: The cop testified under oath that the defendant accepted his money, and the defendant didn't object; my fellow jurors wondered why there was no security camera footage showing the transaction. (On television, there are unlimited security cameras.) For her part, lab tech Kamiko couldn't have been more positive: The substance in the baggie was most definitely heroin. Yet I sense that a couple jurors wouldn't have been convinced of its heroin-ness unless they had been allowed to sample it.

Your Honor, I submit to you that had television been around in 1925, the jury in the Scopes Monkey Trial might have sent Scopes directly to jail—unless Clarence Darrow had rendered a CGI animation depicting the fast-motion evolution of the chimpanzee. I submit to you that David

Brearley was right, in a sense: Six more jurors might have found the smuggler innocent from the start—especially if they were a Nielsen family.

We have, I fear, become a *not-unless-I-see-it-with-my-own-two-eyes* culture. And while a healthy skepticism is one thing, intransigent knee-jerk disbelief based on nothing more than an episode of procedural television starring David Caruso is quite another. It's certainly not what David Brearley fought and died for.*

Therefore I offer my amendment, and I rest my case.

YOUR NEW SIXTH AMENDMENT

In all criminal prosecutions, the accused shall enjoy the right of a speedy and public trial by an impartial jury of his Peers—but only those peers who were smart enough to avoid jury duty yet chose not to, have never watched any of the many *CSI*s, Miami, New York or otherwise, or at least have the good sense to know that the rules are different in Hollywood. If you're gonna nullify a cherished law, do it for a better reason than your TiVo told you to.

---

* Technically, Brearley fought for American independence, and he died of unknown causes having nothing to do with David Caruso. But until we see the evidence exonerating Caruso, perhaps we should bring him in for questioning.

☆ ☆ ☆

THE SEVENTH AMENDMENT
Yes, There Is One

☆ ☆ ☆

RATHER, THERE *WAS* ONE.

The Seventh Amendment to the United States Constitution enjoys only one notable distinction: No one in the history of America has ever read it, cited it, or knows what it does.*

And the last thing we need in our new Constitution is an amendment that no one has read, cited, or bothered to remember.†

Our Constitution deserves better than that. We deserve better than that.

So:

YOUR NEW SEVENTH AMENDMENT
Nulle and Voide.

---

* Upon greater investigation, apparently the Seventh Amendment guarantees a jury trial for any civil case where "the value in controversy" exceeds "twenty dollars." Setting aside whether it's appropriate to discuss money at a time like this—James Madison, have you no sense of occasion? This is a bill of rights, not a bill for lunch—it would seem the update is obvious. "Twenty dollars" in 1787 terms must be, what, a zillion dollars now? (Note to Editor: please check on this.) So there you go: From here on out, everybody gets a jury if they're suing for a zillion dollars.

† Having consulted my editor, I should amend my numbers. Apparently by a "dollar," the Founders meant a *Spanish milled dollar* (if you ask me, they might have made that clear in the first place), which was established by the Coinage Act of 1792 as "three hundred and seventy-one grains and four sixteenth parts of a grain of pure, or four hundred and sixteen grains of standard silver." Or, at today's bullion-to-greenbacks exchange rate, about 23 bucks. So "twenty dollars" of the 1792 variety really means 460 simoleons of the modern sort. But you know what? I'm no fan of juries (for the reasons stated in the previous amendment), so I'm gonna stick with a zillion dollars. A zillion dollars buys you a jury.

THE EIGHTH AMENDMENT

Cruel, I Get; but What's So Wrong with Unusual?

HECADE AGO, I was sent to jail.

I had committed no crime. I had done nothing wrong. No jury of my peers had found me guilty. Yet I had been dispatched to Arizona's Maricopa County Correctional Facility to spend my days with some of that state's most notorious miscreants and convicted criminals. They had robbed banks, stolen cars, kidnapped children. They were in for aggravated assault, indecent exposure, breaking and entering, possession of narcotics, and attempted murder.

My offense? I was a television writer.

The show I was working on, *Politically Incorrect with Bill Maher,* was gearing up to do a week of episodes exploring issues of crime and punishment, and the executive producers thought it would be clever to tape them on location from a jail—because it was fascinating, because it was timely, and, let's be honest, because it was sweeps. Sweeps—that occasional time of year when it seems like a good idea to spend a week on location either on a beach in Hawaii or behind bars in Arizona.

We chose behind bars in Arizona. And we chose me to send there. *Mahalo!*

The panels that week would feature a mixture of inmates and guards discussing what life was like in jail, so it was my job to wander the halls of the jail, preinterviewing the inmates and discerning which among them might be "good on television." Like a casting director—one who, it would seem, had gotten seriously lost—I was looking for people with star quality. I was on the hunt for the few inmates who had "it"—while hoping that "it" wasn't a shiv with my name on it. Mine wasn't an easy assignment; I hadn't been announced, I was barely escorted, and I was outnumbered by men twice my size.

A dozen years later, I still wonder how I had the courage—not to mention the permission—to walk up to perfect strangers who also happened to be convicted criminals and whisper, "Psst. Hey, you. If you had thirty seconds on national television, what would you say?" (It won't surprise you that most answers were a version of "I was framed.") Although it was fascinating, and it made for "good TV," it wasn't my proudest moment. As I saw it (at least, as I ruminated on it later), the whole thing felt a little too exploitative for my tastes. These inmates had been sentenced to do hard time for their crimes; they hadn't signed up to be broadcast to the world doing it. And here I was, asking them to sign up.

While it's true that every inmate we cast volunteered to be on television, I couldn't shake the queasy feeling they hadn't fully considered the ramifications—to, say, their future employment—of leaving such a durable record of their incarcerated selves. I mean, let's be honest: They clearly had trouble weighing the consequences of their actions. They were already in *jail*.

Never mind why a television show would want to exploit the inmates of a jail, or why the inmates would choose to make their star turn while doing hard time. Here's my question: Who is the cruel sadist that would let them?

That would be Sheriff Joseph M. Arpaio.

★ ★ ★

When, at the last minute before the Bill of Rights was ratified, James Madison switched a key word in the Eighth Amendment from "ought" to "shall" (its current version: "Excessive bail *shall* not be required, nor excessive fines imposed, nor cruel and unusual punishments inflicted"), it's hard not to imagine he was thinking of Maricopa County sheriff Joe Arpaio. For a strongman like Arpaio, Madison must have known we'd need an equally strong amendment.

Arpaio gleefully promotes himself as "America's Toughest Sheriff." He is, indisputably, the ACLU's worst nightmare. Since his election in 1992, he has become notorious, earning a reputation for concocting ingenious—some would say diabolical—methods to make sure his inmates know they're being punished. Overcrowding. Beds without pillows. No access to a gym. No smoking. No coffee. He has banned movies, and (ironically, considering my presence, and his permission) almost all television programs. Only G-rated material, the Disney Channel, and the Weather Channel are permitted.

He serves his inmates spoiled, surplus-only food, and not much of it—two meals a day. "It costs more to feed our police dogs than our inmates," he has bragged. According to the ACLU, he abuses pretrial detainees by "feeding them moldy bread, rotten fruit and other contaminated food, housing them in cells so hot as to endanger their health, denying them care for serious medical and mental health needs and keeping them packed as tightly as sardines . . . for days at a time." Three years before I arrived, Arpaio had instituted a punishment most Americans would guess was long gone: chain gangs. And not just for men. Women, too. (And now you know why Arpaio allows the Weather Channel: "I think my chain gang deserves to know how hot it is when they hit the streets.")

The most obvious throwback to a less kinder, less gentler time? Arpaio's inmates must wear the old-timey inmate uniform—they are dressed in wide black-and-white stripes, as if they had just walked out of a Depression-era cartoon. As I wandered the halls, I half expected to see a mustachioed bodybuilder in a suspendered swimsuit lifting a dumbbell with "100 lbs" written on each weight. Or a robber wearing a raccoon mask carrying a bag marked "$$$." (As a "parting gift"—his words—Arpaio gave a few of us our very own black-and-white striped ensemble to take home. It now sits in my closet. I admit that I wore it once—in a pinch, as a last resort, mind you, so don't judge me—as a Halloween costume.)

One of the sheriff's proudest modifications (wait, what's the opposite of modification? Retrofication?) isn't inside his jail at all. It's outside, in the oppressive Phoenix sun—"Tent City," it's called, although even Arpaio has described it as a concentration camp. In the summer, many inmates are housed outdoors, under Korean War–era tents donated by the armed forces—a nice touch, especially since Sheriff Arpaio has justified the housing by pointing out, *Hey, if it's good enough for our military, it should be good enough for our inmates.* When it's 115 degrees in Arizona, Arpaio points out that "it's 120 degrees in Iraq and the soldiers are living in tents, have to wear full body armor, and they didn't commit any crimes, so shut your mouths." A straightforward bit of logic that, while hard to swallow, is hard to refute.

As for me, I can't decide if it is America's "toughest" jail or America's silliest. Arpaio has turned it into a cross between Alcatraz and the Island of Dr. Moreau—a playground for him to test his incarceration theories and experiments.

Because wait, there's more. Under the black-and-white uniform, Arpaio forces inmates to wear pink underwear. To make their meals even more unpleasant, the lunch menu often features "green bologna."

He has launched a contest on his website—"Mug Shot of the Day"—in which members of the general public can vote on which inmate's mug shot they deem most, what, entertaining? Ridiculous? Arpaio insists it's educational.

He stole from *American Idol* to create the "Inmate Idol Con-test" (see what he did there?) in which inmates sing for prizes—to be judged by Arpaio and Alice Cooper. *The* Alice Cooper. The winner got a Big Mac.

He once purchased Republican Newt Gingrich's ten-part, $150 video lecture series (using inmates' canteen funds) to play over the jail's closed circuit television system. That, too, was meant to be educational. Yet when asked if he planned to do the same with a Democrat, he said of the inmates, "Some people might say these guys already got enough of those ideas."*

In 2010, he created an armed citizen "posse" specifically to fight illegal immigration; it counts among its ranks the actors Lou "the Hulk" Ferrigno and Steven "the Hulk?" Seagal.

In a perverse bit of kitsch, the observation tower above Tent City features a blinking neon sign: VACANCY. There's always room for more subjects.

Arpaio, who once was a cop in Vegas, clearly has a showman's disposition. On television, he's a gruff crime dog who enjoys his image as a tough-on-crime lawman. In person, he's actually somewhat cheerful and engaging, even when talking about the miseries he inflicts—the jolly sadist. It's hard not to think of Arpaio as the kind of man who would host a reality show called *Smile, You're Under Arrest*.

Mainly because he *did*.

For two seasons.

On Fox.

(True story.)

Sheriff Arpaio's methods might be cruel. They are definitely unusual. A U.S. District Court judge has deemed some of them officially unconstitutional.

But they are popular. Arpaio has been reelected by the voters of Maricopa County four times, each time by double digits. In 2007, when a group called Arizonans for the U.S. Constitution and the Recall of Joe Arpaio (to some, that would be redundant) tried to recall him, they couldn't collect enough signatures to get on the ballot.

---

* In the decade since, it appears Sheriff Joe has graduated to new intellectual heroes. In the 2012 race for the Republican nomination for president, Arpaio endorsed Texas governor Rick Perry.

The people of Maricopa County (who love the Second Amendment but don't fret too much about the Eighth) clearly like what they see.

Even if this is what they see.

CRUELTY IS IN THE EYE OF THE BEHEADER

YOU MAY RECALL, from the chapter on the Legislative Branch, that just outside the walls of the Constitutional Convention in 1787, hundreds of drunk, smelly, and naked prisoners were rioting, protesting the inhumane living conditions within Philadelphia's Walnut Street jail. (And for good reason. The abusive conditions in the Walnut Street jail make Maricopa County jail look like Knott's Berry Jail.) But you probably wouldn't guess that while the protests at Walnut Street were well within earshot (and sadly, eyeshot and noseshot) of the State House, the Framers hard at work drafting the new Constitution were probably more annoyed by their noise and their smell than inspired by their argument.

Prisoners' rights weren't exactly a common cause in the eighteenth century. In fact, the first organized prisoners' rights group, the Philadelphia Society for Alleviating the Miseries of Public Prisons, was born from the protests of the Walnut Street rioters. (As I've always said, if you want something done right, do it yourself, while drunk and naked.) Even when the phrase "cruel and unusual punishments" was first used, in the English Bill of Rights in 1689, the bar for "cruel" or "unusual" was mighty high.

The acceptable punishment for treason was to hang the culprit until *almost* dead, then disembowel him, then—while he could still watch—burn his innards right before his eyes. The punishment for a woman found guilty of treason was much simpler and more humane: She was burned at the stake.

Chivalry wasn't dead; it was just slightly tortured.

By the time our American Bill of Rights was ratified in 1791, we hadn't exactly turned into Gandhian peaceniks. We still cropped ears and branded skin. We punished everyday larceny with whippings, and we regularly pilloried convicted criminals—which is to say, we bound their neck and wrists and forced them to stand in stress positions in public, often in the center of town.

A few reformers—Benjamin Rush and Benjamin Franklin among them—raised mild objections. A decade earlier, Thomas Jefferson had proposed a "Bill of Proportion in Crimes and Punishments" to the Virginia House of Delegates, in which he suggested replacing the death penalty with a lifetime of hard labor. But his (not-so-) soft-on-crime, (relatively) weak-kneed, and (presumably) tough-on-the-back proposal was rejected.

More so than not, the Framers endorsed extreme punishments. Had they walked across the street to witness the worst Walnut Street prisoners being tortured, they likely wouldn't have speed-dialed the ACLU.

Relatively speaking, then, the Framers might not have been too alarmed by the eccentric (and excessive) Wonka-like punishments of Joe Arpaio. Would they truly have been troubled by the prospect of being forced to wear pink underwear? Doubt it. Some probably *wore* pink underwear.* Would they have taken to the streets over black-and-white stripes, just because they look silly? As Georgia delegate William Pierce once said, "I see your black-and-white stripes and I raise you powdered wigs."† Would they have rioted over having to sweat it out in the heat of a Tent City? Not a chance. Even the reformer Benjamin Franklin wouldn't have cried foul at that; they were hard at work in Philadelphia, in the summer, in a non-air-conditioned, unventilated room while wearing long coats, pink underwear, and silly powdered wigs. As Franklin might have said, "We wrote a Constitution on the face of the sun, and I'm 134 years old, so shut your mouths."

★ ★ ★

---

* Historians disagree on this matter.

† Historians disagree on this matter, too. Though oddly enough, *different* historians.

This isn't your great-great-great-great-grandfather's Eighth Amendment anymore. It's ours. It's mine. It is now up to us, which is to say *me*, to determine just how much cruelty and unusualness we will put up with.* So says Thomas Jefferson: "The question," he wrote to Madison from France in 1789, "whether one generation of men has a right to bind another, seems never to have been started either on this or our side of the water"—clearly, not-so-veiled references to the common punishments of man-binding and waterboarding—"but I set out on this ground which I suppose to be self-evident"—which, as we've learned by now, is the best kind of evident— "that the earth belongs to the living; that the dead have neither powers nor rights over it." Hear that, Gunning Bedford? You can't tell me what is cruel or not cruel. Get the message, Oliver Ellsworth? I'll decide what is unusual.

Even the First Congress, which proposed the Eighth Amendment, saw the writing on the wall: that "cruel" is a matter of taste, and taste is something that constantly evolves. Representative Samuel Livermore of New Hampshire took the House floor and reminded his fellow congressmen, "It is sometimes necessary to hang a man, villains often deserve a whipping, and perhaps having their ears cut off," and then asked, "but are we in the future to be prevented from inflicting those punishments because they are 'cruel'?"

Let's hope that was a rhetorical question. I like to think he was asking for clarification rather than permission.

In the future, yes, we *were* to be prevented. We no longer determine what is cruel or unusual based on the standard that was fixed during the Founders' time—otherwise we'd still be drawing and quartering our men and burning our women at the stake. Representative Livermore was right: Since the Framers left "cruel and unusual" vague and ambiguous, it was up to later generations to interpret just how much pain we'd endure—or inflict.

Not that it's an easy calculation. On the cruelest punishment—capital punishment—we've gone wobbly. In 1972, the Supreme Court halted the use of the death penalty in all fifty states, ruling 5–4 that "arbitrary" procedures employed in the death penalty made it "cruel and unusual." Four years later we changed our minds yet again; capital punishment was back on the menu. But Justice William Brennan, in his concurring 1972 opinion, took the opportunity to try to bring some method to the madness

---

* Rather, up with which we will put.

going forward. He devised a handy cheat sheet: "Four principles by which we may determine whether something is 'cruel and unusual.'" Namely, a "punishment must not, by its severity, be degrading to human dignity"; nor can it be "inflicted in wholly arbitrary fashion"; it can't be one "that is clearly and totally rejected throughout society"; and it can't be a "severe punishment that is patently unnecessary."

I know what you're thinking—it's like he's taking all the fun out of punishing people. And if you're not thinking it, Sheriff Joe is.

But it didn't start with Brennan. The killjoys were upon us a decade earlier. Take the 1958 case of *Trop v. Dulles,* for example. Albert Trop, a natural-born citizen of the United States, had deserted from the army while stationed in Morocco. When he returned to base, he learned he was no longer welcome; not only was he dishonorably discharged, he was essentially banished—although he didn't know it just yet. Eight years later, when he applied for a passport, he was denied. Chief Justice Earl Warren, writing for the majority, declared that revoking someone's American citizenship was too cruel a punishment for desertion from the army. Kick 'em out of the military, sure. But kick 'em out of the country? The Constitution says not so fast.

When I first learned that, I couldn't help but recall that desertion from the army is punishable by the death penalty. So let me get this straight: Losing one's life is fine, but losing one's AmericaCard? That's a fate worse than death? (I thought I was being clever. Turns out Justice Felix Frankfurter used exactly that phrase in his dissent. He asked, "Is constitutional dialectic so empty of reason that it can be seriously urged that loss of citizenship is a fate worse than death?" I'd like to say great minds think alike, but frankly I'm not sure what "dialectic" means.)

Why is such a punishment too cruel? Because apparently we all got together and agreed it was. According to Justice Warren, the Eighth Amendment "must draw its meaning from the evolving standards of decency that mark the progress of a maturing society."

Oh *must* it? Must *we?*

Because if we do, if we *must,* if we are obligated to just make it up as we go along and enact laws as we sit fit in our wisdom as a "maturing" society (which, by the way, is giving us far too much credit), then I can't help but ask: What is the point of having the Eighth Amendment at all? Isn't the Amendment, then, simply saying, *I don't know, you guys figure it out?* (Okay, here, too, I thought I had made a revolutionary brainstorm. It turns out Justice Joseph Story had beaten me to the punch by almost two hundred years. In 1833, he pointed out that if a majority of Americans can define "cruel and unusual," the Eighth Amendment "would seem to be wholly unnecessary in a free government, since it is scarcely possible that any departure of such a government should authorize or justify such atrocious conduct.")

Justice Story makes a compelling dialectic. (What can I say—I'm a quick study. I looked it up. It means "the art of investigating or discussing the truth of opinions.") And upon further investigation, in my opinion, the truth is: We need some guidelines. We can't just roll with it anymore. After all, it was this unsettling sense that, *Hey, things change*—namely, that we "must" determine what is cruel and unusual by "the evolving standards" of our society—that got Justice Scalia so agitated at our lunch, that led him to complain to me, and to others, that his own Court "must be living in another world" and is "busy designing a Constitution for a country I do not recognize." A country that doesn't respect its elders. A country that doesn't say "please" or "thank you." A country that wonders whether torture is unconstitutional.

(Lest we forget, this is a man who didn't want to "revive" the Constitution; he wanted to pronounce it "already dead." Some might say his default position is cruel and unusual. And he might say that's a compliment.)

But I have a solution that might build on Brennan's test, take into account Warren's standard, and put a little spring back in Scalia's step.

Consider the facts of the case: In *Wilkerson v. Utah*, decided in the late nineteenth century, the Supreme Court made plain that drawing and quartering, public dissection, disemboweling, and burning humans alive would all fall under the category of "cruel and unusual." In the early twentieth century, in *Weems v. United States*, it declared that the common sentence of "cadena temporal"—essentially, "hard and painful labor" while being shackled—was cruel, but not, at the time, all that unusual.*

But isn't there another combination we haven't directly considered?

Which is to say: Cruel, I get—but what's so wrong with unusual?

I wonder if, back in 1833, when Joseph Story pondered whether the Eighth Amendment was "wholly unnecessary," he was only *half* right. The

---

* Even today, cruel-but-not-unusual isn't all that unusual. In a recent case, the Court ruled that a corrections officer cannot punch an inmate in the face. Seven justices said it was cruel and unusual. Two dissenters, Justices Scalia and Thomas, said it was *not* cruel and unusual. Any aficionado of basic cable prison dramas would argue: It's cruel, but happens pretty much every third episode.

Eighth Amendment is only *half* unnecessary. I wonder if our evolving standards don't have a problem with unusual, as long as we're not cruel.

After all, we're in the twenty-first century now. Our standards have evolved; they haven't necessarily matured. We are a nation that forbids thumbscrews and guillotines, but we are also a nation that—and I was as surprised as you must be—allows pink underwear and "Inmate Idol." Could it be that in the case of *America's Toughest Sheriff v. the Rest of the Civilized World*, the verdict is in? *Unusual* punishments don't get you arrested, sentenced for violating the Constitution, and thrown in your own "toughest jail."

They get you reelected.

And if our standards of decency have evolved to reflect our new approval of unusual punishment—as alarming as that may be—so should our amendment.

Your New Eighth Amendment
Excessive bail shall not be required, nor excessive fines imposed, nor cruel punishments inflicted. Unusual punishments will be judged on creativity and degree of difficulty.

Some may argue this isn't the perfect amendment, but it *is* a more perfect one. So, respectfully, *shut your mouths.*

THE NINTH AMENDMENT

My Ninth Amendment Is to Ask for a Zillion More Amendments

☆ ☆ ☆

HE YEAR WAS 1944. The country was at war. And President Franklin Delano Roosevelt said the Bill of Rights "can lick my boots."

Although those weren't technically his words—and in retrospect, I probably shouldn't have put quotes around them—the sentiment behind them was most definitely his: After more than a decade spent defending the Constitution as president of the United States, he had looked anew at its first ten amendments and found the rights they guaranteed—his word, I promise—"inadequate." So inadequate, in fact, that when he gave his State of the Union address on January 11, he called for nothing less than a do-over.

His solution? The time had come, he said, for "a second Bill of Rights," a list of economic guarantees the Founders had neglected to include when they had the chance.

In his speech to the nation that evening, he gave the original Bill of Rights its requisite lip service, as any president should: "This Republic had its beginning, and grew to its present strength," he said, "under the protection of certain inalienable political rights—among them the right of free speech, free press, free worship, trial by jury, freedom from unreasonable searches and seizures. They were our rights to life and liberty." (I almost can't bear to tell him what I've been up to.)

Then he got down to business. He declared that the state of our union was not as strong as it had once been. "As our nation has grown in size and stature," he continued, "these political rights [have] proved inadequate to assure us equality in the pursuit of happiness." So he called for "a new basis of security and prosperity . . . for all."

FDR wanted a new deal—over and above the one you may already have heard about.

Conveniently, he had already written it. Among the rights he demanded, right then and there: "the right to a useful and remunerative job," "the right of every family to a decent home," "the right to adequate medical care," "the right to a good education," and "the right to earn enough to provide adequate food and clothing and recreation." Some might say it was a bold vision for a president of the United States; others might say he was the President of Fantasyland. He might as well have said that every child has the right to a pet unicorn.*

FDR had reason to be bold. He had been in declining health for three years. He was war-weary, body-fatigued, suffering from coronary artery disease and congestive heart failure. In just over a year, he'd be dead. That week, he even had the flu. But FDR, despite feeling weak—he gave the speech over the radio rather than in person—believed in his message strongly. So strongly that, after he finished, he invited the newsreel cameras into the Diplomatic Reception Room and recited his new Bill of Rights again. Flu or no flu, he had gone to the trouble of writing a handful of new rights; by gosh, he wanted to be recorded reading them—once more, with feeling. He wanted to go on record.†

"And like I told James Madison, you can't spell 'Founder' without 'FDR.'"

---

* The right to a pet unicorn wasn't officially proposed as a constitutional amendment until nine-year-old Colleen Lawson was elected senator in the Commonwealth of Virginia and ascended to position of Senate majority leader. Her proposal for an amendment to the Constitution failed, 99–1. She cried about it, like a crybaby.

† The video of his delivery—footage oddly enough discovered by documentary filmmaker Michael Moore while researching *Capitalism: A Love Story*—is worth watching. When Roosevelt finishes listing the amendments to his new Bill of Rights, he turns his head and gives a heavy sigh, as if to say, *This rewriting the Constitution business is hard work.* (Tell me about it, Franklin.)

But did he need to? Did Roosevelt have to go to all the trouble of writing new rights to shore up the original ten?

Or rather, was he so busy jawing about a "second" Bill of Rights that he actually failed to make it all the way through the first one? Because by my reading of the Ninth Amendment in Madison's original Bill of Rights, Roosevelt needn't have bothered:

> The enumeration in the Constitution, of certain rights, shall not be construed to deny or disparage others retained by the people.

In other words,

> Chill out—just because a right isn't mentioned here doesn't mean it doesn't exist.

The Ninth Amendment is a solution to a problem the Framers themselves created: When they decided they would list specific restrictions on government in the Bill of Rights, many Founders feared—Alexander Hamilton and James Wilson being the most fearful—that any restriction *not* mentioned would be presumed to have been intentionally overlooked. The Ninth Amendment, then, is an attempt to both cover their bases and cover their arses, much the way an Oscar winner might say, "and to anyone else who I forgot, you know who you are—and *thank you*." That way, when he neglects to thank his wife, he can amend his comments later:

But honey, I didn't forget. It was implied.

Of course, they wouldn't have had this trouble if they hadn't written the Bill of Rights in the first place. But that's not how we do it; unlike other countries that have unwritten constitutions—Israel, New Zealand, the United Kingdom—we write stuff down. We hold written constitutions supreme, especially ours. We feel the need to go on record.

GET YOUR PENCILS READY

BEFORE INDEPENDENCE, American colonists were perfectly willing to get by without leaving a paper trail. Inspired by the writings of John Locke and Thomas Hobbes, we traced the origins of our individual rights not to any piece of parchment, but to something much more intangible, and less flammable: God, or nature, or traditional customs. Our rights were endowed by our Creator—surely He was keeping track of them. As George Mason wrote in his draft for the Virginia Declaration of Rights—which served as the basis for the Bill of Rights—"men are born naturally free," and therefore hold "certain inherent natural rights, of which they cannot, by any compact, deprive or divest their posterity."

Which was a fine approach for 1776. But by 1787, we figured it might be more helpful to list those rights. You know, just to be safe.

Which is why the Ninth Amendment causes problems. It mentions that there *are* unenumerated natural rights, but it doesn't bother enumerating them. For this reason, Judge Robert Bork, during his ill-fated confirmation hearings in 1987, colorfully said the Ninth Amendment is "an amendment that says, 'Congress shall make no' and then there is an inkblot, and you can't read the rest of it, and that is the only copy you have." (It's a shame Bork never made it to the Supreme Court. He might have been given another copy.)

But he was right: The Ninth *is* one big inkblot. That's why neither liberals nor conservatives are happy with it. Liberals are wary of admitting, as the Ninth seems to, that men do have natural rights—we deserve equality under the law, for example—that might trump the laws they'd like to pass, such as affirmative action, or hate crimes legislation. Conservatives are afraid that if we actually start enumerating these rights, liberals might go crazy with that power. They won't *stop* enumerating. They won't be satisfied with what the Ninth Amendment has already provided: a right to privacy, and to move about freely, and to contraception, and to abortion. They'll use the Ninth Amendment to ask for a zillion more amendments. Next thing you know, women will have a constitutional right to play in the NFL. Marijuana won't just be legal, it will be mandatory. Animals will not just be cage-free, they will be eligible for unemployment insurance. And then, before you know it, gay people will be allowed to get married.

What would stop liberals from going on an enumeration spree? Certainly not the courts. As Justice Goldberg put it in his opinion in the contraception case *Griswold v. Connecticut,* "The Framers did not intend that the first eight amendments be construed to exhaust the basic and fundamental rights." Exactly—there are plenty more where that came from.

Shucks, I can think of a handful right off the top of my head. The right to great governance, or to good sex, or to decent pizza. To gorgeous sunsets. To long walks on the beach. To party. To meet someone you can laugh with. To see Air Supply in concert just once more before you die happy. To die happy. In a single speech, Franklin Delano Roosevelt whipped up enough for a "second Bill of Rights." Where would the madness stop?

Or is this all just a Band-Aid? If FDR thinks of eight, and I think of eighty, does that solve the problem? It would—right up until the moment that someone else thinks of eight hundred. The Ninth Amendment isn't set up for that. How could it be—it's only twenty-one words long.

No wonder everyone steers clear, failing to make good use—or any use, really—of the amendment. It is unfinished, incomplete, unrestricted, and despite being vague and nonspecific, is somehow still inflexible. That is in part why, according to constitutional historian Jack Rakove, it "lies inertly in the Constitution, a joker that's never been played." According to constitutional savior Kevin Bleyer, "never been played" is no respectable fate for an amendment.

So then: If written constitutions reign so supreme, and enumerated rights are more helpful than unenumerated ones, perhaps it's time we all pick up a pen. Let's all do the hard work of enumerating these rights. Let's reveal what's behind the inkblots together.

When, ten years ago, Justice Scalia wrote that the Ninth Amendment's "refusal to 'deny or disparage' other rights is far removed from affirming any one of them," he was absolutely correct. The Ninth Amendment doesn't give you the right—or the opportunity—to make up new rights.

But then, he was talking about the old Ninth Amendment.

The new one is a Mad Libs, for both mad libs and mad conservatives—one that can be played over and over again.

YOUR NEW NINTH AMENDMENT

The enumeration in the Constitution, of certain

_____ rights, shall not be
(adjective ending in "alienable")

construed to deny, or disparage, or

_____ others not mentioned here, such
(verb beginning with "d")

as the right to _____, or to _____, or the
                (annoying activity)   (verb)

Freedom of _____, retained by the
                (*very* annoying activity)

_____ people of the United States of
(complimentary adjective)

_____.

(exceptional place)

THE TENTH AMENDMENT

The Amendment to the Constitution That Does Not Amend the Constitution

HENRY ROLLINS, the hypermuscular, aggressively tattooed former frontman of the hard-core punk rock band Black Flag, a self-avowed "curious and angry" man who has bragged that he once tested his DNA for the so-called "warrior gene" that predisposes men to violent behavior, has yet one more distinction that sets him apart from the average non-muscular, non-tattooed, non-warrior American: He reads the Constitution every day.

"Absolutely," he says, "a little bit every day."

While others read a little bit of the Bible, or a little bit of the Torah, or a little bit of the German fetish porn on the Internet, Rollins cozies up to the Necessary and Proper Clause, or the Supremacy Clause, or the part about Bills of Attainder.

Or so he claims. It's hard to believe he keeps such a daily ritual, but frankly, because he is the hypermuscular, aggressively tattooed angry man who has a vested interest in violent behavior, really, who am I to doubt him?

Nor should I. Rollins is an avowed patriot, a prominent humanitarian for global democratic causes, and enough of a celebrity that in September 2011 he was granted entree to a vault deep in the recesses of the National Archives in Washington, D.C. There, he got to take a closer look at the actual parchments of the founding documents that established the basis for the country he loves, lives in, and rocks out to. (If I've learned nothing else in my constitutional journey, it's that Nicolas Cage needn't have been so dramatic. He had to break in; Henry Rollins simply asked.)

Once inside, Rollins read a little bit of the Bill of Rights: the Tenth Amendment.

The powers not delegated to the United States by the Constitution, nor prohibited by it to the States, are reserved to the States respectively, or to the people.

Specifically, Rollins read the 1789 draft of the Tenth Amendment that was passed back and forth between the two houses of Congress as the Bill of Rights hot-potatoed its way to ratification. Language was added; clauses were taken out. And when Rollins took a closer look, he made a startling discovery. "The last words of what became the Tenth Amendment"—*or to the people,* the four words that end the amendment and conclude the Bill of Rights—"were a handwritten addition."* They had, Rollins surmised, been added on the fly.

"Wow!" Rollins wrote later on his blog. "I can't tell you how awesome it was to see that." *Wow, awesome*—a surprising, arguably undignified display of childlike glee, especially from a man who routinely sees handwriting on his own forearms.

It may not have been *his* discovery, but I'll give him full credit for it, for a few very good reasons. One, I hadn't heard or read it anywhere else except from him—and I have read and spoken to *every* serious philosopher on the subject of the Tenth Amendment's rollicking ratification debate (they were both quite nice); two, Wikipedia gives him credit for it, so there's that; and three, and most important, the aforementioned stuff about the muscles and the tattoos and the warrior gene.

Not that we should be impressed. Whether it was his or not, let's not be fooled into thinking this was a profound discovery. Knowing what we know about the Bill of Rights, that they were a bribe to allay the fears of the Anti-Federalists who feared a centralized government, it makes sense—it's obvious, really—that "the people" would be an afterthought added hastily in the margins. Because for all the attention paid to "We the People" when the Constitution began, if we're being honest about the Tenth Amendment, it's not about the people.

The real stars of the Tenth Amendment are the states.

---

* I assume he means they were written hastily in the margin. Seeing as the entire Constitution was, technically, "a *handwritten* addition."

DON'T MESS WITH AXIS

THE WASHINGTON MONUMENT is the first thing one sees when one steps outside the National Gallery. The tallest structure in our nation's capital springs 555 feet, 5 inches into the air from the center of the National Mall, or what was known during its erection as the Grand Avenue, and from most every vista, it draws attention. As monuments go, it is an impressive one, if you're into that kinda thing.

Like Henry Rollins, I'm into that kinda thing, so I'm impressed. On my first visit to the capital as an adult, I was fortunate enough to enjoy a view of the monument from my hotel room, and well, W*ow. I can't tell you how awesome it was to see that.*

It is something that commands attention, as its designers had intended when they conceived it: a grand obelisk that—and I don't think I'm overstating the matter—would spring forth from bedrock so firm, jut into the sky so proudly, point into the heavens so far, and symbolize a clarion call to liberty so global, that the earth would have no choice but to start rotating on its new axis, the poles would reset themselves, Santa Claus would move into the White House, and, given sufficient time for migration from the Arctic, polar bears would soon gather to frolic in the Reflecting Pool—as if God Himself had stuck a push pin labeled "Freedom" into the heart of Democracy City, so that later, when He was looking for it again to help redesign South Africa or the new Baltic states or some other distant planet, He would remember where he last left it.

Okay, perhaps I am overstating the matter.

And if I am overstating the matter, it is only because Washington the monument was designed to resemble Washington the man, and there was no shortage of overstating the man. "A Roman hero or a Grecian god," according to contemporary poet Philip Freneau. A "high-poised example of great duties done," wrote James Russell Lowell. "He stood in all his civic dignity with moral grandeur, erect, serene, majestic," said Pennsylvania's Richard Rush, upon seeing Washington stand in the doorway to the Pennsylvania State House. "Profound stillness reigned. Not a word was heard, not a breath. Palpitations took the place of sounds. It was a feeling infinitely beyond that which vents itself in shouts. All were gazing, in mute unutterable admiration. Every eye was riveted on that form—the greatest, purest, most exalted of mortals."

In other words: *Wow. I can't tell you how awesome it was to see that.*

Washington held, as historian Fergus Bordewich put it, "a stoicism that lent spine to a nation." Just as the monument in his name lent spine to a country. It said, *This is the new center of the universe.*

Not London. Not France. And most definitely not South Carolina or Rhode Island. After a decade under the Articles of Confederation, the country was finally back in charge.

The Tenth Amendment, however, is enough to make the Washington Monument go flaccid. "The Tenth Amendment was simply included in the Bill of Rights," points out author Frank Miniter, "to put an exclamation point on the fact that the federal government is restricted to the powers it is granted by the Constitution." As the Convention in Philadelphia wrapped up, Anti-Federalists were so stunned by the shift back to federal power—Washington had replaced the "rope of sand" that was the Articles of Confederation with a federalized republic on steroids, or what his fellow Virginian Patrick Henry called a "consolidated government" that would render the states meaningless—that they held the Constitution hostage until Washington and Madison agreed to include ten written guarantees to individuals and to states. There would be a Bill of Rights, and there would be a Tenth Amendment, or there would be no Constitution.

So to some, the Tenth Amendment was a necessary check on federal power. It was a reminder that, as President Reagan said, "the federal government did not create the states. The states created the federal government." To others—men like Henry Rollins—the Tenth Amendment isn't just a reminder of the limits of federal government; it is a "states' rights issue" that "often becomes something like, for example, no abortion and no fags. It's *our* state!" Or to men like Georgia congressman James Jackson—the Henry Rollins of the eighteenth century, who would have agreed with Rollins that sometimes the states should defer to Washington, D.C., since Washington "might be compared to the heart in the human body—[the] center from which the principles of life [are] carried to the extremities." In other words, count your blessings, Alabama, or Texas, or Montana. You wouldn't exist without D.C.

It's a chicken-and-egg problem: Which comes first, the states or the federal government? And it's a dilemma the Tenth Amendment was supposed to help clear up.

Yet it doesn't. It doesn't say what's what. Worse: It doesn't say *anything.* Despite taking up marquee placement in the Bill of Rights—what should be the grand finale, the big showstopper, the *drumroll, please*—the Tenth Amendment, according to constitutional expert Jack Rakove, "is commonly described as a 'truism' that does not alter or amend the Constitution in any way." It says merely that "powers not delegated are not delegated; powers not prohibited to the states are not prohibited; and if any powers are left over, they belong either to the people or the states."

What a waste of ink. Be it resolved: *Up is up, down is down, and every other direction points somewhere else.*

Even the Supreme Court has found the Tenth Amendment officially useless, ruling in 1931 that it "added nothing to the [Constitution] as originally ratified." Ten years later it again called the Tenth "but a truism" stating "that all is retained which has not been surrendered." Your Honor, if I may: *Well, duh.*

No wonder we have responded to this "exclamation point" with a resounding *question mark.*

Huh? What's the point?

Even when he first introduced the Tenth Amendment to Congress for ratification, James Madison had to admit the obvious: that the words of the Tenth Amendment "may be considered as superfluous. I admit they may be deemed unnecessary: but there can be no harm in making such a declaration, if gentlemen will allow that the fact is as stated. I am sure I understand it so, and do therefore propose it."

To hell with it, he was saying. *Let's just get this country started already. Forgive me*—United States. *Let's get these United States started already.*

YES, VIRGINIA, THERE IS (STILL) A COMMERCE CLAUSE

IT'S NOT THAT JAMES MADISON didn't try to put some teeth in the Tenth Amendment. In fact, he considered an addition that wouldn't make it merely a "truism" that doesn't alter the Constitution "in any way," but tweaks the Constitution in at least one significant way: It would have weakened the federal government. One of his early drafts of the Amendment had included an artifact from the version in the Articles of Confederation: the word "expressly." As in,

Each state retains its sovereignty, freedom, and independence, and every power, jurisdiction, and right, which is not by the Confederation expressly delegated to the United States, in Congress assembled.

Had it stayed, that word would have eliminated any thought of *implied* powers for the federal government. But Madison's heart wasn't in it. After all, this was a man who, in one of his many failed proposals for the Constitution, had wanted to give the government a "national veto" over all state laws "in all cases whatsoever." Of course Madison wanted the federal government to be powerful. Heck, he had just spent months designing it.

Thomas Jefferson, on the other hand, was a fan of states' rights. When he saw Madison's list of proposed amendments for the Bill of Rights, he could only muster a tepid endorsement. "I like it as far as it goes," he wrote to his friend, "but I should have been for going further." He had seen the list of restrictions on government, and he wanted more.

In one of the first tests of federalism—the question of whether the United States should (or legally could) establish a national bank in 1791—Jefferson pulled no punches. He told Madison he thought the bank—which Alexander Hamilton had been promoting as secretary of the treasury—didn't simply violate the Tenth Amendment, it was actually treason. *Exclamation point.* "For any person to recognize a foreign legislature in a case belonging to the state itself"—and in this case the foreign legislature was no less than the federal government—"is an act of treason against the state." Maybe so, but Hamilton got his national bank—a bold first strike in a steady expansion of federal power.

Since then, the Tenth Amendment has proven no match for the rest of the Constitution. States, on their own, have had a hard time competing with the powers of the federal government, whether it be the Necessary and Proper Clause, which permits Congress to make all laws necessary and proper to enforce all the other laws—and which even a die-hard Federalist would have to admit is a pretty big loophole*—or the Supremacy Clause, which establishes the Constitution as "the Supreme Law of the Land"—over and above piddly state laws—or the Commerce Clause, which allows Congress "to regulate Commerce . . . among the several states." It didn't matter that some states claimed to be doing just fine on their own, thank you very much.

Thanks to the weak Tenth Amendment—an amendment that, let's remember, "does not amend"—Hamilton got his precious national bank. President Franklin Roosevelt won the right, contrary to state wishes, to regulate the growing of wheat even though the wheat was only for "home consumption" and not interstate commerce. (On this position, no doubt

---

* One that even a muscular, tattooed punk rocker might fit through.

Roosevelt received the wise counsel of the undersecretary of the Department of Agriculture, "nutball" Rexford Guy Tugwell. I could look it up, but like all things regarding Tugwell, I can't be bothered.)* More recently, President Obama has made the case that his national health care reform can include an individual mandate, despite the Tenth Amendment—and even though some states, such as Virginia, filed suit to stop it.

Cue the backlash. After two centuries of watching the feckless Tenth Amendment be ignored like the feckless amendment James Madison himself suggested it was, a movement of limited government advocates—so-called Tenthers—are hard at work finding deep meaning in something Madison called "superfluous" and "unnecessary." They have inspired the creation of the Tenth Amendment Center, a think tank whose purpose is to "preserve and protect the principles of strictly limited government" and "the decentralization of federal government power as required by the Constitution." They have persuaded more than three dozen state legislatures to propose nonbinding "Tenth Amendment Resolutions" to remind their residents that there *is* a Tenth Amendment. No word on whether they somehow got God to trigger the earthquake that cracked the Washington Monument in 2011, putting it out of service as the nation's metaphorical epicenter—although many liberal Democrats wouldn't put it past them. I bet Henry Rollins thinks so.

So who's right? Who's to say.

The Tenth Amendment (merely) reminds us that the powers not given to the federal government are reserved for the states. Beyond that, the Framers left us hanging. Should that mean that *every* power not listed—especially powers that couldn't have been conceived when the Tenth Amendment was conceived—must be left for the states to wield? The power to restrict Internet access? The power to bend spoons with your mind? The power to make a right turn at a red light?

If even Madison and Jefferson couldn't agree, it's hard to imagine all fifty states agreeing with the federal government. For the country's sake, we can only hope that by amending the Tenth Amendment—the amendment to the Constitution that "does not amend" the Constitution—I can finally amend the Constitution in ways that mend the country.

---

* It certainly helped that all but one of the Supreme Court justices called to weigh in on the constitutionality of the measure had been appointed by FDR.

YOUR NEW TENTH AMENDMENT

The powers not delegated to the United States by the Constitution, nor prohibited by it to the States, are reserved to the States respectively, or to the people. But for any other powers the Founders didn't foresee or predict or previously distribute, the United States and the respective States should talk it out respectfully and come to some kind of a mutual understanding. Because—wow, I can't tell you how awesome it would be to see that.

Exclamation point!

FOOTNOTES TO HISTORY

*Seventeen More Amendments to Address
Three More Problems: Booze, Servants, and Suffrage*

KNOW WHAT YOU'RE THINKING RIGHT NOW: Holy crap, there are seventeen more of these?

It's true. There are twenty-seven amendments to the United States Constitution: ten in the Bill of Rights—well, nine now*—and seventeen more that have been added in the two centuries since ratification.

Although those twenty-seven amendments, taken collectively, easily justify my grand enterprise here—any four-page document with twenty-seven things wrong with it deserves to be tossed out and started from scratch—they do present a problem. Namely: Well, *now* what? How should we deal with the messy jumble of jury-rigged Band-Aids our predecessors applied to keep this clunky thing intact? How do I amend the amendments, without adding more amendments? Should I replace them? Rescind them? Redact them? Cover them in Wite-Out?

It's tempting to overlook them entirely. What are amendments, after all, but official apologies? They are our predecessors, *making amends* for the mistakes of our forefathers. It's okay to apologize once or twice—so I'm told, having never tried it myself—but twenty-seven times? That's just pathetic. As a patriot, then—the good kind, the kind who always presumes the greatness of America and never makes any apologies for it—I'm inclined to sweep the remaining amendments under the rug and pretend they never happened. Nothing to see here. Move along.

Oh, look, over there! The Emancipation Proclamation![†]

Yet that would be dishonest. Pretending the amendments never hap-

---

* Ever since the overdue eradication of the Seventh Amendment.

[†] Come to think of it, perhaps the Emancipation Proclamation isn't the best distraction. It, too, is a rather profound apology.

pened—or were written merely for kicks, or were just some fever dream of James Madison's—would be to deny the basic facts of history. And that's not my style. I'm not a revisionist. I'm a visionist.

So, how then to address the seventeen issues my predecessors thought so important they made a federal case out of each and every one? How to honor appropriately the many concerns they deemed so vital they went through the torturous labyrinth that is Article V (their version, not mine) to amend the Constitution seventeen times? If we were to grapple with each amendment on its own, we'd be here all decade.

Not to mention that such a Herculean labor, especially hard on the heels of so many Herculean labors, would exhaust a lesser man. It would crush a mere mortal.

Fortunately, I am no lesser man. I am a greater man. So it is not true, what you may have presumed, or heard from people who have spent time with me lately, or deduced logically from the basic laws of physiognomy and the effect of fatigue on human anatomy: that just the thought of having to address each and every remaining amendment individually makes my eyes roll back into my head, my eyelids slam shut, and my brain stage a protest by going into REM sleep without my blessing or permission.

It's not true. I swear.

I'm not tired.

I'm not.

I'm just resting my eyes.

I'm just eqio qnkd;z zkzzzzzzzzzzzzzzzzzzz.

[Dog bark!]

Luckily, we don't have to. Even better, *I* don't have to. My cursory scan was enough to reveal a pattern that will help me make short (or shorter) work of the leftover amendments. By my reckoning, all the essential remaining amendments concern three easily digestible subjects: alcohol, voting, and slavery.*

In other words: *No sweat.*

We can do this.

More important, *I* can do this.

---

* Okay, okay, a couple deal with taxation, but I'm a visionary, not an accountant. So, only because I promised to cover everything:

YOUR NEW AMENDMENT ADDRESSING TAXES
If ya wants to sit at the table, ya gots to ante up.

Most important, I *will* do this.

So: If the previous chapters were the meticulous redesign of a new, fundamentally improved republic, consider this the lightning round.

Every bit as insightful, every bit as revolutionary. Only quicker.

NEXT ROUND'S ON ME: THE AMENDMENTS INVOLVING ALCOHOL

FIRST YOU GET DRUNK, and *then* you sober up. That's the way it's supposed to go. But with the Eighteenth and Twenty-first Amendments, the United States of America flipped the script: We started a tab at the founding of the country, cut ourselves off in 1919 with the ratification of the Eighteenth Amendment, sobered up during fourteen years of Prohibition, and then, in a bizarro reverse intervention known as the Twenty-first Amendment, decided that we're more fun when we're drunk. Uncle Sam woke up to the harsh light of day and announced, "Oh, man, you should have seen me last decade. I was *so* sober. I totally remember how I got home last year. This suuuucks."

Such was the attitude of the United States as it ended Prohibition: The first step is to admit that you don't have a problem.

If you recall from our trip to 1787 Philadelphia, we are a country that was founded by problem drinkers. Drunks, really. The ship that brought John Winthrop and his fellow early American settlers to the shores of Massachusetts carried with it ten thousand gallons of wine and, despite the dangers of dehydration, three times as much delicious beer as clean water—they may have been Puritans, but they weren't prudes. Our Constitution was written by men who owned breweries, imported whisky, drank beer with their breakfast, and tried to hump cows in the streets of Philly. In the 1790s, the per capita consumption of alcohol was two and a half times greater than it was even in the decade before Prohibition. So prevalent was alcohol in the lives of the Framers that, in his spare time, Benjamin Franklin compiled a list of 228 synonyms for "drunkenness," more than an Eskimo has for "snow." "In the Sudds," "Topsy Turvey," "Like a Rat in Trouble." James Madison drank a pint of whisky every day. George Washington made certain his soldiers got four ounces of the good stuff with their daily ration, insisting that "the benefits arising from moderate use of strong Liquor have been experienced in all Armies, and are not to be disputed." By the 1820s, liquor flowed so freely it was less expensive than tea. We were, it's been said, an "alcoholic republic."*

Suffice it to say, the amount of staggering was staggering.

Attempts to deny us our alcohol were futile—a lesson James Madison himself learned when he tried to run for reelection to the Virginia Legislature. During the campaign he had refused to offer voters what they had become quite accustomed to: free liquor, and plenty of it. Although a fan himself, he thought bribing voters with booze was "inconsistent with the purity of moral and republican principles." The voters in turn thought Madison was being a cheapskate. He lost the election, but on the bright side, he gained an excuse to drown his sorrows, like a Rat in Trouble.

Madison eventually sobered up to the reality that alcohol was a winning strategy. As president, you'll recall, he tried to establish a National Brewery. He asked for a position in his cabinet for a Secretary of Beer. He got neither, but he wasn't wrong to ask. By the time alcohol was outlawed by the Eighteenth Amendment, it had become the fifth-largest industry in the country. Today we don't outlaw beer; we have "beer summits" at the White House.

To think that the Eighteenth Amendment—declaring that "the manufacture, sale, or transportation of intoxicating liquors within, the importation thereof into, or the exportation thereof from the United States and all

---

* Even our national anthem, written by Francis Scott Key to commemorate the resilience of the American flag during the Battle of Baltimore in 1812, owes its resilience to alcohol. Key wrote the poem in a hurry, as bombs were bursting in air—he didn't have the time to set it to music. But within days, the words of "The Star-Spangled Banner" were being sung all over Baltimore—to the tune of a popular drinking song. Think of it: After a rousing rendition of our nation's cherished anthem, it would be just as proper to shout "Last call!" as "Play ball!" (*Oh, say, can you see? Because I'm seeing double.*)

territory subject to the jurisdiction thereof for beverage purposes is hereby prohibited"—would ever last is to deny a self-evident truth about America: We have very clear purposes for our beverages. Namely, we intend to drink them.

And not just some of us. Almost all of us. If there was one mathematical proof that *We the People* simply won't do without our intoxicating liquors, it has to be this: The thirty-sixth state to ratify the Twenty-first Amendment, thereby officially making it official and retapping the national keg, was Utah—a state that won't even drink caffeine.

Of course Prohibition failed. The Eighteenth Amendment is the only amendment that sought to restrict the rights not of the government, but of the people. As might have been pointed out by Thomas Jefferson—a man who amassed a renowned wine collection and made rye whiskey, yet still managed to spell "injuries and usurpations" in his letter to King George— it's not really about the alcohol. It's about free will. It's about unalienable rights to life and liberty. It's about, in Jefferson's words, "the pursuit of happiness," via—my words—the pursuit of hoppiness. No wonder the Eighteenth Amendment lasted barely a decade. It is, or rather was, perhaps the only amendment that skipped right past the Constitution and messed with the Declaration of Independence.

Not only was it doomed, it backfired. "Today," Jacob Weisberg points out, "*prohibition* is a byword for futile attempts to legislate morality and remake human nature."

Prohibition can also make a guy thirsty. When FDR signed the bill that made 3.2 percent alcoholic lager legal once again—an early step toward the full repeal of Prohibition—he put down his pen and held his hand out for a cold one. "I think this would be a good time for a beer," he said.

I'll drink to that.

Your New Amendment Addressing Alcohol
Please drink responsibly.

SUFFRAGING FOOLS GLADLY:
THE AMENDMENTS ABOUT VOTING

Who should be allowed to vote?
Quiet, I wasn't asking you. I make the decisions here.

I brought it up just to pose the question. Not to let you answer it. You don't get a vote on the matter.

I'd like to think the Framers would applaud me for my antidemocratic stand—seeing as they never mention the word "democracy" in their Constitution and many had very little patience with the concept. Although it is hard to overlook one particular fact: If the Founders had had their way, even *I* wouldn't be able to vote. I am a grown white male a few years over eighteen—okay, I'll admit, a few years over twenty-one—with no felony convictions that anyone knows about, who was born here, raised here, and assigned my own Social Security number here. Yet even I fail to meet their original criteria.

Never mind blacks and women—*Wait, that sounded wrong*. Never mind that many of the Framers of the original United States Constitution denied the concerns of blacks and women;* they denied the vote to a group of people who must never have thought they'd be left out on election day: anyone who rents an apartment.

I am a non–hedge fund manager who lives in Manhattan; in other words, I still rent. And if it were up to Gouverneur Morris and others who thought the vote should be the privilege of property owners only, I'd have no vote. His reason is surprising: "Give the votes to the people who have no property," he said in 1787, "and they will sell them to the rich who will be able to buy them." I might have thought he would suggest that property owners have more at stake in America—more land in the game, as it were—but Morris's concern was that apartment owners like me, who rely on landlords to put a roof over our heads, are simply deficient, unqualified to make the difficult decisions. "The ignorant and the dependent," he said, speaking of anyone without a mortgage, "can be as little trusted with the public interest [as] children." And "children," he helpfully pointed out, "do not vote."

John Adams agreed. When Adams's friend suggested that Massachusetts abolish all property qualifications for the vote, Adams would not hear of it. He knew what would happen: "There will be no end to it. New Claims will rise. Women will demand a Vote. Lads from twelve to twenty-one will think their rights not attended to, and every Man, who has not a Farthing, will demand an equal Voice with any other in all Acts of State." Can you imagine such a thing? Women, teenagers, and renters—oh, my!

Adams was especially intent on denying women the right to vote. He

* That still sounds wrong.

said he had no plans to trade the tyranny of King George III for "the despotism of the petticoat." This despite his wife, Abigail Adams, sending him a letter in 1776 and asking, famously, that "in the new code of laws which I suppose it will be necessary for you to make, I desire you will *remember the ladies* and be more generous and favorable to them than your ancestors." Oh, he remembered the ladies, all right—with their petticoats and their despotism—and he chose not to give them the vote. No wonder Abigail was wary of letting men rule the world—she was married to one. "Do not put such unlimited power in the hands of husbands," she had warned. "Remember, all men would be tyrants if they could."

Actually, Abigail, that's not entirely true. Not all men are tyrants. In fact, one man is responsible for giving women the right to vote, as Abigail had requested. Although despite her famous admonition, it wasn't her tyrant husband John.

Ladies, meet Harry T. Burn. He was the Tennessee lawyer who finally stepped out of the way of the Nineteenth Amendment and endorsed suffrage for the women who had suffered so long. But he, too, needed a little feminine encouragement. In 1920, when Tennessee was debating whether to become the thirty-sixth state to ratify the amendment—thereby making it the law of the land—Burn was the deciding vote in the Tennessee General Assembly. He had decided to vote against it; that is, until he, too, received a long letter from someone he loved: his mother. "I have been watching to see how you stood," she wrote, "but have not noticed anything yet. Don't forget to be a good boy."

Unlike Adams, Burn was a good boy. He changed his mind. He voted "yea" so that, in the years to follow, millions of women could as well.

The Constitution now grants the right to vote to almost every adult American. African Americans can vote, thanks to the Fifteenth Amendment—as can citizens of every race. Women can vote, thanks to the Nineteenth Amendment. (They can also thank the Eighteenth Amendment, establishing Prohibition. Women wanted saloons closed down, and they began to demand their right to vote on the matter; the so-called temperance movement ushered in the suffrage movement.) The Twenty-third Amendment grants the vote to people who, in a shocking display of lack of judgment, choose to live in Washington, D.C. The Twenty-fourth Amendment says you can vote even if you elect not to pay a fee for the privilege. With the Twenty-sixth Amendment, naïve eighteen-year-olds can indulge in a constitutional right previously reserved for worldly-wise twenty-one-year-olds.

The steady march to full suffrage has led to some absurd proposals. Some parents have suggested they should be allowed to vote on their children's behalf, the theory being that since we're burdening our children with so much debt in the future, they should have a say in how we govern in the present. Other ideas—lowering the voting age to sixteen, lowering the voting age to thirteen, giving pregnant mothers two votes, three if she's having twins—have been floated as well.

But we don't need more voters—especially ones that can't drive, let alone crawl, to the voting booth. We're already lousy with voters.

The problem is that we're lousy at voting. Despite aggressive Get Out the Vote campaigns—"Vote or Die," "Vote or Contract Syphilis," "Vote or I'll Shoot This Puppy"—barely half of the people who have been afforded the basic right—nay, great privilege—of voting for their representatives in national elections actually do so. For much of the nineteenth century, it hovered around 80 percent. In the twentieth century, some elections enjoyed almost 65 percent turnout. In the giving-a-damn sweepstakes, our century, the twenty-first century, comes in third. As the country gets older, we get more indifferent.

We act like it's a burden, when it's a privilege. One that took half a dozen amendments to secure.

It's a privilege that can be revoked. We forget that although the Constitution requires that representatives and senators be elected by "the People," it never quite explains which people it's talking about. It leaves that chore to the states. And in fact, as long as a state doesn't directly conflict with anything in the Constitution, it can withhold the right to vote from anyone it so wishes. Some states deny convicted criminals a vote. Some states deny the vote to anyone deemed mentally incompetent.

Who's to say we can't deny the vote to anyone deemed obviously apathetic?

If we can deny the incarcerated and the insane, why not the indifferent?

The way I see it, if you don't care, you shouldn't count.

So there you are: If you don't vote in this election, you don't *get* to vote in the next one. Use it or lose it.

Do I worry that such a rule would mean that elections would become the reserved playground for right- and left-wing extremists who'll vote every time? Not really. They'll vote every time anyway. That's what makes them extremists.

But perhaps—and I realize this is something of a bank shot—by making voting a valuable commodity that can be repealed, the average nonextremist American who took it for granted might take it more seriously, if only because they'll never know what hot-button issue or unacceptable candidate might be on the ballot next time. And they won't be able to bear the thought of missing out.

Like Abigail Adams and Harry T. Burn's mom before me, I'm crossing my fingers that moderates will see the wisdom of my not-so-gentle reprimand and recognize the value of their voice.

I say it's worth a try.

And like I said, you don't get to vote on the matter.

Your New Amendment Addressing Voting
Be a good boy (or girl): Vote.

JUDGE US NOT BY THE COLOR OF OUR SKIN, BUT BY THE CON-TEST OF OUR CHARACTERS: THE AMENDMENTS ADDRESSING SLAVERY AND DISCRIMINATION

Which brings us to slavery.

And, um, gosh, wow, there's not much to say on the subject.

Some have said that slavery wasn't intended to be so evil. Small states with large slave populations merely wanted to shore up their ranks in the census, so that they'd have greater representation in Congress, and therefore were eager to dignify slaves as full Americans—just not full humans. So really, they say, slavery was about voting.

But I think it has more to do with Prohibition. Because frankly, it must have been an idea we had when we were drunk.

Fortunately, others have already diagnosed the problem. Supreme Court Justice Thurgood Marshall said that the Framers' willingness to condone slavery was proof that "the government they devised was defective from the start." Abolitionist William Lloyd Garrison called it "A Covenant with Death and an Agreement with Hell." To others, it reveals the promise that "all men are created equal" as nothing but "a self-evident lie."

A defect isn't something you tinker with. A covenant with hell isn't something you tweak. A lie isn't something you repeat or defend.

It's something you make amends for.

So actually, this amendment isn't all that difficult:

Your New Amendment Addressing Slavery

What the—? Involuntary servitude? We actually *did* that?! That's terrible. Let's not do that.

★ ★ ★

There you have it.

One Preamble, seven Articles, and twenty-seven Amendments. The long-overdue fulfillment of Thomas Jefferson's dream: that the Constitution be rewritten every nineteen years by "the living generation." That it not be treated like "the ark of the covenant, too sacred to be touched." That "each generation . . . choose for itself the form of government it believes most promotive of its own happiness."

The *living* generation. That's me.

And I just touched it.

And I gotta say: I'm pretty happy about it all.

Mainly because—and don't tell him I said so—there's no way James Madison could have done what I have done here. He wouldn't have had the stomach for it. He may have been "the Father of the Constitution," but this was a man who described shepherding just the first ten amendments through Congress as a "nauseous project." Imagine what he would think of having to contend with seventeen more.

I can tell you, James: *It's not so bad.* I managed to get it all done, and I didn't vomit once.

Even while "researching" the section on Prohibition.

Come to think of it, maybe *I* should be president.

☆ ☆ ☆

POSTAMBLE:
SIGNED, SEALED, DELIVERED

FROM PREAMBLE TO ME-AMBLE:

*or, One Man's Successful Quest to Save
the Constitution, and Why, in the End,
No Thanks Are Necessary*

☆ ☆ ☆

THEIR BELOVED STAMP WAS IN JEOPARDY.

It had been designed carefully and artfully, graced not only with the stately visage of an adored and enduring national icon, but also with a denomination chosen to reflect just how long it would last. Nay, how long it *should* last.

"Forever."

It was 2011, one hundred and twenty-five years after the statue it featured had been dedicated as a gift from France as "a memorial to independence"—*Liberty Enlightening the World*—and to honor her long journey across seas and centuries, three billion stamps had been printed by the patriots at the United States Postal Service. Two billion had already been issued. Countless licked—or peeled and stuck—and sent far across town, across the country, and around the globe to enlighten the world one envelope at a time.

Alas, "forever" wouldn't last forever.

One eagle-eyed philatelist, armed only with a jeweler's loupe, a rabid obsession with detail, and way too much time on his hands, made a shocking discovery. The lady on the stamp wasn't the 305-foot copper and iron neoclassical figure standing sentry on an island in New York Harbor.

No, sir.

The lady on the stamp was the pint-sized knockoff on the Las Vegas strip, overlooking not New York, New York, but the New York, New York casino.

She hadn't welcomed the huddled masses yearning to breathe free in the New World; she welcomed obsessive gamblers yearning to sidle up to the $3.99 All-You-Can-Eat Buffet. Less the stuff of immigrants' hopes and dreams—a real-life Lady Liberty—more the stuff of fiberglass and Styrofoam: a replica Lady Luck.

In other words: *Oh, fuck.*

And we've got three billion of these?!

A small discolored rectangle that mars her crown's most prominent center spike—the real Lady wouldn't be caught dead with such a blemish—was the telltale giveaway: Someone, somewhere, had merely raided a stock photography service and thought, *Yeah, seems about right. It must be her. And if it's not, I doubt anyone will notice.*

Someone noticed.

Once alerted to its gaffe, the United States Postal Service released an official statement. But not of apology; of adoration. "We still love the stamp design and would have selected the photograph anyway." They admitted no defeat, made no excuses, announced no recall. They also, it must be said, made me proud to be an American, where at least I know I'm free . . . to pretend *I totally meant to do that.* Even when I *totally screwed up.*

After all, what was the Postal Service to do? Should it deny it made a mistake, as original author James Madison might have wished in that summer of 1787, and as originalist Antonin Scalia would still advise today?

Should it recall the stamp and continue living in the past? That was the unfortunate choice Jonathan Dayton made in his later years when he, the youngest delegate at the Constitutional Convention, stayed so fixated on his participation in Philadelphia that he never once updated even his manner of dress—"the last of the cocked hats," they called him—a walking example of arrested development.

Should it waste decades redesigning every feature of the imperfect stamp, following in the small footsteps of Nutball Guy Tugwell, who everyone knows is a nutball who wasted decades redesigning every feature the Constitution?

Or should it make a bold wholesale makeover in a staggering, miraculous flurry of glorious inspiration—as I, Kevin Bleyer, your hero and humble servant, have done in these pages?

Even if it *should*, it didn't. Instead of promising a More Perfect Stamp, the postal service insisted the stamp *was* a more perfect stamp, one that—despite the injuries and usurpations brought on by a sloppy postal researcher—still secures the blessings of the Liberty as we know her, life-size and in full. It interpreted the advice of Thomas Jefferson—that we not look at stamps, or anything really, "with sanctimonious reverence, and deem them like the ark of the covenant"—and of James Madison too—that we not suffer a " blind veneration for antiquity"—as something slightly different: That we should just get over ourselves, stick with the program, and meet up at the craps table. *Baby needs a new pair of shoes.*

The lesson shines forth as bright and unmistakable as the flame in Lady Liberty's outstretched hand: Sometimes, in order to honor an icon that defines us as a nation—whether it be a giant green woman holding a torch or a Constitution of the United States of America—we just have to roll with what we've got.

Because it's still pretty damn awesome.

USA FIRST CLASS FOREVER!

☆ ☆ ☆

ACKNOWLEDGMENTS
Giving Full Faith and Credit
Where Credit Is Due

☆ ☆ ☆

> The summer soldier and the sunshine patriot will, in this crisis,
> shrink from the service of their country; but he that stands by
> it now, deserves the love and thanks of man and woman.
>
> Thomas Paine, 1776

As with any project of this magnitude, there are so many people to thank me. Sadly, these few pages cannot possibly begin to express how grateful they must be for my tireless efforts in making such an obvious contribution to their lives. However, under the assumption that a representative sampling is better than none at all, I'll do my best to give them a voice.

Mine.

It's the least I can do.

To those who believed in the merits of this project from the very beginning—and you know who you are—holding this book in your hands is, let's be honest, reward enough. Those sunshine patriots who doubted me, rest assured no one will *ever* know who *you* are. You will die alone.

First and foremost, to my editor, Andy Ward, who knew he was latching himself to a shooting star—in choosing to work with me he proved early on that he is a man of impeccable taste. Luckily, so am I; not only is he the best editor a writer could ever ask for, and now a great friend to boot, but when he approved my *second* deadline extension, I finally realized, *I can work with this guy*. Point is, I'm very glad I worked with this guy.

To our many collaborators and colleagues at Random House—to Susan Kamil, Tom Perry, Gina Centrello, Benjamin Dreyer, Evan Camfield, and Emily DeHuff, and to London King, Liza Eliano, Avideh Bashirrad, and Erika Greber, and of course to Kaela Myers—I don't have the words to thank you. Because you took them all away from me. And then you *published* them. I'll never forgive you for that.

To John McElroy and Kelly Gildea, for giving my voice the platform it deserves, and for having profound patience with my plosive *p*s.

To Jon Stewart and Stephen Colbert, and to all my friends at *The Daily Show with Jon Stewart*, with whom I've had the great pleasure of laughing every day for the past seven years—what can I say? It remains an honor for you to work with me.

To the master Nelson Shanks, and of course to Leona Shanks, Dodge Thompson and David Pettibone, and to all the artists who welcomed me, their humble subject, into their worlds to witness their creative genius first-hand. You can't know how inspired I am to know that you're inspired by me. It's very—there's no other way to express it—inspiring.

To Associate Justices Antonin Scalia and Stephen Breyer, for not kicking me out of their chambers. Your Honors, your clear judgment on the bench of the Supreme Court is eclipsed only by your lack of judgment in agreeing to talk to me about it.

To Bob Clark, the supervisory archivist at the Franklin D. Roosevelt Presidential Library in Hyde Park, New York, who effortlessly fielded all my impertinent questions about Rexford Guy Tugwell, who is a nutball. Thank you for overlooking my excessive antagonism and abundant use of curse words.

A few devoted patriots read early drafts of this manuscript; my only regret is that more didn't have the chance.

Leslie Farrell, Jon Prinsky, Peter Greenberg, Randy Cohen, Michael Breyer, Mark Goffman, Gideon Yago, Noralen Curl, Garrick Utley, Richard Rampell, Lisa Ellman, John Hlinko and Leigh Stringer, Ian Bremmer and Ann Shuman, Scott and Caroline Simon, and of course Gabby and Mark, who frequently came to my aid and rescue when I was having trouble realizing my full potential, helped me realize my full potential. Let that be your thanks.

To Charles Duhigg and A. J. Jacobs, who both recommended several significant changes to chapters I was already perfectly happy with, for chrissakes. Gentlemen, I'll never forget you. Remember the good times, before the ugliness.

And to Colleen Lawrie, who insisted that my caustic, bullying sense of humor was charming even when it was directed at her. Colleen, you were invaluable to this process. Perhaps someday you'll be valuable to one. (Boom! Who's charming now?)

Of course, I can't wrap this up without mentioning my crackerjack team at William Morris Endeavor—a stipulation in the contract they negotiated, apparently. So, to Erin Malone and Suzanne Gluck—but only because you made me—*thank you*. Thanks as well to Cara Stein, Tom Wellington, Greg Hodes, Dan Shear, Christian Muirhead, Lisa Harrison, Theresa Brown, Jeff Lesh, Henry Reisch, and Ari Emanuel, who have always had my best interests at heart. I look forward to meeting you someday.

To my mother and father, there wouldn't be *Me the People* without *me, the person*, so I owe *you, the parents*, a sizable debt of gratitude. Since you're family, I'm sure we can work out a mutually agreeable financial arrangement to get that monkey off my back as soon as possible.

I didn't hire an assistant, not because I didn't need one, but because I thought it would be unfair to all the assistants I *didn't* hire. So here, where I would have thanked, let's call her "Vanessa," I'll instead use this space to point out to all the naysayers who said I'd never write this book that, whaddya know, I wrote this book. I'll have Vanessa send you a copy.

And speaking of books: To the many historians, academics, and constitutional experts from whose numerous works of scholarship I have drawn so liberally and so skillfully herein—you are the Jeffersons to my Madison. Together we have changed the entire world forever, and I say that without the slightest bit of exaggeration.

Finally, to the signers of my Declaration of Independence from the Constitution of the United States, we must, indeed, all hang together, or most assuredly we shall all hang separately. And hey, let's all hang out once in a while, okay?

To those who aren't mentioned here, to the summer soldiers and the sunshine patriots who did shrink from the service of their country and this Constitution, please know—and be reassured that *I* know—just how unlucky you are.

"Look on this picture and weep over it! And if there yet
remains one thoughtless wretch who believes it not, let him
suffer it unlamented!

THOMAS PAINE, 1776"

—KEVIN BLEYER, 2012

APPENDIX

The Declaration of Independence from the Constitution of the United States

In Congress, assembled.

The Unanimous Declaration of the fifty United States of America (Revised!)

When in the Course of Human Events, it becomes necessary for one man to dissolve, dismantle, and discarde the Political Bands which have, let's face it, been duteously discredited and duly discounted - no disrespecte - and offer his Boundless Wisdom, Unique Insight, and Rhetorical Eloquence on behalf an entire nation, thereby ensuring, through the labor of one man, one giant statutory leap for Mankind - and hey, not for nothing, but you're welcome, Mankind - necessity demands - nay, requires - that he rewrite the Constitution of these United States of America. Single-handedlye.

Ask ye, Why be it Kevin so entrusted?

He holds these truths to be self-evident, that all men are created equal, that all women are created even equaller, that together they are endowed by their Creators with certain unalienable Rights, or "inalienable" Rights depending on who you ask, that among these are the Rights to Life; to Liberty; to the hot pursuit of Happiness; to cry if you want to, be it your party or not; to letting your Flag fly, be it Freak or otherwise; to the unfettered freedom of expression, to the fettered freedom from the use of emoticons ;), and to Rights yet untold and unforeseen - mainly because he hasn't thought of them yet but, like, totally will by the time we go to print with this thing - and that, to reaffirm and restore these Rights for Eternitye, a new Covenant need be written, and should be written, and shall be written, and that Kevin J. Bleyer, affirmed gentleman, scholar, penman, wordsmith, mathlete, World Traveler, prospective homeowner, hopeless Romantic, deep thinker, infamous scribbler, Award-Winning Satirist, Penultimate Fighting Champion, Peerless Leader and humble servant, shall be the one to write it.

So, help him, God. (Oh God, please help him.)

Therefore, on this day, We the Undersigned, appealing to the Supreme Judge of the world, do, in the Name, and by presumed Authority of the good People of these United States, solemnly publish our Signatures in big, floppy Cursive and declare their implied deed; namely,

John Hancock ~ actual Gentleman named John Hancock ~	John Hancock ~ a spare John Hancock ~	"The" Kevin Bleyer ~ humble servant ~	Ed Begley, Jr. ~ Savior of the Earth ~	Randy Cohen ~ World-Renowned Ethiciste ~
Amy Dickinson ~ The Most Trusted Advice Columniste ~	Juliette Fretté ~ Playboy Playmate ~	Taylor Hicks ~ American Idol, 2006 ~	A.J. Jacobs ~ The Smartest Person in the World ~	Bob Mankoff ~ Cartoon Editor, The New Yorker ~	Merrill Markoe (the big expert!) ~ Award-winning Satirist ~
Father James Martin, S.J. ~ Jesuit priest, Chaplain de Colbert ~	Craig Newmark ~ Founding Father, Craigsliste.com ~	John Oliver ~ bona fide English person ~	Lawrence O'Donnell ~ yellow journalist ~	Jane Poynter ~ original crewmember, the Biosphere ~
Rob Riggle ~ Lt. Comedian, United States Marine Corps ~	Gideon Rose ~ pamphleteer, Foreign Affairs ~	Scott Simon ~ host, National Publick Radio ~	Jimmy Wales ~ Founding Father, Wikipedia ~	Jim Wallis ~ Authority on Matters Religious ~	Gideon Yago ~ voice of the MTV generation ~

additional prominente patriots to follow...

About the Type

This book was set in Caslon, a typeface first designed in 1722 by William Caslon. Its widespread use by most English printers in the early eighteenth century soon supplanted the Dutch typefaces that had formerly prevailed. The roman is considered a "workhorse" typeface due to its pleasant, open appearance, while the italic is exceedingly decorative.